FILM COMEDY

FILM COMEDY

GEOFF KING

WALLFLOWER PRESS
LONDON AND NEW YORK

First published in Great Britain in 2002 by Wallflower Press
5 Pond Street, London NW3 2PN
www.wallflowerpress.co.uk

A catalogue for this book is available from the British Library

ISBN 1-903364-35-3 (pbk)
ISBN 1-903364-36-1 (hbk)

Printed in Great Britain by Antony Rowe Ltd., Chippenham, Wiltshire

contents

list of illustrations

acknowledgements

introduction: taking comedy seriously 1

one: comedy and narrative 19

two: transgressions and regressions 63

three: satire and parody 93

four: comedy and representation 129

five: comedy beyond comedy 170

notes

filmography

bibliography

index

list of illustrations

1   *Les Visiteurs*   6

2   *Liar Liar*   35

3   *Good Morning Vietnam*   41

4   *A Day at the Races*   46

5   *Bringing Up Baby*   52

6   *There's Something About Mary*   66

7   *Monty Python's The Meaning of Life*   76

8   *Brats*   79

9   *The Strong Man*   80

10   *A Night at the Opera*   89

11   *Ruka*   98

12   *Britannia Hospital*   103

13   *Bob Roberts*   109

14   *!Three Amigos!*   113

15   *Scary Movie*   127

16   *Some Like It Hot*   135

17   *48Hrs*   151

18   *Passport to Pimlico*   159

19   *Local Hero*   165

20   *La Vita è Bella*   191

21   *C' Est Arrivé Près de Chez Vous*   194

22   *The Bostonians*   200

acknowledgements

Thanks to Tanya Krzywinska for numerous conversations and suggestions relating to various aspects of the book during the period of writing. I am also grateful to Paul Wells for reading the manuscript and offering a number of useful suggestions. Leon Hunt provided guidance and materials relating to comedy from Hong Kong. Dave Bessell helped to translate my inexpert understanding of the use of music in comedy into technically more appropriate terms.

I would also like to thank Yoram Allon at Wallflower Press for agreeing to allow this book to be expanded from its originally planned format in the *Short Cuts* series: I could not possibly have kept it down to that length without suffering severe frustration!

Much of the material contained in this book was developed in conjunction with my teaching on the Comedy module in Film and TV Studies at Brunel University.

Finally, I would like to dedicate this book to Alison, Jordan and Maya, for tolerating a rainswept camping holiday in France in the summer of 2001 while I stayed at home completing the first draft.

introduction

taking comedy seriously

From slapstick to satire and subtle innuendo. From the grotesque to the carefully mannered. From madcap anarchy to the darkly deadpan. Film comedy comes in a wide range of forms. For as long as film has existed as an entertainment medium, so has film comedy. The film generally acknowledged to be the first work of fiction on screen was a comedy: the Lumière Brothers' *L'Arroseur arrosé* ('The Waterer Watered', 1895). Comedy was one of the most popular formats in the early years of cinema and has remained so ever since. Rarely one of the more prestigious or award-winning forms, and often subject to critical neglect, comedy has provided a reliable source of income for cinemas around the world. It has many attractions. Comedy is generally a relatively inexpensive form, capable of producing healthy profits at low cost. In Hollywood, for example, in the summer of 1998, a number of $100 million plus special effects-oriented blockbusters were outperformed by the modestly budgeted *There's Something About Mary*. An audience survey in 1982 showed comedy to be 'by far the most popular genre with both sexes, irrespective of age'.[1] Most of the top 20 in a survey of US video rentals in 1999 were either comedies or action-adventure titles.[2] Successive records for top-grossing British films in recent years have been monopolised by comedies of varying kinds, examples including the romantic comedies *Four Weddings and a Funeral* (1994) and *Notting Hill* (1999), the star-comedian vehicle *Bean* (1997) and *The Full Monty* (1997). Comedy has also been a staple in the cinema of many less wealthy nations across the globe.

1

One quality that most, if not all, comedy has in common, and that helps to explain its widespread appeal, is that it is usually considered to be relatively 'safe' and unthreatening. Some forms of comedy, such as political satire and black comedy, can be sharp, controversial and, in some cases, commercially or politically risky for those involved. In general, however, comedy is often taken to be the epitome of light relief or 'just entertainment' on film. Comedy, along with the musical – and sometimes in combination with it – is one of the types of film that has often been allowed to flourish in the most oppressive political regimes, under a number of dictatorships in the history of Latin America, for example.[3] Comedy, by definition, is not usually taken entirely seriously, a fact that sometimes gives it licence to tread in areas that might otherwise be off-limits.

But what exactly is film comedy? What are its main forms, themes and characteristics, and what kinds of issues are raised by the presence of the rather strange dimension of the comic? A comedy might initially be defined as a work that is designed in some way to provoke laughter or humour on the part of the viewer. This is the dominant definition in contemporary usage, although that has not always been the case. Comedy, in this respect, has something in common with forms such as horror and the 'weepie': defined to a significant extent according to the emotional reaction it is intended to provoke. This is not an exhaustive definition, however, if only because comedy has also to be understood from the point of view of consumption. Intended comedy might fall flat; or, alternatively, comedy might be found where it had not been intended by the producers. It is a relative rather than an absolute phenomenon, dependent on a range of specific contextual factors. It also appears in many works that might not clearly be defined primarily as comedy films or 'comedies'. Its function in such cases will be examined later. The appeal of comedy is such that it is often found as one component of films that fall into other categories. Comedy can figure as a minor element in otherwise more 'serious' material. It might be a substantial component, perhaps equal with one other, in which case a film might be termed a hybrid: a 'comedy thriller', for example, in which the thriller element is not entirely subordinated to the comic. To be clearly defined as a comedy, a film should be dominated to a substantial extent by the comic dimension – and this will be the main basis for inclusion in this study of film comedy – but the exact balance varies considerably from one example to another.

Comedy in film, generally, is probably best understood as a *mode*, rather than as a *genre*, if these various different degrees of comedy are to be taken into account. Comedy is a mode – a manner of presentation – in which a variety of different materials can be approached, rather than any relatively more fixed or localised quantity.[4] Any genre might be treated as a subject for comedy. A variety of possibilities exist. A western might include some comedy without altering its primary definition as a western. *The Searchers* (1956), for example, directed by John Ford, contains sequences of rather foolish knockabout comedy that do not usually undermine the film's reputation as a serious exploration of the dark side of the frontier hero. All-out spoofs such as *Blazing Saddles* (1974) and *Carry On Cowboy* (1965) are clearly in the domain of comedy, first, and the western only secondarily; the western is used as material for a particular brand of comedy rather than comedy being worked into the western. Some westerns-with-comedy occupy a less clear-cut space somewhere in between.

A term such as 'comedy' can be used either as an adjective or as a noun, another way of exploring the relationship between mode and genre.[5] In its adjectival use, comedy is modal, an inflection of a noun-object, as in the case of 'comedy western': a western presented in a comic mode. In its use as a noun, comedy seems to suggest the relatively more solid object of a genre. 'Romantic comedy', for example, suggests a particular adjectival take (romantic) on the noun-object, comedy. Comedy can function at either level. Historically, Rick Altman suggests, the adjectival form usually comes first: '*comedy* itself did not start as a noun, but as one of a set of adjectives designating the possible types of theatre or song: the word *comedy* comes from the kind of singing associated with reveling (Greek *komoidos*: *komos* = revel + *aiodos* = song)'. To become a noun, in its own right, an adjectival form has 'to commandeer entire texts and demonstrate a clear ability to pilot them independently' (1999: 51).

At its broadest, comedy remains a mode that can be applied to any object, in film or elsewhere. Film comedy is so widespread as to be difficult to locate as a single or stable generic noun-form. The descriptive or analytical category 'comedy', as a noun, seems rather vague. If a film is categorised in these terms alone we are likely to require additional information to get a sense of its more specific identity. A number of adjectival qualifications of 'comedy' are usually in general use in any particular time and place. These might be seen either as genres in their own right or as comedy sub-genres or more short-term cycles; such distinctions, again, are never fixed or exact but subject to historically-specific qualifications. Romantic comedy, for example, examined in Chapter One, has demonstrated sufficient longevity, as a form with distinctive conventions, to have earned widespread industrial, critical and audience recognition as a genre or sub-genre. A form such as 'gross-out' comedy, considered in Chapter Two, is of shorter historical provenance. It might, as a result, struggle to gain recognition as an identifiable sub-genre. Other forms have achieved the movement from adjective to noun outlined by Altman as part of his broader account of the process of change within and between genres and generic components. Examples include satire and parody, although the uses of these terms have their own complications, as will be see in Chapter Three.

But the question still remains: what *is* comedy, regardless of whether one manifestation or another is defined as a mode, genre, adjective or noun, or whether the effect is intentional or not? We all, probably, have some sense of what makes us laugh. But what is the basis of this effect? Comedy often appears to be a very obvious quality: a particular gag or plot situation is just 'funny' or 'comic' – or it falls flat, does not work. But why? This is one of the broadest questions considered in this book. In what does the comedy actually lie, what makes something comical in film, and what are the implications of this? Why do we not always agree about what is or is not comic? To describe film comedy as 'just comic', or otherwise, is to beg the real question. Nothing is *just* comic: things are comic in particular ways and for particular reasons. Comedy in film, as elsewhere, plays upon a variety of elements to achieve its effects. It can only be understood in relation to a number of specific contexts, including many of our basic expectations and assumptions about the world around us.

We are not usually encouraged to take comedy very seriously. Producers of comedy often argue against analysis of their work. To analyse comedy, the cliché goes, is to destroy it. To seek to understand comedy through weighty theoretical speculation is to fail to grasp the nature of the beast, it is claimed. A similar prejudice against academic analysis is found in most forms of popular entertainment, as argued by Richard Dyer (1992) in the context of the Hollywood musical. Such defensiveness might be understandable from the point of view of practitioners, for whom excessive analytical probing might threaten a form of creativity that draws on a range of unstated and unselfconscious assumptions. To take comic forms apart in order to understand exactly how they work might be to undermine some of the pleasures they offer, but this need not always be the case. Understanding can add to the pleasure – or be a source of pleasure in forms of comedy that are less appealing in themselves. Either way, this is a risk that has to be taken. Film comedy is widespread, as a part of the culture of its time and place; as such, it merits serious analysis.

This study pays close attention to particular forms of comedy, as manifested in particular contexts, including some examples taken from beyond the more familiar Hollywood, British or other European, 'Western' or English-language traditions. But it also returns frequently to these general questions about the nature of comedy: what it means for something to be comic; how we might explain the very particular effect of comedy, something that often affects us bodily, making us react physically. A number of broad theories of comedy, jokes and laughter are encountered along the way. Theories of comedy date back at least as far as the world of ancient Greece. Many of the 'great thinkers' in our intellectual tradition – from Plato and Aristotle to Kant, Nietzsche and Freud – have pondered on the nature of comedy at some stage, as have numerous other commentators. Some of these contributions are outlined here, but only as they appear useful in the understanding of particular issues. This is not a history or summary of general theories of comedy.[6] Instead, the book is organised around a number of key issues, themes, approaches and forms of comedy that have loomed relatively large in the specific arena of film (which, generally, here, means works originally shown in the cinema, rather than strictly applying to the medium of use: television comedy shot on film is not included, for example).

Comic modality: departing from the norm ... but not too far

There is no single adequate theory of comedy, despite various efforts to produce an all-embracing account. Various different theoretical approaches are available and of differing degrees of use, depending on the precise nature of the comedy involved in any individual case and the different questions we might seek to answer. As Murray Davis suggests of humour more generally:

> It is fruitful to apply Hobbes' superiority theory to aggressive jokes, Bergson's mechanization theory to farce, Freud's sexual theory to dirty jokes, and Northrop Frye's anthropological theory to Aristophanic Old Comedy ... But humor is too complicated to be comprehended by such single-factor theories, no matter how well they explain one of its aspects. (M. Davis 1993: 7)

The issue is complicated by shifts in the criteria that have been used, historically, to define comedy. Steve Neale and Frank Krutnik outline two different sets of divisions that cut across the field: between the rival criteria of the happy ending (a defining feature for some theorists in the past, especially, which need not entail the generation of laughter) and the generation of laughter (which need not require narrative dimensions such as the happy ending), and between narrative and non-narrative forms: 'Although there tends, within neoclassical theory, to be a coincidence between them, the two kinds of division are logically distinct. Moreover, they do not always, in practice, correspond with or accompany one another' (1990: 15).

A recurring theme of this book, however, and the nearest it comes to a general conclusion, is that comedy tends to involve departures of a particular kind – or particular kinds – from what are considered to be the 'normal' routines of life of the social group in question. In order to be marked out as comic, the events represented – or the mode of representation – tend to be different in characteristic ways from what is usually expected in the non-comic world. Comedy often lies in the gap between the two, which can take various forms, including incongruity and exaggeration. Incongruity features in a great deal of comedy and is the basis of one major branch of comedy theory drawn upon here.[7] Comedy can result from a sense of things being out of place, mixed up or not quite right, in various ways. One set of examples is found in films that derive much of their comedy from temporal, geographical or other forms of displacement.

In *Les Visiteurs* ('The Visitors', 1993) an eleventh-century knight and his vassal are mistakenly transplanted into contemporary France. At first, the signifiers of the world around them seem congruent enough: a forest, open grassland, a glossy black horse that offers suitable transportation for the knight, Godefroy the Hardy (Jean Reno). But then there is a road and a car, the latter attacked by Godefroy and Jacquasse the Crass (Christian Clavier), with sword and other medieval implements. Further incongruities are a major source of the film's comedy as knight and vassal, unfamiliar with the amenities of modern life, proceed to wreak havoc in the home, castle and various institutions of their descendants. Similar kinds of comedy are found in other time-travel films, including the *Back to the Future* series. *Back to the Future: Part III* (1990), for example, in which the principals travel back to the 'wild west', offers incongruities such as horses towing a broken-down DeLorean sports-car/time-machine across an open western landscape. What is involved here, in the language of semiology, is a combination of *semantic* elements (units of meaning: DeLorean/horse-drawn, western setting) that would normally be expected to belong to different generic territories (those of the western and science fiction). Geographical displacement can offer similar fish-out-of-water effects, as in *Crocodile Dundee* (1986), in which American reporter Sue Charlton (Linda Kozlowski) is transplanted to the Australian outback and, in complementary fashion, the eponymous star (Paul Hogan) finds himself in the urban jungle of New York City; and in *Okno v Parizh* ('Window to Paris', 1994), in which a magical portal in a St Petersburg apartment leads from the shortages and scavenging of post-Soviet Russian society to the material abundance, romantic escape and temptation offered by the French capital.

A more radical sense of geographical-cultural juxtaposition is found in *The Gods Must Be Crazy* (1981), a comedy from Botswana that revolves around

Figure 1 Incongruity attack: *Les Visiteurs* (1993)

a series of misunderstandings between a Bushman from a remote part of the Kalahari desert, a scientist conducting research on elephant dung and a reporter who gives up her job to become a schoolteacher at a remote Kalahari settlement. One strain of comedy results from the defamiliarised view of modern 'civilisation' offered by a third-person voice-over commentary from the perspective of Xi (Nixau), the innocent Bushman who comes into contact for the first time with the outside world. A rifle, for Xi, is 'a funny stick' and he cannot understand why its owner puts his hands up and then flees (comically speeded-up, a technique used regularly in the film) when Xi points it at him. The schoolteacher, Kate Thompson (Sandra Prinsloo), depicted on numerous occasions in states of semi-undress, is, for Xi, 'the ugliest person he had ever come across … as pale as something that had crawled out of a rotting log'. An almost equal degree of misunderstanding is generated between the clumsy-with-women scientist, Andrew Steyn (Marius Weyers), and Thompson, suggesting the difficulties (and comic potential) offered by what might be expected to be narrower cultural divides. He jumps on top of her twice, the first time when she is scantily clad, to protect her from a pack of warthogs and from a rhino that charges through their camp. She, unfamiliar with the terrain, does not accept his protestations of innocence of any improper intentions. He tells her that two passing locals will confirm his explanation of the presence of the rhino, which she did not see; they shake their heads, a gesture understood by Steyn as an act of confirmation in their culture, but one that adds to his difficulties in convincing Thompson.

One of the pleasures offered by comedy is the freedom vicariously to enjoy departures from the norm, a dimension examined from a variety of perspectives in this book, especially in Chapter Two. Comedy can be seen as a form of disruption, such as that unleashed by Godefroy and Jacquasse in *Les Visiteurs*. The film offers a glorious assault on the fabric of well-heeled bourgeois life. By contemporary standards, Godefroy and Jacquasse are clumping and unwashed oafs, bringing chaos to the immaculate surfaces of a luxury home and a castle that has been turned into an overpriced hotel. We are invited to enjoy their depredations: the flooding of the house and the destruction of china, the incineration of a joint of meat skewered on an umbrella in the fireplace and a series of assaults on the fabric of the castle/hotel run by the vain and arrogant Jacques-Henri Jacquart (also played by Christian Clavier). A similar effect is offered by the presence of the backwoods figures of Dundee, Xi and, to some extent, the transplanted Russian figures in *Okno v Parizh*. All four films offer the spectacle of figures coded as more raw, authentic and 'noble', in their own ways, cutting through the pretensions of 'decadent' civilisation.

Dundee, for example, seeks and often achieves a level of human contact untypical of big city life, establishing relationships with numerous 'lowly' background figures, such as those of the serving classes. Having learned a lesson about the deceptive nature of appearances (chatting up a 'woman' who turns out to be a man in drag), Dundee takes a direct approach on his next such encounter, grabbing a 'suspect' figure by the balls to confirm his suspicion. Actions such as these are a recurrent source of comedy-through-incongruity, but they are also presented as more honest, 'natural', enlightened and liberating than the usual state of alienation experienced in the metropolis. The same goes for the raucous and opportunistic behaviour of the second-string troupe of Russian characters unleashed in the decadent Paris of *Okno v Parizh*. Comically disruptive characters are granted freedom from the constraints that usually prevent such behaviour. They can also be unsettling, in some cases, depending on the perspective of the viewer. The scope for disturbance in most forms of comedy is limited, however, by the fact that disruption is not meant to be taken too seriously. If we can 'let go', enjoying the experience of a realm not restricted by the usual rules, we can do so with the provision of a safety net. We do not have to worry too much about the consequences. The close combination of these two effects appears to be one of the main attractions of the comic mode, enabling us to have the best of both worlds. Comedy has the potential to be both subversive, questioning the norms from which it departs, and affirmative, reconfirming that which it recognises through the act of departure; or a mixture of the two. Two different conceptions of comedy are often combined: comedy in the sense of laughter, anarchy and disruption of harmony, and comedy in the sense of a movement *towards* harmony, integration and the happy ending.[8]

The same is true to some extent of other modes or genres that have the potential to offer wholesale departures from the conventions of everyday life. In horror and science fiction, for example, ruptures of normal expectations are usually motivated and underwritten by both specific generic conventions and those of 'escapist' popular entertainment in general (the narrative structure of mainstream Hollywood-type films tends to revolve around the creation followed by the resolution of a specific kind of emotional tension, as Ed Tan suggests (1996: 35)). The specific effect of comedy may partly be explained by the fact that the two components of this process seem to interpenetrate more closely. A moment of horrific departure from normality might be recuperated by its presence as a to-be-expected ingredient of a horror film; but, by definition, it is still intended to create an horrific *frisson*, or discomfort, to some extent, in its moment of deployment. Consumption of horror films is considered by some critics to entail elements of masochism.[9] In comedy, the moment of potential disruption, liberation or transgression and that of disavowal of any real distur-bance can occur more or less simultaneously and in a context that is coded in advance as unthreatening. Horror invites us to take its departures a degree more seriously, even if they are contained by the generic framework (how some elements of horror might be *combined with* comedy, to potent effect, is consid-ered in Chapter Five). Broad forms of comedy generally entail a larger step back from potential seriousness, tension and anxiety. A situation is established that might, in other circumstances, have more serious implications, but these are undermined in one way or another. Any serious engagement is relaxed, as

Elder Olson puts it, 'due to a manifest absurdity of the grounds for concern' (1968: 16).

As a mode, comedy implies a particular *modality*, in the sense in which the term (from linguistics) is used by Robert Hodge and David Tripp, to suggest 'ways of situating messages in relation to an ostensible reality' (1986: 43). Different kinds of texts are coded in different ways to suggest different degrees of reality or plausibility, from documentary 'authenticity' or news footage (themselves constructs in their own ways, of course) to the most outlandish fantasy.[10] The modality in which a text is placed – in acts of production, reception and intermediary forms such as publicity or reviews – shapes the kind of impression it is likely to make on the viewer. Modality markers specific to the broader forms of comedy establish a sense of clear distance from reality or seriousness in any particular film or sequence, although subtle shades of variation and shifts of modality are possible. Susan Purdie puts this in terms of degrees of 'implication' offered to viewers, the extent to which they are encouraged to sympathise or empathise with characters and to treat the represented events as 'real' – at some level, relatively – within the fictional frame (1993: 78); a quality that can vary across a range from dark comedy or satire (taken seriously, as having reference to objects in the real world) to all-out farce (usually taken to be of lesser, if any, obvious consequence). Many comedies occupy a space somewhere in between, offering a shifting balance between implication in the experiences of central characters – a modality in which we are encouraged to 'care' about what happens to them, to follow their fortunes with a degree of emotional investment in the outcome – and the more distanced perspective from which we can sit back without emotional consequence to enjoy the comedy of their incapacities and set-backs as well as their often unlikely triumphs.

The enjoyment of knockabout farce or slapstick often depends on the establishment of distance from comic figures who are not represented as 'rounded' characters. In this respect, Kathleen Chamberlain suggests, some screen clowns have much in common with their forebears in the *commedia dell' arte* of the Italian Renaissance. The latter wore stylised masks, which put the emphasis on the creation of limited but intensely presented character 'type' rather than the development of 'anything resembling realistic behaviour' (2001: 55). An equivalent to these masks, Chamberlain suggests, is found in the trademark appearances of figures such as Buster Keaton, Harold Lloyd, the Keystone Kops and the Three Stooges. The result is the creation of 'the intensity, extremity, and simplicity that is essential to farce. The audience remains distanced, removed from that sort of emotional identification that can destroy the tone of farce' (57). The same might be said of later generations of screen comics. Distancing qualities can be mixed with devices that invite a greater degree of implication, however, as in the combination of iconic image, slapstick and sentimentality found in many of the films of Charlie Chaplin. At the other end of the scale, formats such as contemporary romantic comedy tend to establish a dominant modality that encourages a strong degree of emotional implication in the fate of characters, verging on the (melo)dramatic.

Discrimination between the precise modalities that might be in play – from moment to moment, or from one type of comedy to another – helps to explain how a real sense of suspense and, in some cases, discomfort, can still be generated in films that are clearly in the domain of silly-comedy-fantasy. To take one example, the bank robbery sequence in *The Parole Officer* (2001) is hardly likely to be mistaken for anything other than entirely comic silliness. It is clear from the opening moments that the film is little more than a vehicle for the distinct persona of the British comic performer Steve Coogan. The plot into which he is inserted is a familiar/conventional unlikely-heist narrative. At the same time, however, the film is structured to encourage a significant measure of sympathy for, and emotional allegiance with, the plight of the wronged central character played by Coogan, the parole officer Simon Garden, who is set up by a corrupt detective. The threat posed to the character and his collaborators is placed at several removes by the use of particular comic devices during the robbery sequence and by the broader assurance, offered by the comic mode, that all will turn out well in the end. Elements of suspense and tension persist, however, even in this comically-coded context; a result of the balance established between comic and less comic forms of modality.

As Raymond Durgnat puts it, detachment from the consequences of actions is often a feature of comedy but not, in many cases, the source of its most potent effects: 'It's surely not because we're detached from the comic action that we laugh until we choke or cry, or till our ribs ache, or our sides split, or we laugh ourselves sick, or roll in the aisles, or die laughing. We seem to relish comedy best when it makes us participate to the point of hysteria' (1969: 22). Theories of humour or comedy based on the notion of superiority – that we laugh at the misfortunes or incapacities of others as a way of asserting our own, distanced, superiority – fail to account for this dimension.[11] For all the comic unreality, Durgnat suggests, we are often 'half-aware' that we have traits in common with the fictional characters on screen, 'that their weakness, rather than their immunity, is ours' (22). However absurd the idiom of a film, 'there can be no jokes without a dramatic undertow, for there can be no incongruities if there is no emotional tension' (50). Many films begin in a lighter mode before taking a more sober and dramatic turn towards the end 'before a final, reassuring release' (45).

A good example of the dynamic described by Durgnat is found in *La Crise* ('The Crisis', 1992), a crazy tragi-farce in which the central character Victor (Vincent Lindon) struggles to find sympathy for his plight (his wife leaves him, seemingly unaccountably, on the same morning that he loses his job, apparently unfairly) amid the travails faced by everyone to whom he turns. The comic hysteria generated by the film is based on a combination of attachment and detachment. Structurally, the film uses familiar devices to draw the viewer towards Victor, but also to qualify this: both 'alignment' (proximity to the character and access to his feelings, although his figure is sometimes pushed to the margins of the screen or excluded on occasions when his problems are being eclipsed by those of others) and 'allegiance' (sympathy, based on a moral evaluation of character, although the viewer is also invited, increasingly, to accept a degree of critique of his self-centred attitude).[12] Comic impact is created through a mixture of frustration, shared with Victor, in his thwarted efforts to find anyone not immersed in their own problems, and the measure of distance and delight created by the absurd exaggeration of the situation (the fact that *everyone* to whom he turns is in a state of crisis, with the exception of the seemingly most disadvantaged, the unprepossessing barfly Michou (Patrick Timsit)). A manic sense of snowballing emotional and relationship chaos gives way, in the latter stages, to the more serious strain that runs through the film, a meditation on the destructiveness of concern only with the self; the ending is 'happy' – Vincent reunited with his wife – but distinctly in the mode of drama rather than comedy.

How exactly this balance of modality works out varies from one example, or one form of comedy, to another. Godefroy the Hardy and Jacquasse the Crass in *Les Visiteurs*, for example, and the situation in which they are projected into the future, are marked out from the start as the stuff of knockabout farce in the guise of atmospheric period drama. The first image of the film is a pair of pointy amour-protected feet, clanging along a wooden walkway. The length of the foot-armour is excessive, a point emphasised by close framing; the delicate points to which the armour comes seem incongruous, given the heavy weight of the footfall, especially when bouncing slightly in motion as the wearer taps one foot in a sign of impatience. A voice-over provides historical context-background marked as comic in its initial reference to King Louis VI, 'known as "The Fat"'. The mock-serious modality suggested by the weighty intonation of the voice-over – and a pensive, slightly troubling theme on the soundtrack – continues to be undermined, as we cut to an extreme long shot of a mountain vista with a medieval castle in the distance, by the presence of the toe-tapping armoured feet, and the accompanying legs (but, incongruously, no upper body), framed in the upper right-hand corner of the screen. This builds into a scene marked, initially, as one of tension and edginess, until it is established, quite quickly, that the behind-enemy-lines encounter we have joined is of an amorous nature – and therefore already incongruous in the circumstances – between the King and an English princess. The broadly comic nature of the dalliance is underlined when it climaxes in the 'shocking' revelation to the former of a glimpse of the latter's ankles and knees (hardly the fruits for which, from a modern viewer's perspective, a potentially hazardous encounter might be likely to be risked). In terms of modality, the opening moves offer a blend of comic silliness, in words and action, and the more 'substantial' resonances of 'period' reconstruction. Armour, weapons, settings, theme music and the overall urgency of events have a certain solidity that lends 'realistic' texture against which elements of comedy are played.

Modality can be complex and multi-dimensional, different elements contributing to a range of potential impressions. Music, and sound more generally, is an important and often neglected ingredient, contributing textural 'solidity' in the case of the opening of *Les Visiteurs* but often used as a key marker of comic modality. Music can be one of the strongest indicators of modality, particularly in establishing or confirming basic qualities of tone from the start, whether the unsettling edginess of a thriller or the extra degree of fictional/fantastic insulation offered by the comic mode. Introductory or credit-sequence music often has this effect, examples including the 'Cuckoo Waltz' associated with Laurel and Hardy and the Henry Mancini theme used in the *Pink Panther* series (from 1964), each of which has become synonymous with the respective brand of comedy involved.

Opening sequences are especially privileged moments of modality-setting more generally, along with posters and other publicity materials that precede the experience of the main text. The English-language poster for *Les Visiteurs* establishes the basic incongruity of the film, depicting a knight in armour standing on a road, modern buildings in the background, wielding a 'Stop' sign in place of a more suitable historical weapon. Title or poster typefaces are often crooked or uneven, or otherwise mixed, exaggerated or distorted, to signify comic modality. In the satirical comedy *Serial Mom* (1994), the first line of the title on the videocassette box is picked out in uneven 'cut-out' letters, a signifier of criminality but given a comic twist by their cheery bright colours. On screen, the main title slides into frame from screen-right, the letters rotating into their correct position, a novelty effect that would be unlikely to be devised for an entirely 'straight' film. The wording of the title itself establishes the identity of the film as a comedy of some kind, of course, through the incongruous juxtaposition of 'serial' – implying nasty mass killers – and the ultimate cosiness of 'mom'. Poster and video-box tag-lines and quotations pulled from friendly reviews serve further to underline dominant modality, or sometimes to shift it in directions that might appear more commercially attractive. The latter was the case in the UK poster tagline for the bitter-sweet coming-of-age comedy *Diner* (1982) – 'The one thing they were looking for wasn't on the menu' – which associated the film with a more exclusively sex-oriented brand of contemporary youth comedy.

A light, or otherwise comic, tone on the soundtrack can be used to indicate the modality according to which we are encouraged to receive events that might, otherwise, be open to different modes of reception. The opening music of the animated *Gulliver's Travels* (1939), for example, offers a mixture of lush, full-blown Romantic orchestral scoring and snippets of lighter and more playful ditties. The effect is to create an impression of epic scale, important to the context in which the film appeared, but emphasises the fact that this is Jonathan Swift's potentially biting satire in safely child-friendly cartoon-comic mode. A number of musical techniques can be used to suggest comic modality, including, as elsewhere, the generation of incongruity. Staccato rhythms played on instruments such as the bassoon or tuba, for example, can result in a comically clumsy or ungainly effect, the result of a mismatch between the capabilities of the instrument and the qualities it is asked to reproduce.[13] Exaggeratedly high or low pitch, or incongruous shifts between the two, might also emphasise comic modality. In Laurel and Hardy's rendition of 'The Lonesome Pine' in *Way Out West* (1937) it is Stan Laurel's move into an improbable bass (especially incongruous given his slight physical stature, compared with that of his partner), followed by the falsetto that results from a corrective hammer blow to the head, that moves a more straightforwardly musical routine back into the register of knockabout comedy. Squeaky high pitch, together with jazz-influenced, slightly uneven or dotted rhythm, and the accompaniment of the cuckoo-clock sound itself, helps to account for the comic effect produced by the 'Cuckoo Waltz'. A similarly off-centre and lopsided rhythm is developed in the tip-toeing opening of the Pink Panther theme. Comic resonance can also be associated with the use of major as opposed to minor chords, as a result of their lower position in the harmonic series.

Complex modality can be produced through the combination of different musical effects. The scores of Danny Elfman offer notable examples, often combining darker notes and diminished chords – usually used to generate unease – with more comic, staccato, 'plinkety-plonk' rhythms, to create the distinctive dark-fantastic-comedy resonance of some of the films on which he has worked; in the opening theme of *To Die For* (1995), the result is a blend ideally suited to its black comedy of murderous career-obsession. Music can also be used to shift modality between one part of a film and another, as in the comedy-thriller *Kindergarten Cop* (1990). Urgent action-movie strains accompany the opening and subsequent sequences in which the action-thriller element is to the fore, with lighter and jauntier tones taking over when the central character, played by Arnold Schwarzenegger, faces the different, comically-coded challenge of keeping order in a class full of young children. Shifts in musical modality markers are also used to highlight the unambiguously comic world of Laurel and Hardy. *Blockheads* (1938) begins with dark, urgent, doom-laden tones, to accompany its initial First World War setting, as Stanley is left behind to guard a trench while Oliver joins an assault. The urgent mode is maintained during battle scenes, shifting to lively, celebratory strains over post-armistice footage of returning troops. As a series of annual date-captions leaps forward twenty years to 1938, however, and we return to the disheveled figure of Stanley, still pacing up and 'guarding' his territory, comic absurdity is figured in a silly, woozily high-pitched violin theme. Alternatively, the absence of music associated with comedy, where it might be expected, can be a source of awkward or uncertain modality, as in some of the darker forms of comedy examined in Chapter Five.

Non-musical sound can also be used as an indicator of comic modality, through incongruity and other effects. When the door of a packed lift opens in *Blockheads*, a deep, resonant voice from somewhere at the back says 'out please' – and what emerges, saying 'thank you' in the same voice, is the diminutive figure of a child in adult-style clothes. In *Snatch* (2000), the growling and barking of a dog picked up by a trio of hapless crooks is undercut because it also emits a silly squeak, having swallowed a plastic toy. In both of these cases, and many others, comedy results from a form of incongruity in which displacement occurs in a downwards direction, undercutting that which might be expected to be larger or more impressive; a dynamic in keeping with Kant's absurdity-based definition of laughter as 'an affection arising from the sudden transformation of strained expectation into nothing' (1790/1892: 223). Sound can also be used comically for commentative purposes, whether foolish (the horse whinny that accompanies each mention of the name of Frau Blucher (Cloris Leachman), the sinister housekeeper in *Young Frankenstein* (1974)) or more seriously satirical (the shrieking nonsense emitted by Chaplin's Adenoid Hynkel in *The Great Dictator* (1940)). Off-beat, exaggerated, distorted or otherwise eccentric sound is a major source of the deadpan comic texture of the films of Jacques Tati, examples including the incomprehensible railway station announcements and the repeated plucked-bass-chord note of the hotel restaurant door in *Les Vacances de Monsieur Hulot* ('Mr Hulot's Holiday', 1953).[14]

The comedy experience is pleasurable, Olson suggests, because it involves a relaxation of any tension that might be created by taking the events more seriously; a relaxation usually guaranteed in advance by audio-visual and extra-textual markers of modality. A blend of the plausible and the implausible often characterises the modality of comedy, as Jerry Palmer argues. The events might be plausible enough at some level to have a basis in possibility. This is true of *Les Visiteurs* in the sense of the logic of some of the events that follow once the ridiculous-fantasy premise is accepted. The precise balance may vary but, Palmer suggests, the emphasis is usually on the implausible and absurd. It is for this reason 'that we "don't take it seriously", that we have the emotional certainty that all will be well immediately after' (1987: 56). Many forms of comedy-through-incongruity or exaggeration can be understood in this way.[15] Substitution of objects often results in a form of incongruity in which implausibility outweighs, but does not entirely displace, plausibility. It is clearly implausible for a character to sit down to eat a leather shoe, even when starving, or to treat a faulty alarm clock as an organic object (listening to its innards with a stethoscope) as the figure played Charlie Chaplin does in celebrated scenes in *The Gold Rush* (1925) and *The Pawn Shop* (1916), respectively. The comic effect of these substitutions, in which objects are treated as if they were items of an entirely different order, is based on incongruity combined with an element of plausibility or twisted logic. Chaplin's character acts *as if* the objects were edible or treatable, persisting in a sustained engagement that is logical in its own terms, as in *Les Visiteurs*, once the initial absurdity is accepted. As the animator Chuck Jones, creator of many comic absurdities, put it: 'We must believe in a *logically illogical* way that this is really happening to a character' (quoted in Sandler 1998: 7).

It is the simultaneous presence of the two frames of reference – absurd and plausible/logical – that is central to the creation of the comic effect, a phenomenon termed 'bisociation' in a useful elaboration offered by Arthur Koestler. A great deal of comedy, Koestler suggests, results from the perception of a situation or an idea in two mutually incompatible associative contexts: an alarm clock, for example, as both inorganic mechanism and as an object the inner workings of which bear some *metaphorical* resemblance to those of the body; or a pun, in which two different meanings of the same term are put into play. As Koestler puts it: 'It is the sudden clash between these two mutually exclusive codes or rules – or associative contexts – which produces the comic effect. It compels us to perceive the situation in two self-consistent but incompatible frames of reference at the same time; it makes us function simultaneously on two different wave-lengths' (1982: 328). The comedy-effect lies in 'the delightful mental jolt of a sudden leap from one plane or associative context to another' (328). The emotional dynamic that leads to the production of laughter, in response to this logical structure, Koester suggests, is the result of a disjunction between the operations of emotions and reason. Thought processes can change direction, nimbly, at a moment's notice; emotions, possessing greater inertia, cannot. Laughter, for Koestler, is the mechanism through which emotion is released after a shift of association deprives it of its original object: 'It is emotion deserted by thought that is discharged in laughter' (333).[16]

In order to be comic rather than disturbing, incongruities and other departures from the norm found in comedy do not usually go too far. As Elder Olson suggests, terms 'expressing purely *logical* relations – such as "incongruity", "inappropriateness", "discrepancy", "contradiction", "paradox", and the like' are insufficient for a definition of comedy because they are ambivalent, 'or rather multivalent, for they may be involved as much in one emotion as another' (1968: 9–10). They are not exclusive to the realm of comedy. Incongruity is also found in the bizarre juxtapositions found in works of surrealism, for example. The films of Luis Buñuel contain much that is comical as a result of incongruity or inversion of convention: the constantly interrupted dinner parties of *Le Charme Discret de la Bourgeosie* ('The Discreet Charm of the Bourgeoisie', 1972); the blandishments exchanged around a table surrounded by toilet seats from which the participants excuse themselves to eat singly in a small room down the corridor in *Le Fantome de la Liberté* ('The Phantom of Liberty', 1974). The operative modality, however, includes a sense of greater seriousness or substance: the satirical treatment of bourgeois society or artistic-philosophical statements of Absurdity (the capital 'A' distinguishing this from 'mere' comic silliness). Both films offer a subversion of normal expectations intended to unsettle and disorient to a degree greater than that usually associated with comedy alone. Examples include the dreams-within-dreams structure of *Le Charme Discret*, periodically undermining the narrative-reality status of the preceding events, and the manifest illogic of the world of *Le Fantome*. The latter includes sequences in which a girl is treated as 'missing' by school, parents and police, despite the fact that she is clearly present before them, and in which a mass-killer gunman is found guilty, sentenced to death and then allowed – unaccountably, with no explanation, and no behavioural or representational indicators of comic modality – to walk free from the court.

Comedy usually involves a particular blend of the unlike and the like. Excessive implausibility, Palmer suggests, departing too far from recognisable norms, tips comedy in the direction of nonsense (including, potentially, the weightier absurdities of Buñuel). Excessive plausibility tips it towards seriousness, at the risk, variously, of creating dullness, offence or embarrassment. Or, as Durgnat puts it: 'Too little shock, and a joke is feeble or tame; too much, and it's drama' (1969: 24–5). This is partly a matter of the perspective or disposition of the viewer.[17] What is comic for some might be silly, tedious, impressively absurd or offensive for others. The wholly unlike – that which departs radically from the norm – verges on the 'monstrous', in Olson's terminology, a territory closer to that of horror. This might be the ground occupied by a figure such as Godefroy the Hardy were he shown to enact on screen much of the violence of his time to which he refers verbally (a great deal of summary disemboweling, essentially). That he does not, and that the differences depicted between his world and that of his descendants are restricted to safer material, helps to ensure that the film remains in the realms of broad and often slapstick comedy.

A number of parallels are established in *Les Visiteurs*, as well as differences between the two eras, and it is here, arguably, that the comedy is most effective, in the play between like and unlike. We are invited to laugh at the obvious incongruity of medieval-knight-attacking-car-with-sword, but a more subtle effect is created in a stand-off between helmeted sword-and-shield-wielding Godefroy and a unit of national guardsman equipped in same-but-different manner, with their riot shields, helmets and batons. The juxtaposition provides a form of comedy that might also undermine some assumptions about differences between the worlds of 'barbarism' and 'civilisation'. Comedy is sustained through further uses of similarity-within-difference. Godefroy's modern female descendent Béatrice (Valérie Lemercier) closely resembles his medieval fiancée (played by the same performer). Jacquart proves to be a descendant of the lowly Jacquasse; the latter, in turn, begins to enjoy the freedoms available in post-Revolutionary France.

Three main approaches are used to tackle such issues in this book, in various combinations: formal, social-historical-political, and industrial. Some central issues in the understanding of film comedy relate to the formal dimension, including film structure, style and aesthetics. A major example, the subject of the Chapter One, is the relationship between comic moments and the broader narrative frameworks in which they occur. This perspective plays a particularly important part in understanding the place of comedy in the early development of some of the fundamental characteristics of mainstream cinema. Social, cultural and historical – and more specifically political and ideological – perspectives inevitably loom large in any attempt to understand film comedy, both in general and in more specific contexts. Film comedy, like all popular cultural products, is rooted to a large extent in the societies in which it is produced and consumed. Many different kinds of analyses can be located within these broad social-cultural-historical approaches. Particular forms of comedy, or particular tendencies within more general forms, can be understood in the context of the specific times and places in which they appear. The norms from which departures are dramatised in comedy are defined to a large extent at the social-cultural level. Such acts of comic departure can provide revealing insights into the underlying and often taken-for-granted assumptions of the society in question.

Film comedy also remains the product of an industrial process that has its own impact on the forms of comedy produced in one moment or another. The formal question of the relationship between comic moments and narrative structure, for example, can only fully be understood in the context of industrial developments in the early decades of film and, with continued relevance today, the commercial significance of central star performers. Particular kinds of comedy might engage with a variety of social-cultural issues, which might help to account for their existence; but the prevalence of one form or another is also determined by industrial considerations. Certain varieties of British comedy might tell us something about the construction of notions of 'British' identity, for example. But they might say as much about the particular constructions deemed most likely to sell either at home or in the all-important American market. The fact that comedy can, simultaneously, be both subversive and affirmative is of importance to an appreciation of its social-cultural and ideological role. But this is also a substantial source of its attraction as an industrial product that can appeal to a range of potential audience groups. An adequate understanding of film comedy (and, indeed, of most other aspects of film) requires analysis from a combination of these different perspectives.

This book starts with an examination of several aspects of the relationship between comedy and narrative, from early gag-based films and contemporary comedian-centred comedy to the strongly narrative-framed format of romantic comedy. The first chapter also includes an examination of different ways of 'framing' comedy, both literally, in terms of issues of placement within the frame and editing strategies, and in the more specifically narrative dimension of structures through which knowledge is distributed, on-screen and off, in the staging of comedy. Chapter Two, 'Transgressions and Regressions', enters into more broadly social-cultural territory, drawing partly on the general notion that comedy can offer a form of escape or 'release', of one kind or another, from the pressures or norms of everyday life, whether understood at the social or social-psychological level.[18] The first part, 'From Grotesque to Gross-out', takes as its principal object the contemporary gross-out comedy, which is examined principally in the light of the theory of carnivalesque inversion of social norms developed by Mikhail Bakhtin and other more general socio-cultural and anthropological perspectives. Examples range from the mainstream Hollywood productions of the Farrelly Brothers to the extreme represented by the early films of John Waters. The second part of this chapter, 'A Space Outside: Childishness, Play and the "Pre-Oedipal"', combines socio-cultural and Freudian psychoanalytical approaches to consider the recurrence of forms of comedy and comic performance that seem to offer a return to an innocent state of early childhood.

The subject matter of Chapter Three, 'Satire and Parody', is more self-explanatory. Satire is examined as a form of comedy with a political edge, examples including recent Hollywood satires of the American political system and satirical visions produced in the former Soviet Union, Eastern Europe, Cuba and other parts of Latin America. Parody, a form that has become ubiquitous in film comedy in recent years, is distinguished from satire largely in terms of a change of comic target, from the social-political arena to that of film forms and conventions, although the distinction is far from always entirely clear. Chapter Four, 'Comedy and Representation', considers the role of comedy in the politics of the representation of particular social groups, focusing on the dimensions of gender, race/ethnicity and national identity. Chapter Five, 'Comedy Beyond Comedy', returns in more detail to some issues considered above: specifically, the role and effect of elements of comedy used in films that are not defined principally as comedies, including the use of comedy as light relief and darker and potentially more disturbing blends of the comic and non-comic.

Comedy is a huge subject, even when confined to the single medium of film. The aim of this book is to explore a number of central issues, but it does not pretend to achieve exhaustive coverage. An effort has been made to include as wide a range of geographical and historical examples as is possible in a single volume but the dominant Hollywood tradition retains centre stage and many varieties and examples of comedy are, inevitably, omitted from consideration. Comedy has suffered from relative critical and theoretical neglect in Film Studies; largely, it seems, as a result of its apparent lack of weighty respectability and, perhaps, its sheer ubiquity in the routine commercial mainstream. A number of works in recent years have sought to redress this imbalance of attention,[19] although it remains surprising that, at the time of writing, no up-to-date single-authored volume focused on a wide range of comedy in film alone is in existence; a fact that this book seeks to rectify.

one

comedy and narrative

Gags vs. narrative in early slapstick

'This is a very importance conference and I do not wish to be interrupted,' demands the smooth and scheming Sylvanian ambassador, Trentino (Louis Calhern), in *Duck Soup* (1933). He is promptly subjected to an outrageous series of gags and disruptions as he attempts to get any sense out of his two 'spies' Chicolino and Pinky (Chico and Harpo Marx) on their surveillance of the newly installed Freedonian leader Rufus T. Firefly (Groucho). To give just one extract from a rapid-fire series of silliness: 'Did you bring me his record?' asks Trentino. Harpo produces a gramophone record from under his coat. 'No, no,' protests Trentino, flinging it into the air, to which Harpo responds without missing a beat by drawing a gun and shooting it down like a clay pigeon. Chico rings a bell on Trentino's desk and presents Harpo with a cigar, trapping the ambassador's fingers in the box as he shuts it. Trentino persists, valiantly, demanding 'a full, detailed' report of their investigation; more nonsense, word-play and physical abuse ensues.

Comedy is often disruptive. It messes things up and undermines 'normal' behaviour and conventions. This has a range of potential social-cultural or political implications that will be considered at numerous points in this book. Comedy in film sometimes works through the disruption of dominant expectations about the ways of the world. It can also play havoc with conventions more specific to film itself. Narrative, or story development, is often subject to

19

the kinds of frustrations faced by Ambassador Trentino. 'Gentlemen, we are not getting anywhere,' he protests, a complaint that might be shared by those who dislike this particular style of comedy.

What, then, is the relationship between comedy and narrative? It varies. Some comedy is closely integrated with narrative, emerging quite smoothly from narrative situations. But not all. Many film comedies have been seen as little more than strings of gags tied only loosely together by narrative thread. Even comedies that invest more highly in narrative development are often freed from some of the constraints usually associated with narrative, particularly its the dominant incarnation: the 'classical Hollywood' form of narration. Classical Hollywood narrative is usually characterised by the telling of a largely coherent story. A series of events is presented, each of which is meant to be linked in a more or less clear pattern of causes and effects. Other features are supposed to be subordinated primarily to the main task of telling the story. Characters are meant to be reasonably believable, their actions generally explained by coherent motivations. Qualifications such as 'largely', 'more or less' and 'reasonably' are required in the description of this kind of narrative style because the coherence of 'classical' narrative is only approximate, not always subject to closer examination. Gaps and unmotivated coincidences are rife in classical Hollywood cinema, but they are usually passed speedily over by sheer assertiveness, emotion and forward momentum.

Different modes or genres obey different conventional rules of plausibility. Gaps and implausibilities are often allowed in the fast-moving contemporary action cinema, for example, that might not be acceptable in a more 'serious' or 'substantial' drama. Horror, science fiction or fantasy have generically motivated scope for departures from the norm, as suggested in the Introduction. So does comedy, and perhaps more so. Genres such as horror, science fiction and fantasy are expected to maintain a reasonable level of narrative coherence *in their own terms*, given the premise that allows for 'abnormal' events such as intrusions from and into other dimensions (they tend to come in for criticism if they do not). Comedy, by its very nature, can be given freer reign. Absurd behaviour is permitted, expected even. Outrageous coincidences or *deus ex machina* devices are acceptable to a greater extent than elsewhere (Neale & Krutnik 1990: 102). This can be a source of comedy in itself, as in many Buster Keaton two-reelers, where actions have a habit of coming back around in unlikely boomerang effects whose logic owes more to the fantastic realm of comedy than anything found in the real world. In *The Goat* (1921), for example, Buster is being chased by police. He takes care of one contingent by locking them in the back of a truck. The action continues until later, when walking freely down a street, he comes upon a (the) truck being unloaded – and out tumble the police right in front of him. Where lack of plausible explanation is generally glossed over in other modes,[1] it is something to which our attention is often drawn in comedy. In *Road to Morocco* (1942), the Bob Hope and Bing Crosby characters are deposited in the desert, trussed and tied up in netting. Next scene, they are free. 'Say, how did we get loose with our hands and feet tied and everything?' asks Hope, to which Crosby replies: 'If we told anybody they'd never believe it.'

Normal rules of physiological causality do not always apply, as in an early sequence in *The Patsy* (1964) in which the Jerry Lewis character, Stanley Belt, falls from a hotel window (continuing his fall in a series of still cut-out images over the opening credits) only to land on a diving board and bounce back up through the window. This style of comedy owes much to that of animated cartoons, where the world can take on a fantastic plasticity in which both normal narrative plausibility and the laws of physics can be overridden at will. In the classic routine in which cartoon characters keep running in midair, until the moment of realisation that no ground lies underfoot, the rule of the subjective comes to dominate over objective reality. The physical consequences of actions are frequently ignored, including those involved in the vertiginous drop that follows the running-in-the-air gag in Road Runner cartoons and elsewhere. Bodies spring back into shape after being subjected to every conceivable distortion. Logical sequences of events are prone to all sorts of short-cuts and subversions. In *Devil May Hare* (1954), for example, Bugs Bunny disposes of a Tasmanian Devil by telephoning the Tasmanian Post-Dispatch, placing an advertisement seeking a Devil bride; no sooner has he replaced the receiver than the sound of a plane is overhead, the bride lands and the antagonist is safely contained by marriage.

The real and the illusory undergo a process of continual transformation. In *Hot Rod and Reel* (1959), Wile E. Coyote sets up a fake railroad crossing – a short length of track, a sign, a recording of train sounds – in his latest attempt to capture the Road Runner. As he stands on the track and is about to capture his prey ... he is mown down by a real train. A similar gag occurs in *Gee Whiz-z-z-z* (1956) when he falls down the gap in a painted illusion of a broken bridge. In Tex Avery's *Happy Go Nutty* (1944), a dog paints a bomb red – disguising it as an apple – and gives it to his quarry, Screwy Squirrel. The latter takes a bite and proceeds to eat it as a real apple, while the fuse continues to burn. He discards the core; it is picked up by the dog and – predictably, in this context – explodes, reverting to its original status. The status of animation, an extra degree removed from any pretense at representation of the 'real' world, establishes a modality in which greater extremes of comic craziness are licensed. This kind of transformation is also a frequent source of gags in the slapstick tradition, however, as in a routine in *Long Pants* (1927) in which Harry Langdon's character mistakes a ventriloquist's dummy for a policeman but then gets into trouble by throwing a brick at the 'dummy' after it has been replaced by a real officer. Such are the departures of the cartoon-comic world that a gag can also be made from a reversion to something half-way closer to normal logic. In *Fast and Furry-ous* (1949), Road Runner produces a notice saying, reasonably enough, 'Road Runner can't read', to account for ignoring Coyote's fake 'School Crossing' sign.

A direct translation of the cartoon style is found in some live-action features, including aspects of the work of Frank Tashlin, who began his career in animation, and Preston Sturges (see Henderson 1991). Laws of biology and mechanics are contravened: the impossible contortion of the body of Jerry Lewis at the hands of a masseur (leg bent back behind head, legs tied in a knot) in *Artists and Models* (1955) and the magically implausible cartoon route taken by a runaway golf ball in *Who's Minding the Store* (1963) (Henderson 1991: 154). A typically cartoon-style reversal occurs in *Bananas* (1971), in which Fielding Mellish (Woody Allen) does the standard military-idiot routine of blowing up his hand after pulling the pin from a grenade and throwing the pin; next time, he ponders a moment, gets it right, keeps hold of the pin and throws the grenade and … the pin explodes, the kind of painful illogic that constantly befalls the schemes of Wile E. Coyote. A more thoroughgoing merger of animated and live-action forms occurs in *The Mask* (1994), in which the central character played by Jim Carrey gains cartoon-like qualities of extreme action, literal eye-popping, jaw-dropping and other forms of distortion. The whole point, for many comedies, is to be unconstrained by the usual limitations created by demands for sanity or narrative coherence. Comedy can be a 'spanner in the works' as Frank Krutnik (1995) puts it, authorising all kinds of disruption and silliness.

Much debate on film comedy has revolved around this issue, the relationship between comic moments, gags and pratfalls and broader narrative structure. The kind of comedy that disrupts, or has little investment in, narrative coherence has been both celebrated and criticised; seen as either a wonderfully free-form and potentially anarchic force or as an inadequately developed or 'immature' comedy. One way to avoid such polarised judgements, and to gain a more detailed understanding of the relationship between comedy and narrative, is to look more closely at the historical context in which film comedy developed. This is a reason for starting with a focus on this particular formal perspective: it takes us back to the origins of both film comedy and film itself.

In the beginning was the gag. The first film comedies, such as *L'Arroseur arrosé*, were single jokes, their narrative dimensions minimal beyond a rudimentary process of cause-and-effect (boy stands on hosepipe: water stops; boy removes foot when man looks down pipe: man soaked). *L'Arroseur arrosé* provided a model for many of the short, one-shot films made from 1896 to 1905, a period in which comedies and trick films were the most common fictional productions (Gunning 1995a). According to one authoritative calculation, comedies accounted for 70 per cent of fictional films in the period before 1908 (Bowser 1990: 179). Comedies began to extend in length through the elaboration or repetition of the basic gag. *That Fatal Sneeze* (1905) offers a good example. A mischievous boy exacts revenge by impregnating a man's handkerchief with pepper. The man sneezes violently, causing chaos and destruction wherever he goes. The comic action of the film is comprised of a simple repetition of the gag, narrative development existing only in the increased number of outraged victims in pursuit and a climactic sneeze of such violence that the protagonist disappears.

Cinema as a whole was characterised in its first two decades by a development of more extended narratives. As films became longer, eventually reaching feature length, events tended to become more integrated and less episodic. This was true of some comedies, particularly in the development of more 'genteel' forms in the 1910s, films that located their comedy within a 'respectable' world of middle-class characters and institutions such as the marriage and the family (Neale & Krutnik 1990: 115; Bowser 1990: 180). Examples include *A Cure for Pokeritis* (1912) and *Foxtrot Finesse* (1915), featuring the early comic stars John Bunny and Sidney Drew, respectively. Comedy emerges from situation in both cases, from scenarios of hen-pecked husbands devising ultimately unsuccessful ploys to escape the attentions of domineering wives (narratives that bear a close resemblance to more recent generations of television sit-com). Others resisted this tendency, continuing to offer sequences of 'crude' slapstick incidents rather than more logically developed plots. The best-known examples are the crazy antics of the world of Mack Sennett, creator of the legendary Keystone Kops.

Many comic shorts from the 1910s and 1920s display a mix of slapstick and narrative, the balance of which varies from one example to another. Chaplin's *Shoulder Arms* (1918), for example, starts out as a series of comic sketches of 'life in the army' and in the trenches, without any real narrative development beyond the establishment and exploration of aspects of that situation. An episodic sequence-of-gags effect is underlined by the movement from one skit to another though a series of fade-outs. A plot begins to develop half way through the film. Chaplin's character gains in confidence, nonchalantly allowing the enemy to open his wine bottle and light his cigarette by holding them up into the line of fire. He takes an enemy trench single-handed and is volunteered for a mission behind enemy lines. Numerous incidents of basic slapstick humour are inserted more or less arbitrarily into these adventures (including anal assaults with a hot poker). They culminate with the capture of the Kaiser, before being deflated by the dénouement in which it all turns out to have been a dream.

A more substantial narrative framework is established from the start of *The Pilgrim* (1923), in which Chaplin plays an escaped convict mistaken for the new preacher in a western town. Some of the gags arise directly from the narrative situation. So, when Chaplin bluffs his way comically through a church service, much of the comedy comes from inappropriate behaviour rooted in the character's real identity. His foot reaches, instinctively, for the 'bar' when he stands at the pulpit; he takes out a cigarette in front of the congregation; sits and twiddles his thumbs when he should be giving the sermon. But some are closer to arbitrary and unmotivated slapstick. An extended sequence of foolery ensues between Chaplin and a pesky child, at the house where he is lodging. It climaxes with the destruction of a man's bowler hat that becomes mixed up in a pudding. This sequence could, quite conceivably, have been made of direct relevance to the Chaplin character's masquerade. It could have been structured to lead to his recognition and potential unveiling by the wronged owner of the hat, for example. But it does not. It serves little purpose other than its own slapstick appeal, as do numerous other incidents.

Each of these films can be located in a period of transition, in which Chaplin is attempting to solve the problems posed by fitting an established comic character into longer narrative frameworks (Kerr 1975: 161–3). They were produced under the terms of an eight-film contract between Chaplin and First National. *Shoulder Arms* (1918) is a three-reel film in which narrative is developed but seems to remain secondary to the sequence of gags. *The Pilgrim* (1923) – at four reels, technically a feature – is a move further in the direction of narrative integration. Chaplin had also starred in the first feature-length comedy, *Tillie's Punctured Romance* (1914), directed by Mack Sennett, a film that offers a distinctly uneven balance of gag and narrative elements. On the one hand, it is a longer film with a sustained plot, charting the ups and downs of the Chaplin con-artist's attempt to obtain the savings or inheritance of a country girl (Marie Dressler). On the other, its debt is more clearly to the Sennett tradition, moment-by-moment activity dominated throughout by violent slapstick routines culminating in the obligatory Keystone Kops chase.

A number of factors helped to shape the different forms taken by comedy in this period. Narrative was becoming more central to the cinema. So was the feature-length film, a factor that itself encouraged a move towards a greater degree of narrative integration. A series of gags could be sustained with little other support in the one- or two-reel short; a more substantial framework seemed to be demanded by the full-length feature. But the continued existence of non-narratively organised comic incident was not simply a disruption of, or failure to achieve, narrative coherence, however much that might appear to be the case in an early feature such as *Tillie's Punctured Romance*. It had its own specific dynamic and roots. Debates about the relative merits of slapstick and narrative integration are less helpful than a recognition of two distinct *modes* of cinema that were involved, each driven by particular historical and institutional contexts.

Gag-based slapstick comedy, like much early cinema, has its roots in popular theatrical forms such as variety, vaudeville, music hall or burlesque. None of these forms are characterised by the development of sustained narratives. The variety or vaudeville bill consisted of a group of short acts, skits or routines following one after another. Individual acts might contain minor elements of narrative organisation. A structure of sorts might exist from one act to another, balancing one variety with another and building towards a climactic finale. But there was no overarching structure of a specifically narrative kind. The brand of comedy favoured by this context was slapstick and gag-based, 'instantly intelligible, full of powerfully marked effects designed to produce an instant (and audible) audience response' (Neale & Krutnik 1990: 113). Much comedy continues to bear the marks of this inheritance. Institutions such as vaudeville and music hall contributed many of the stars of film comedy in the first half of the twentieth century, including figures such as Chaplin, Keaton, the Marx Brothers and W. C. Fields in America, and George Formby, Gracie Fields and the Crazy Gang in Britain. Comedy films often included direct translations of these acts onto the screen. A comic drunk act perfected on the vaudeville stage was employed by Chaplin in films such as *Mabel's Married Life* (1914), *One A.M.* (1916) and *The Cure* (1916). Keaton's films use a variety of stunts and skills developed from his background as part of a stage comedy-acrobat act ('The Three Keatons'). Film performances by W. C. Fields drew on routines for which he had gained fame in vaudeville, including a pool-hall act used, among others, in the early short *Pool Sharks* (1915).[2] The early films of the Marx Brothers were translations of full-length Broadway shows that built, in turn, on their earlier vaudeville performances. The films of Formby and Fields were organised to a large extent around the musical-comedy personae and performances developed by the stars in music hall and variety; the antics of the Crazy Gang, similarly, were translated largely intact to the screen in films such as *O-Kay for Sound* (1937) (Medhurst 1986). Subsequent generations of comedy have drawn on performers with reputations established in radio, television or stand-up comedy, also often in variety or sketch-based rather than narrative-led formats.

The mode that governs this type of comedy is described as 'performative' or 'presentational', based on a performance played directly out to the audience, whose presence is openly acknowledged. Thus, the waterer of *L'Arroseur arrosé* brings the miscreant up to the foreground of the image to *display* his chastisement; the mischievous boy of *That Fatal Sneeze* makes a self-conscious *show* to the camera of the act of filling his target's handkerchief with pepper. In Tom Gunning's (1990) influential account, early films in general, until 1906, constitute a 'cinema of attractions', designed to stimulate and excite viewers in the manner of a fairground attraction. This is contrasted with a narrative mode, in which performance is directed inwards, as part of a self-sufficient fictional world in which the presence of the viewer is not explicitly acknowledged.

Comedy based on sequences of gags performed with little or no concern for their place in any larger narrative has its own history and rationale, in other words, rather than being either inherently disruptive or in some way deficient. The merits of this kind of comedy have been questioned by some critics, writing from the perspective of the later period in which narrative integration was often taken for granted as a basic assumption of 'artistic' film quality. Gerald Mast, for example, labels the slapstick of Sennett as 'primitive'; whatever its merits, in terms of 'exuberance' and 'vitality', it is found wanting for its lack of attention to human motivation or psychology (1979: 43). The early work of figures such as Chaplin and Keaton is examined less on its own terms than from the perspective of their later, more narratively-integrated work. The past, here, is understood teleologically, in terms of assumptions developed after the fact. This was the fate of early cinema in general until relatively recently: judged as crude and 'primitive' rather than being understood in its own specific context. A turn towards a closer analysis of historical context in Film Studies in the 1980s and 1990s helped to correct this tendency.[3] But the more 'crude' variety of slapstick comedy also came in for plenty of criticism in its own time, within the industry, for reasons closely allied to the factors that drove the wider movement towards a cinema of greater narrative integration. Particularly at issue here was the question of the audience and cultural position sought by cinema owners in the United States.

A number of factors encouraged the movement towards narrative-centred formats, in comedy and more generally. Changes occurred throughout the film business as it became an increasingly large-scale industrial enterprise. The precise shape in which films were seen by audiences had been subject to considerable influence by the individual exhibitor. In the early years the exhibitor could buy or rent many films on a scene-by-scene basis, or even decide in what order they should be screened. This business arrangement lent itself to the modular, gag-centred form of comedies such as *That Fatal Sneeze*, in which individual gags or sequences could be added or removed without undermining the overall effect. Control gradually shifted to the production end of the business during the 1910s, partly as a result of the growth of the industry and the dominant position gained by the feature-length film. Features offered the prospect of larger profits and required a more centralised and rationalised mode of production, distribution and exhibition. The development of the feature film was, in turn, tied up with a strategy of seeking to attract a more middle-class audience to the cinema.

Slapstick comedy came in for criticism in the American film trade press during the late 1910s and early 1920s because of its low standing among the classes the industry was seeking to attract.[4] Middle-class audiences were more affluent and so could support higher admission prices. To attract them, the emphasis of the industry moved – partially, at least – towards the production of films with more culturally 'respectable' associations, based on novels, short stories and legitimate theatre: the primary sources of what was to become the 'classical' narrative form. Slapstick and gag-based comedy was deemed to be a 'lower' cultural form, filled with 'crude' and violent behaviour (including a propensity for assaults on the lower regions of the body, especially the backside); more suited to less affluent audiences from lower-class backgrounds. It was also subject to criticism from reform movements, to which the film business felt obliged to respond to avert the threat of censorship or other forms of regulation.

Physical slapstick remained a popular source of profits, however, as Peter Kramer suggests, leading the industry to adopt a somewhat Janus-faced approach to these issues. Displays of slapstick, especially those of a violent nature, had to be justified by an emphasis on narrative context and a location within publicity and critical discourses emphasising the respectability of any individual title. At the same time, in a case such as *The Butcher Boy* (1917), the violent antics of the stars Fatty Arbuckle and Buster Keaton were highlighted as the main attraction in trade adverts designed to play up the qualities thought most likely to sell the film to distributors. A divergence is suggested, as Kramer puts it, 'between a discourse of effectivity primarily driven by a concern for audience pleasures and industry profits, and a discourse of respectability' (2001: 110). A trade-off between the appeals of 'respectable' narrative-led drama and 'crude' spectacular attraction (from the lunatic ballet of violent slapstick encounters to contemporary gross-out, action and special effects) has been a characteristic of Hollywood cinema ever since. A temporary compromise was reached at the level of exhibition during the 1910s. Comedy in general, and slapstick in particular, underwent a revival from 1911, its previous dominance having been undercut by a shift towards more dramatic forms and towards more 'polite' character and narrative-based varieties of comedy (according to Bowser, the previously favourable ratio between comedy and drama was reversed between 1907 and 1908). This was the moment at which Sennett came into his own with the formation of the Keystone company. One reason for the revival, as Kramer suggests, was the consolidation of an exhibition strategy in which comedies were relegated to the role of shorter supporting acts. The pleasures of slapstick could thus be acknowledged, indulged and given a place on the bill, as a sideshow, without detracting from the claims of moral respectability attached to the main feature (111).

This put slapstick in a commercially marginalised, secondary position, however, at a time when the feature-length film was becoming the industry standard and the greatest source of profits (Neale & Krutnik 1990: 119). As a result, key figures in the tradition of short slapstick comedy such as Harold Lloyd, Buster Keaton and Charlie Chaplin began to move into features during the late 1910s and early 1920s. The wilder antics of slapstick were often discarded in favour of comedy that fitted more easily into the feature-length format (and that, in the process, helped to meet some of the demands of those seeking an image of greater respectability). Keaton himself wrote of the abandonment of 'what we called impossible or cartoon gags', suited to comic shorts but out of place in the 'full-length' picture (quoted in Neale & Krutnik 1990: 121).

A variable balance between slapstick/gag and narrative continued to characterise many of these films. Narrative might have become of greater overall importance, but the precise degree of emphasis was subject to shifts that did not entail a simple one-way 'evolutionary' development in its favour. The Keaton feature *College* (1927), for example, has a largely episodic structure. The centre of the film is comprised of a series of gags in which Keaton's character demonstrates his comic inability to perform at baseball and track-and-field sports. It is repetitive and rather predictable. But it is narratively motivated: he has to achieve at sports, rather than remaining brilliant only as a scholar, if he is to win the girl he loves. And the series of comic-failure actions is mirrored, structurally, in the character's eventual success: after an unlikely triumph as coxswain to the college boat crew, he rushes to the rescue of the girl, triumphantly running, hurdling, jumping, pole-vaulting and hurling various discus and javelin-type objects in the process (comedy resulting at least partly from the under-motivated and, by normal standards, highly implausible transformation in his abilities).

Keaton's earlier *Our Hospitality* (1923) has been celebrated as an example of more consistently narrative-integrated silent feature comedy. It develops a linear narrative in which the Keaton character, Willie McKay, gets caught up in an ancient Southern clan feud. It also deploys a number of recurring motifs and other devices that help to achieve an effect of visual and comic unity between one sequence and another (Bordwell & Thompson 1997: 200–5). Some of the gags pick up on and play around with images produced in earlier sequences. One involves Keaton's character and a fishing rod (he catches a tiny fish); it is mirrored later when his diminutive body dangles hazardously on a rope suspended on a log (more small fry). Patterns such as these give the film a rich and self-allusive texture. But there remain plenty of gags and gag-sequences that exist primarily for their own sake, including a lengthy and playful series during McKay's trip south by train that could be omitted without any significant narrative consequences. Comedy grows out of the basic narrative situation, which undergoes some development (McKay's realisation at one point, for example, that the people with whom he has become involved are members of the deadly rival Canfield clan). But it is questionable whether the narrative is developed very far beyond the scope found in two-reel Keaton shorts such as *The Goat*, in which his character is mistaken for an escaped murderer, or *My Wife's Relations* (1922), in which a language mix-up leads to accidental marriage to a large Irish woman and her loutish family, or many others. An initial narrative premise provides the basis for a series of comic routines in each case; some narrative progression occurs, but not a great deal and not with the kind of forward-driving 'classical' momentum that outweighs the impact of a more performative dynamic that delights in the antics of the star.

In the 1920s and 1930s narrative-centred romantic comedy forms began in more concerted fashion to displace slapstick as the most prevalent form of comedy, a subject to which we will return later. But slapstick and gag-based comedy did not disappear, even if it was usually reigned in to a greater extent by the constraints of narratively-situated plausibility. Comedy, along with the musical, is singled out by Tom Gunning as one of two forms in which the cinema of attractions most clearly persisted in the face of the requirements of classical narrative integration. Comic routines, like musical numbers, constitute potential ruptures in the narrative fabric, harking back to the performative traditions of vaudeville and variety. Comedy performers have continued to occupy a performative as well as a narrative role, even in more narratively-sustained feature productions. They are often permitted the freedom to break the fictional frame, for example, through direct address to the audience, a characteristic trait of performers ranging from Groucho Marx and Bob Hope to Woody Allen, each of which can be rooted in aspects of pre-cinematic performance. Plenty of comedy from the 1910s to the 1930s is narratively situated, narratively framed, of greater-or-lesser direct narrative relevance. But, within this context, scope remains for the comic performance or gag sequence that is largely detached from narrative motivation. The combination of slapstick and narrative-integration offered by many films in this period can be explained in part by an industrial strategy of trying to appeal to a range of audiences (Jenkins 1992). A degree of sustained narrative combined with more subtle and nuanced gags, such as many of those found in the films of Chaplin and Keaton, was likely to appeal to the 'respectable' middle-class element. The 'mass' or lower-class audience remained important, however, and was catered for by the provision of healthy doses of slapstick, farce and pratfall.

Duck Soup is one of the most extreme examples of what could still be achieved in Hollywood by the end of the 1920s, a brand of lunacy described by Henry Jenkins as 'anarchistic' comedy, in which narrative momentum is constantly undermined by the madcap activities of the comic stars. Specific historical developments might also help to account for this particular outbreak of narratively-disruptive comedy, in the early 1930s. A fresh burst of performative comedy appears to have resulted from the advent of the sound film, which prompted the recruitment by Hollywood of a new wave of performers from vaudeville and Broadway. The anarchistic variety in full flow proved short-lived, the product of a transitional period. A combination of pressure from studio heads and the declining box-office success of the format led to greater conformity to classical norms in the second half of the 1930s (Jenkins 1992). The Marx Brothers themselves were subjected to greater constraints in their later films: madness continued, but it tended to be mobilised to some extent in the service of, rather than in opposition to, narrative developments. In *A Night at the Opera* (1935), the mayhem is used in pursuit of, as well as alongside, the principal non-comic narrative goals established at the start: the achievement of romance between the singers Rosa (Kitty Carlisle) and Ricardo (Allan Jones), and the recognition of the latter's talent. A number of classic Marx Brothers routines revolve around the effort to smuggle Ricardo, along with Fiorello (Chico Marx) and Tomasso (Harpo) into the United States. Some of the chaos of *A Day at the Races* (1937) works, similarly, in support of the efforts of a young couple, Judy (Maureen O'Sullivan) and Gil (Allan Jones), to raise funds to maintain her ownership of a debt-ridden sanitarium. The usual panoply of Marx Brothers mayhem is used in the climactic sequences of these films but in both cases it operates to further narrative ends: to give Ricardo his chance to perform on stage in *A Night at the Opera* and, in *A Day at the Races*, to delay the start of a race long enough to enable the horse owned by Gil to escape capture and join the race in order to win the prize money required to save the sanitarium. Goal-oriented narrative still remains largely in the background in both films, however, and can hardly be said to come close to dominating films organised around numerous lengthy comic and musical routines.

The balance between gag- and narrative-centred formats underwent a similar process of change in the animated sector, although the cartoon short held onto its place in the cinema longer than its live-action equivalent, creating greater space for less narrative-centred approaches. Comedy cartoons had roots in vaudeville similar to those of the slapstick tradition. Cartoons of the early sound era were often anarchic, their crazy antics lacking much in the way of coherent motivation or logical sequence. From 1934, Norman Klein (1993) suggests, a move away from the gag-based format can be identified, a tendency driven by the market leader, Disney. Characters became more stable, their activities required to be integrated into the development of more focused narrative dynamics. Anarchy was replaced by a moralistic tone, although the struggle between the two became a theme of many Disney cartoons. The shift was a product of numerous factors, Klein suggests, including but not limited to the constraints imposed by the creation in 1934 of the Production Code Administration to enforce voluntary regulation of content in Hollywood. Disney was also seeking, largely for economic reasons, to give its products qualities closer to those of live-action cinema, a more elaborate illusion in terms of both quality and 'depth' of animation and of more developed (sentimentalised, melodramatic) narrative structure.

A return to an antic, fast-paced gag style is found in many animated shorts from the later 1930s, however. Animators such as Tex Avery, Chuck Jones and Bob Clampett developed a format characterised by a highly ritualised and reductive adversary structure, such as that found in innumerable Bugs Bunny and Road Runner cartoons, in which the moralising of the Disney tradition is often directly undermined (see Klein 1993). Classic fairy-tales were given a raunchy and distinctly amoral twist by Tex Avery in *Red Hot Riding Hood* (1943) and *Swing Shift Cinderella* (1945), two almost identical scenarios in which the usually innocent heroine is transformed into a curvaceous and scantily-clad siren, singing in nightclubs. The wolf becomes an urbane suitor, pursuing Riding Hood/Cinderella but himself subject to the sexual designs of Grandma. In neither case are the strong, seductive female figures placed in any conventional or punishing moral/narrative frame. A conscious rejection of the Disney-type tradition is made at the start of *Red Hot Riding Hood*. A conventional version of the story is interrupted by the complaints of the characters: 'I'm fed up with that sissy stuff,' says the wolf. 'It's the same old story over and over. If you can't do this thing a new way, I quit.' Greater space for this kind of material was provided by the wartime context, in which the need for entertainment (including the amusement of troops serving overseas) was sometimes given higher priority than moral regulation.

Shifts and changes in the formative years of American comedy were to have wider implications in the world of film comedy, the later 1910s being the period in which the US industry gained international economic dominance that has never seriously been challenged. Slapstick or gag-based comedy has continued to offer the potential to undermine the conventions of classical-style narrative. But it is often mobilised alongside or within reasonably coherent and ordered plots. How exactly the two dimensions interrelate remains variable and open to differing interpretations. It is certainly the case that comedies have often been *constructed around* gags as much as plots, in terms of the genesis of individual projects in the production process. Where the story outline was developed first in the silent era, it was often adjusted to fit the selected gags, as the director Frank Capra, who worked as a joke writer for Mack Sennett, recalls; and 'it was not unusual to reverse the general order of story preparation and work out plots to embody a series of gags which had been worked out independently' (Capra 1927: 64). The 'gag man' – as distinct from the writer or director – was a key creative figure in the silent and early-sound eras, generally unrecognised in the critical canon (for an account of the career of one such figure, Al Boasberg, who helped to shape the work of film comedians including the Marx Brothers and Bob Hope, see Schwartz 2001).

The extent to which narrative 'contains' or is 'disrupted' by the gag has been much debated, especially in studies of American silent comedy.[5] As Henry Jenkins suggests, gags may be more or less integrated into the causal structure of narrative but they retain 'an affective force' apart from any narrative functions; 'gags remain a source of audience fascination that competes directly with plot and character development' (1992: 104). Jenkins offers a useful and balanced account of the relationship between gag and narrative that might result. Up to a point, the distractions of the gag or slapstick incident can be absorbed by the classical Hollywood style of narrative 'without substantial disruption to its coherence and clarity; it may even benefit from the momentary "relief" from narrative consequences such elements provide' (106). Once a certain critical mass is reached, however, 'once the gags develop in sufficient number and demand sufficient interest apart from their consequences, these comic details cease to be servants of the narrative; they instead assume a greater affective charge than the storyline within which they are embedded' (106). At this point, narrative causality becomes subordinated to the appeal of the gag or other forms of comic spectacle. The operative modality here is likely to be one in which implication plays a lesser part. Implication – the extent to which the viewer is encouraged to sympathise or empathise with character – is a function primarily of the narrative dimension; it is in the realm of narrative that grounds for sympathy/empathy are most likely to be developed. It is for this reason, without the maintenance of a very high standard of gags, that the heavily gag-centred comedy can struggle to maintain audience interest and commitment at feature length.

Gags are often dependent for their effects on narrative preconditions, as Neale and Krutnik suggest. Particular incidents or lines of dialogue are comic in many cases only or largely because of the context in which they appear. Jokes, gags or wisecracks are rarely *integral* to forward-moving plot development, however, 'because they require formal closure, often in the form of a punchline. Because of this degree of closure, they are structurally unsuited to narration' (Neale & Krutnik 1990: 47). Gag sequences can be structured in their own right, with different implications in terms of their relationship to narrative. An isolated gag – physical or verbal – might represent only a brief interruption, compared with that constituted by a repeated gag or the working out of a complex series of variations on a theme, a style often found in the comedy of silent stars such as Chaplin or Laurel and Hardy.[6] More than occasional outbreaks of the particularly episodic, gag-based form can usually be explained by specific contextual factors. A spate of epic, sprawling, wide-screen, multi-star/character gag-centred comedy in the 1960s, including *It's a Mad, Mad, Mad, Mad World* (1963), *The Great Race* (1965), *Those Magnificent Men in Their Flying Machines* (1965) and *Monte Carlo or Bust* (1969) can, for example, be seen as part of the broader attempt to use big-screen spectacular forms (including the musical, another highly performative mode) to stem falling audience numbers in the post-war decades. The relationship between gag and performative comedy and narrative can be examined further in the format known as 'comedian comedy', one that has proved popular from the 1910s to the present.

Comedian comedy

Roger Cobb (Steve Martin) struggles, in spasms, for control of his body; one leg fights its way forward across a pavement, the other dragged crazily behind in protest. Daniel Hillard (Robin Williams) reels off a series of quick-fire impressions, from Ronald Reagan to a hotdog. Fletcher Reede (Jim Carrey) contorts his mouth, emits strange noises, wheezes, spits, growls and blubbers his lips before holding them back, putting out his tongue and making more nonsense sounds. These are characters within fictional worlds. Their zany performances have a place and meaning within a sustained narrative situation. One half of Cobb has become possessed by the spirit of the wealthy Edwina Cutwater (Lily Tomlin), the major narrative device in *All of Me* (1984). Hillard has been established as a brilliant-but-unreliable improvisational performer, seeking to impress a stern-faced court official of his suitability to have joint custody of his children in *Mrs Doubtfire* (1993). Reede has been placed under a spell by his young son and is unable to mouth his usual smooth-talking deceptions in *Liar Liar* (1997).

But only partly. Much of what we are offered is the immediacy of the performance of the star comedian, regardless of plot contrivance. The films exist primarily as showcases for these performances. How far are we expected *really* to be very interested in the narrative plights of Cobb, Hillard and Reede rather than the thinly-veiled comic personae of Martin, Williams and Carrey?

Are these just an excuse for the main attractions, the crazy performances of comic stars doing their inimitable stuff? Steve Martin 'does' a Steve Martin; Williams a Williams, Carrey a Carrey; as have previous generations of film comedians. The name of the comic performer, and the promise of the routine, is usually the main box-office draw.

These films do have carefully developed narrative frames, however. They obey the dominant conventions of the 'classical' Hollywood narrative format to a large extent. The central characters are strongly goal-driven: Cobb seeks a more meaningful existence than his life as a lawyer relegated to dealing with the idle rich; Hillard is desperate to regain access to his children after being rejected by an exasperated wife; Reede is torn between the demands of legal career advancement and the needs of his son. The main plot is entangled, in each case, with a heterosexual romance sub-plot of one kind or another. The movement of comic events is generally driven forward quite briskly through a succession of causes-and-effects. These are the basics of 'classical' Hollywood narrative style and seem to play a stronger role in these films than they do generally in the feature-length productions featuring comedian stars of the silent or early sound era. Films such as *All of Me*, *Mrs Doubtfire* and *Liar Liar* are structured with the intent to ensure that we do, actually, care about characters as well as star comedy performance. The operative modality is not just that of comic inconsequentiality. Familiar Hollywood devices are utilised, sometimes melodramatic – especially in the case of *Mrs Doubtfire* and *Liar Liar*, which play on the needs of 'vulnerable' children – to seek the emotional allegiance of the viewer, to draw us towards the narrative situation of the central protagonists. The viewer is offered a significant degree of implication as well as the distance and 'insulation' provided by comedy. This is a blend found in many comedian comedies but to varying extents; little if anything in the way of implication is found in the films of the Marx Brothers, for example, especially as far as the thinly-disguised, almost non-characters played by the brothers themselves are concerned.

The result might be described as a hybrid form, a mixture of 'classical' narrative integration and the performative/presentational. The existing comic persona of the star is used to shape the fictional character. Cobb is painted from the start as an eccentric in the legal profession, taking his shaggy pet dog with him to the office and playing jazz in a band at night. Hillard's unconventional performing abilities and his nonconformist character are also established in the opening scenes, in which he is fired for inserting his own subversive lines into the voice-overs he is providing for an animated film. Reede's fast-talking legal performances are earning success in the business but his style and initial cynicism are painted as extreme. The comedian is taken *into* a fictional universe; or, rather, a fictional universe is built around the comedian. The process of integration in these cases is considerable; but it is not total. Comic persona is worked into the on-going depiction of events and character, but there are moments or sequences in which it remains more overtly on display, when the forward-moving dynamic of narrative is disrupted, challenged or rivaled by a focus on comic performance that can be appreciated for its own sake. This is partly a matter of staging, the effects of which are variable.

Steve Martin's extraordinary bodily antics occur on a pavement outside the offices of the legal firm for which he works: within a fictional space. Some interaction occurs with bemused passers-by, but not a great deal. To a large extent, he could be on a stage, performing from his one-man show. Little else matters than the struggle going on within, and being expressed through, the writhing body of the performer. This is a crucial narrative moment, setting up the entire premise of the film, yet also one of the performative high points: the perfect combination, perhaps, of the two dimensions typical of the comedian comedy. The Robin Williams impression sequence also occupies a position that seems partly inside and partly outside the fictional (or diegetic) space of the film. The narrative situation, again, is a significant one. Much rests on the ability of Daniel Hillard to impress the court official. Yet the staging is at least half-way in breach of the classical Hollywood norm. One departure that is often permitted in comedian comedy is the direct address of the performer to the viewer, as we have seen, an inheritance of the vaudeville-type aesthetic. This does not quite happen in this instance.

Williams/Hillard is framed in mid-shot from the chest upwards. The shot is taken from slightly over the shoulder of his interlocutor, but it intrudes only partially into the frame. He occupies most of the picture. His body faces more or less towards the viewer. His look, however, is just off towards screen left. He faces his fellow character in the diegetic universe, according to the rules of narrative integration, but *almost* faces the viewer as well. This is a familiar classical Hollywood strategy: framing and editing bring the viewer close to a position as if 'inside' the fictional world while maintaining a distinct degree of more 'objective' separation. The balance in this sequence is perhaps a shade closer than usual to a directly presentational style, the over-the-shoulder shot rotated into an open position that offers the performance of Williams a little more directly to the viewer. The decisive indicator of a break from classical convention lies in the way the sequence is edited. The impressions are not given in a single shot or edited according to the usual continuity conventions. Instead, they are separated by jump cuts, the position of the performer shifting slightly but abruptly in each case, a clear marker of a movement into a different register. The effect is to emphasise the virtuoso skills of the performer. The form of editing highlights Williams' quick-fire style and the separated, performative nature of the sequence.

Carrey's 'excessive' performance in *Liar Liar* is more fully integrated into a conventionally-edited fictional space. Part of the sequence is framed in a manner similar to that of the Williams impressions. Carrey appears in upper-body-and-head mid-shot, his body facing the screen while his head and gestures are directed towards another character (a rival lawyer) on screen

Figure 2 Comedian performance integrated into fictional space: Jim Carrey confronts the opposition in *Liar Liar* (1997)

left, the back of whose head and shoulders are included in the shot. But the sequence also includes half a dozen shots from a reverse angle, over Carrey's shoulder, showing the reaction of his colleague, along with two cutaways to the reactions of other protagonists. The montage-heightened and performative impressions given by Robin Williams in *Mrs Doubtfire* are displayed uninterrupted to the viewer. The facial contortions of Carrey are not. He has his back to the camera part of the time and is out of frame in two shots: our view is sacrificed to some extent to that of the other fictional characters.

The comedian performer can be quite tightly integrated into the narrative and into the diegetic space, but retains a license to break the rules, if only on occasion. Most of *Mrs Doubtfire* is edited more conventionally than the sequence described above, integrating the performer more smoothly into the fiction. Steve Martin does a number of heightened 'Steve Martin' routines in *All of Me*, moving at other times into a more 'naturalistic' or conventional acting mode. Even Jim Carrey slows and calms down to something approaching normality. A familiar comic persona is brought to and enacted within these films, along with the construction of fictional character. There may be some variation, but generally this occurs around a central type of comic act associated with the individual performer: Martin's physical contortions, Williams' high-velocity verbal gymnastics, Carrey's facial plasticity. This is far from unique to the comic performer or the format of comedian comedy. Stardom in general often works this way. Many films are designed as vehicles to showcase a particular star performer, and in many cases the performance is based around the enactment of a familiar persona or routine that breaks out of the purely narrative frame. The difference in comedian comedy is generally one of degree, the comedian – like the protagonist of the musical – being permitted greater scope to move towards the domain of outright performativity.

Contemporary comedian comedy is a part of a tradition that dates back to the 1910s, to much the same period as the advent of film stardom as an institution. Comedian comedy, as Douglas Riblet suggests, 'requires not only a recognisable star but also a consistent comic persona from film to film, with the comedy designed specifically around and for this persona' (1995: 182). Film comedies made before 1907 featured neither. Series built around consistent comic personalities were produced from about 1907 in France and Italy, the biggest star being the internationally famous Max Linder. A move towards a comedian-centred format began in America in the early 1910s (see Riblet 1995). The major names to emerge in America were Sidney Drew and John Bunny. Bunny established an identifiable comic persona sustained from one film to another, that of a frustrated and henpecked husband. The identification of role and character was underlined by the use of titles such as *Bunny All at Sea* (1912) and *Bunny's Birthday Surprise* (1913).[7] A general movement towards a focus on the personae of individual performers mirrors to a large extent the development of more extended narrative formats.

Star names such as Mack Sennett and Roscoe 'Fatty' Arbuckle featured in the Keystone shorts produced at the same time as Bunny's films, but in this case the slapstick style of the studio produced a focus on comic action rather than characterisation (Kramer 1988: 101). Keystone moved towards a more personality-centred format, although to a lesser extent than most of its contemporaries. The distinctive Keystone brand was based on a madcap ensemble type of comedy that continued to be produced alongside more comedian-centred films (Riblet 1995: 186). A major impetus towards the wider adoption of the latter was the enormous success of Charlie Chaplin. By 1914, Riblet suggests, Chaplin's name had become the major draw for audiences. His Keystone films began to be promoted under his name more than that of the studio. Posters and other promotional materials depended on recognition of the familiar persona indicated by costume and make-up. The other major figures of the Hollywood silent era, whose fame followed that of Chaplin, are also usually understood in terms of the construction and repeated deployment of a distinct comic appearance and persona sustained from one film to another: the blank and 'stone-faced' persistence of Buster Keaton, the upwardly striving clean-cut 'glasses' figure of Harold Lloyd, the baby-like otherworldly figure of Harry Langdon. Likewise the comedian-stars of the sound era, from the distinct styles of each of the Marx Brothers to figures such as W. C. Fields, Bob Hope, the Abbott and Costello and Jerry Lewis and Dean Martin partnerships, the solo Jerry Lewis, Woody Allen and the performers considered at the start of this section.

The comedian-centred comedy form has proved highly popular in film comedy around the world. Notable British performers include George Formby and Norman Wisdom, typical examples of the hapless 'everyman' character who manages to prevail against overwhelming odds. A more recent manifestation of this unprepossessing figure is the character played by Steve Coogan in *The Parole Officer*, an earnest fool who blunders his way towards success in both the main narrative and the romantic subplot, the style of performance drawing strongly on the comic personae developed by Coogan on television. Other European examples include the distinctively gangling out-of-place figure of Jacques Tati's M. Hulot character in films such as *Les Vacances de Monsieur Hulot* and *Playtime* (1963), and Roberto Benigni's blithely innocent clown in *Johnny Stecchino* ('Johnny Toothpick', 1991), in which the star's naïve school-bus driver, Dante, is set up as a deadringer for a mafiosi (also played by Benigni), a scenario that results in multiple misunderstandings through which the central character passes in total ignorance of the reality of his hazardous situation. The Mexican comedian Cantinflas (Mariano Moreno) achieved superstar status in the Latin American world in a career spanning several decades from the 1940s, another version of the lowly everyman, 'the *pelado*, the scruffy street-wise *pícaro* who deflates the pomposity of political and legal rhetoric' (J. King 2000: 50). Cantinflas specialises in the use of a 'nonsense' language that is almost entirely untranslatable: 'In *Ahí está el detalle* ('There's the Detail', 1940), in a final court scene, he so disrupts the proceedings that the judge and the officials end up using the same nonsense language' (50). Another exponent of nonsense-language comedy is Stephen Chiau, who achieved major-star comic status in Hong Kong in the 1990s, specialising in the role of rural bumpkin achieving unlikely success in the big city.[8] Preceding Chiau as a comedian comic star in Hong Kong is the 'everyman' figure played by Michael Hui in the 1970s and 1980s.[9] Other international examples include the Egyptian version of this figure played by Adel Imam in a series of films starting in the 1960s, in which he triumphs over big-city corruption, and Iran's Alireza Khamseh and Akbar Abdi. Kiyoshi Atsumi, playing the wandering peasant Tora-San, has featured in a long-running series of comedies in Japan, while the top film comedian in Nigeria is Jagua, a conman-trickster figure.[10]

The appeal of comedian comedy, in so many different national contexts, might be explained on both socio-cultural and industrial grounds. The comedian-comic figure tends to be a lowly or relatively ordinary sort, as far as social position is concerned (if not always so 'ordinary' in terms of quirky behaviour). Many of those cited above are scruffy and/or unprepossessing figures, not usually noted for 'star' qualities such as conventionally handsome looks or strong build. Benigni in *Johnny Stecchino* is a typical example; a somewhat rumpled figure, his jacket sleeves a little too long for his arms, his hair untidily tousled, his nose prominent and his hairline receding. Comedian stars are often distinguished on such grounds from straight romantic or action-based heroes. As such, they might offer a more plausible basis for identification or allegiance on the part of the viewer. A smaller gulf exists, generally, between the kinds of worlds they inhabit, and their initial ability to manipulate or adjust to the environments in which they find themselves, and those of the typical spectator. They are less likely to be objects of desire or figures to whose status we might aspire as something superior, distant and exotic.[11] The viewer, potentially, can identify with the predicaments faced by the hapless 'everyman' character, or feel a pleasurable sense of superiority. Our response might be a combination of the two: an element of sympathy or empathy mixed with more distanced comic insulation. In the terms used by Northrop Frye, the mode in which such figures operate is a combination of the 'low mimetic' ('the hero is one of us') and the 'ironic' ('so that we have the sense of looking down on a scene of bondage, frustration, or absurdity') (1957: 34). At the same time, however, it is important to note that the comedian-comic character usually prevails in the end, against the odds, through a fantastic combination of luck, innocence, invention or guile. The combination of relative 'ordinariness' and these magically transformative qualities – associated with 'romance' or the 'high mimetic', in Frye's typology – might be a major source of audience appeal. From an industrial point of view, comedian comedy has proved extremely successful in a range of national, regional and international markets. Generally a lower-budget format, with the exception of the salaries paid to some key performers, it offers the benefits associated with star-led recipes: a product clearly marketable and pre-sold on the basis of a star or central character presence that lends itself strongly to the economies of on-going series production.

The creation of opportunities for the blatant display of the familiar persona/routines of the comedian performer can, of course, occur at the expense of narrative coherence. Far from all comedian-centred films integrate the performers into the narrative dimension as thoroughly as the examples given at the start of this section. The exact balance varies from one case to another. Limited space is left for narrative development in some films featuring the partnership between Jerry Lewis and Dean Martin, for example, given the need to show off the separate performative skills of both comic and crooner; the same goes for the Marx Brothers films, with their obligatory musical as well as comic routines. Narrative tends to be a minor component in the films of Jacques Tati, largely displaced in favour of extended and deadpan comic business involving Tati and his ensembles of performers. *The Bellboy* (1960), a solo Lewis feature, is an extreme example, making a gag out of its own status as little more than a pure sequence of gags. The film starts with an introduction by the 'executive in charge of production' at the studio, who declares it to be 'just a little different, in so far as there is no story and no plot. That's right, I said no story, no plot. It is actually a series of silly sequences; or you might say it is a visual diary of a few weeks in the life of a real "nut"'. The same might be said of many other comedian-centred comedies, including the *Pink Panther* series, featuring Peter Sellers as the bungling Inspector Clouseau; plotting tends to little more than an obligation to be endured while awaiting the next in a series of performative routines such as Clouseau's extended engagement with a vacuum cleaner in *The Return of the Pink Panther* (1975).

It is not always helpful, however, to understand star comic performance as something essentially separate from narrative that can subsequently be integrated – or not – to varying extents. The star comic persona can function effectively as *part of* the narrative infrastructure. Established stars of comedian-centred comedies, like most other stars, bring with them sets of associations and expectations rooted in their distinctive comic personae. Films designed to showcase such performers usually draw on these expectations at the level of both linear plot development and underlying themes. The characteristics associated with the performer play a central role in the moment-by-moment shaping of our anticipation of what is or is not likely to happen. We expect the established figure of Charlie Chaplin to win out, in the end, against larger and potentially oppressive forces or figures, as in his tussle with the overbearing waiter (Eric Campbell) in *The Immigrant* (1917), even if many of his films do not have upbeat endings. We expect Keaton's blithe unawareness to carry him innocently through various travails, as when he stands chopping wood on the tender of a locomotive in *The General* (1927) while rival armies retreat and advance behind him in the background; or, later in the same film, when the blade of his sword flies off, killing an enemy sniper, an event to which he remains entirely oblivious. We expect a degree of unreconstructed mayhem from the Marx Brothers, especially in their earlier films at Paramount. We expect Bob Hope to blunder and bluff his way through an assortment of institutions or film genre conventions, such as those of the chiller in *The Ghost Breakers* (1940) or the western in *The Paleface* (1949). We expect Jerry Lewis, Norman Wisdom or Roberto Benigni characters to prevail, one way or another, despite, or as a result of, their childlike displays of innocence or incompetence. Expectations such as these are a significant aspect of the narrative experience of the films, a major factor in guiding viewers familiar with the star persona through the developing events on screen.

The expectation of eventual success, however haphazardly it might be achieved, can enable the viewer to enjoy the complications almost certain to occur en route. So we – and its historical audience in the cinema – can enjoy the hazardous spectacle of Harold Lloyd's famous ascent of a department store building in *Safety Last* (1923), safe in the knowledge that the Lloyd persona has been established on the basis of his ability always to come out (in this case, literally) on top. Film comedy often involves the display of negative qualities such as failure, incapacity, stupidly, inadequacy and sheer bad luck. The ability of viewers to take pleasure from such qualities might be predicated on the expectation that they will not be unredeemed; that the seemingly incompetent or outgunned 'little guy' will eventually prevail in his own terms (comedian comedy is, generally, a male-dominated form, an issue to which we will return in Chapter Four). Comedies play with such expectations in the same way as many other films, including action movies, for example, in which it is often obligatory for the action superstar to undergo a period of ritual pain, humiliation and suffering to underline the extent of the eventual triumph. The specific effect of comedy here can be to reinforce the 'safety net' of expectations-likely-to-be-realised found in most forms of popular cinema, a guarantee in many cases, as suggested in the Introduction, that we need not take too seriously material that otherwise might sometimes be potentially disturbing.

The expectations and associations rooted in the persona of the individual comedian performer can also come into play at another narrative level: in the articulation of the thematic issues and oppositions around which many film comedies are organised. A common feature is the pitching of the central performer against unsympathetic formal institutions. The fictional character played by the comic is often cast as a rebel or nonconformist, either through active choice or misfit incompetence. In either case, what is usually asserted narratively by comedian comedies is the value of creative individuality in the face of dehumanising abstraction, classic examples including Chaplin's struggle with mechanisation in *Modern Times* (1936) and Tati's more gentle satires of modernity in *Jour de Fête* ('The Big Day', 1949) and *Playtime*. The eccentricity of Roger Cobb in *All of Me* and that of Daniel Hillard in *Mrs Doubtfire* and Fletcher Reede in *Liar Liar* are played off against the stuffiness of institutions such as the law (in all three cases) and the corporate world (in *Mrs Doubtfire*, the domain of Hillard's estranged wife). The wacky personae of Martin, Williams and Carrey play an important part in the establishment of these dynamics. If there is sometimes a problem in the 'fit' between comedian stars and the orderly institution of classical film narrative, the same goes for the ability of their characters to fit into what are often presented as repressive social situations within the fiction; 'disruption' at one narrative level is to some extent the condition of integration at another.

Chaotic trails of destruction have been left through many of the institutions of modern society, from the domestic scene to services such as hospitals and the police. None more so, perhaps, than the military, the regimented ranks of which offer the perfect playground for the disruptive antics of the film comedian. Military institutions are all about precise order, rules and the suppression of individual quirks: the antithesis, usually, of the star comic persona. From Chaplin to Williams, military discipline has existed in comedy in order to be subverted. Witness the hapless attempts of the former to march in step at the start of *Shoulder Arms*, or the anarchic presence of the latter as the disc jockey Adrian Cronauer in *Good Morning Vietnam* (1987).

Good Morning Vietnam opens by establishing the absolute dullness and lifelessness of the military, in the conventional shape of Armed Forces Radio, Saigon, during the Vietnam War. The first voice we hear is that of one of the regular presenters, a ploddingly over-literal and amateurish effort filled with misplaced stress patterns. Cronauer is very different, as the presence of

Williams would lead us to expect. He gives a series of lighting *tour de force* performances, packed with improvised wit, impressions and satirical outbursts guaranteed to earn the anger of his tight-assed immediate superiors. The existence of the key performative sequences *as* performance is legitimated by the fact that the fictional character is himself a noted comic performer, a device used in many comedian comedies in which motivation is provided in much the same way as that found in the back-stage musical. The Cronauer-DJ performance sequences are set off from, and interrupt, the development of linear narrative momentum. They function very much like the 'numbers' of the musical, a quality underlined by the fact that they include the spinning of discs (another disruption of the rules of the diegetic world, given Cronauer's preference for contemporary music outlawed by the military hierarchy).

Numerous clown performers have disrupted the ranks, other examples including Bob Hope in *Caught in the Draft* (1941), Jerry Lewis in *Jumping Jacks* (1952) and *At War With the Army* (1959), and more recently Goldie Hawn in *Private Benjamin* (1980) and Bill Murray in *Stripes* (1981). A notable feature of

Figure 3   To camera: Robin Williams in performative mode in *Good Morning Vietnam* (1987)

all these films is that the initially foolish or incompetent character played by the comedian eventually comes out on top. A typical device is the inclusion of a key action sequence, an exercise or manoeuvre of some kind, in which the central figure gains the opportunity to prove his or herself. Thus, the cowardly and narcissistic movie star Don Bolton (Bob Hope) comic-bravely rides into the path of live artillery fire to warn an approaching column in *Caught in the Draft*. The hapless Hap Smith (Jerry Lewis) blunders into 'enemy' lines during the exercise that ends *Jumping Jacks* and, innocent of any such intention, manages to destroy a key strategic bridge and capture the rival general. The sometimes dizzy blonde Judy Benjamin (Goldie Hawn) and her team get lost during war games in *Private Benjamin*, only to succeed in taking prisoner the entire enemy force. In *Stripes*, the slobbish John Winger (Bill Murray) leads a rescue mission behind the Iron Curtain after making off in a new and top secret urban assault vehicle. A similarly unlikely, and largely unwitting, triumph on a 'real' battlefield is achieved by the clownish and accident-prone Jar Jar Binks in *Star Wars: Episode One – The Phantom Menace* (1999).

Figures such as these often achieve success in terms both of their own anarchic qualities *and* those of the military itself, even if the latter is sometimes the result of accident or misrecognition. A good example is found at a narrative turning point in *Stripes* when Winger's platoon of no-hopers get through the graduation parade they seem destined to fail by presenting what we assume to be a technically correct drill performance with an extra dimension of idiosyncratic swagger and flair. They conform, at the last minute, turning up late after a night of practice, but in their own creative and entertaining terms (and in another of those narratively implausible comic transformations). In ideological terms, comedian comedy can be read as a celebration of the individual in opposition to restrictive social or collective institutions, a theme to which we will return again. In some cases, however, what is offered is also a degree of reconciliation between the two. A common feature in many Hollywood films and other products of US-dominated Western/capitalist popular culture is the suggestion that the quirks and foibles of the eccentric individual hero do not just stand against but also provide valuable lessons for, and evidence of the value of flexibilities within, larger institutions. The particular role played by comedy in the achievement of such reconciliations will be considered below, in the context of romantic comedy.

Framing comedy

The development of early comedian comedy in the 1910s had implications for the staging and cinematic construction of comic action. The earliest films were shot primarily in single long-shots: the camera pointed at an action and kept rolling until the film ran out. The comedy of some early films was based on tricks achieved with editing and other devices, using the distinctive formal dimensions of the medium to manipulate the world to comic effect. The Lumière Brothers' *Demolition d'un mur* ('Demolition of a Wall', 1895) moved into comedy from the staid representation of 'actuality', for which the French pioneers were known, when the film was stopped in exhibition and shown in reverse, the wall 'magically' reassembling itself. Early experiments with transitional devices were used to create identical comic effects in *Let Me Dream Again* (1900), by George Albert Smith, and the Pathé Brothers' *Rêve et réalité* ('Dream and Reality', 1901). In each case, a man is shown enjoying revels with drink and a woman, only to wake to find himself in bed with less attractive company; a movement out and back into focus and a dissolve, respectively, are used to achieve the transition from dream to reality.

Trick editing was a staple of early comic effects. *Explosion of a Motor Car* (1900), by Cecil Hepworth, is one of many films to exploit the ability of the camera to be stopped and objects to be substituted to comic effect during filming. A cloud of smoke obscures the moment at which a car full of people is replaced by a pile of wreckage, an assortment of body parts, limbs and other objects subsequently falling back to the ground from the sky. Double exposure superimposition was another early technique, pioneered in the fantasies of Georges Méliès, that could be turned to comic effect. In *The Dream of a Rarebit Fiend* (1906), from the Thomas Edison Company, superimposed panning shots are used, along with a tilting camera, to create an impression of the drunkenness of the title character. An experiment with unconventional framing is used to heighten the comedy of Robert Paul's *A Chess Dispute* (1903), making creative use of the stationary camera position of early cinema. A game of chess, in a single mid-shot, degenerates into a tussle between the players, who end up on the floor, beneath the lower edge of the frame. A more mobile camera might have followed the movement of the protagonists but a stronger comic effect results here from its passivity, the struggle being represented obliquely as the viewer witnesses items of clothing and the occasional leg or foot being thrust up into the frame.

Editing featured in the Keystone style of slapstick, which used cutting (along with occasional under-cranking of the camera) to create its furiously-paced madcap world. Analysis by Douglas Riblet points to a progressive speeding up of the editing rhythms used at the Keystone studio, particularly in the crazier second-half action sequences of its output: 'Whereas the Sennett Biographs and early Keystones generally employed crosscutting to give the viewer an omniscient perspective on comic narratives, the rapid editing in the later Keystones exceeded any narrative function, and created a more frantic, visceral effect' (1995: 179). *Double Crossed* (1914) is calculated to have an average shot length of 4.2 seconds, including a second-half chase sequence clocking in at less than 3 seconds per shot, a rate comparable to that found in today's most frenziedly edited action films. Comedian comedy generally entailed a move back to the more leisurely pace of the longer take, which provided the time needed for the development of more subtle nuances of character and for the showcasing of comic star performance. In some cases, such as at Keystone, the two styles were combined, as Riblet suggests, with shifts from longer takes highlighting the performance of a single comedian to the feverish editing patterns of chase and other action sequences.

The visual dimension of film comedy can be constructed according to either of two rival virtues of cinema celebrated by early film theorists: those of montage or of the long take. For some theorists, especially those such as Lev Kuleshov, associated with the Soviet montage style of cinema, the essence of the medium lay in the unique effects that could be created through editing. Others, most notably André Bazin, championed a style of film-making that relied on the ability of film to capture a more substantial reality of events staged in front of the camera.[12]

Montage effects are created through the juxtaposition of different images. The meaning of one image is shaped, created or transformed through the act of juxtaposition. Editing is used not to heighten existing effects but to create distinct effects of its own. This technique is one potential source of film comedy. Gags can be created through cutting to a reverse-angle perspective that changes the expectations established in the previous shot. The opening image of *Cops* (1922), for example, presents what appears to be a forlorn Buster Keaton in a prison cell, his hands clutching the bars, a plain brick wall behind him, and his girl, upset, shaking his hand and moving out of frame. A cut to a longer shot from the reverse angle reveals that, in fact, he is standing outside the gates of the mansion in which the girl lives, she parting with the line that she will not marry him until he makes a success of himself. The same gag is elaborated further at the start of *Safety Last*. An iris-focused close shot gives us Harold Lloyd's character behind bars. The iris opens to a full-screen image that reveals a noose hanging in the background. The camera pulls back, introducing the presence of two tearful women in the foreground (Lloyd's girl and mother, we are likely to assume, correctly). A slight pan to the left accompanies the movement into the scene of a uniformed man who gestures to Lloyd in the direction of the noose. A formally dressed man (priest, prison governor?) enters, shaking Lloyd's hand. The party moves off to the rear, as if to perform the execution, but a reverse angle cut again undermines the impression that has been created: the scene is set at a railroad station from which Lloyd's character is setting off to seek success in the big city, the noose revealed as part of a device used to communicate with passing train drivers.

In *Parenthood* (1989), a reverse angle is used to reveal the comic (although also partly serious) incongruity of the pressure put on children by their father, Nathan (Rick Moranis). Father and mother, Susan (Harley Kozak), are expressing concern at the academic performance of their daughter, Patty, who has not yet been seen by the viewer, with specific reference to the standard of university to which she is likely to secure access. Father is giving daughter a serious talk on the subject. 'I don't know,' he observes, as he is joined by his wife, 'sometimes I feel we want it more than she does.' Susan appeals to her daughter to make an extra effort. The viewer is then supplied with the reverse shot that has been conspicuous by its absence during the sequence, a punch-line revealing Patty to be only about four years old.

Probably the most celebrated example of comedy created through the instant transformations made possible by editing is a reflexive sequence in *Sherlock Jr.* (1924) in which a sleeping Buster Keaton's dream-self enters the world on screen at the cinema where he works as a projectionist. Cuts are used comically to transform the nature of the on-screen reality he inhabits: stepping down a series of steps, he finds himself falling from a garden seat; sitting down on the seat, he falls off a kerb; walking along the road, he almost goes off the edge of a cliff; peering over the cliff, he finds himself looking close up at a lion; wandering around, he is relocated into a desert and suddenly a train rushes closely past; he sits on a mound, which is transformed into a wave-hit rock in the sea; he jumps off and lands, disappearing, all but his legs, into deep snow; leaning onto a tree, he falls over, transported back into the garden.

Assumptions of audience familiarity with the conventions of continuity editing, a style used to achieve apparently 'seamless' transitions between shots, are drawn upon implicitly in the construction of many of the comic effects in *Dead Men Don't Wear Plaid* (1982), a film-noir spoof in which sequences from classic examples of the genre are inserted into the fiction. Techniques such as eyeline-matches and shot/reverse-shot alternations are brought to our attention and rendered comic when used to integrate the detective protagonist Rigby Reardon (Steve Martin) into exchanges with characters such as Alicia Huberman (Ingrid Bergman) from *Notorious* (1946) and Walter Neff (Fred MacMurray) in *Double Indemnity* (1944), the comedy of the latter example increased by the fact that Reardon, in drag, is playing the Barbara Stanwyck role.

Any conventional formal devices, used to excess, can have comic effect. Hyperbolic editing, zoom and pan effects – to an aggressive, fast-driving music track – are used, among other techniques, to create a madcap cartoon impression in a diamond heist in the opening of Guy Ritchie's stylised gang-ster comedy-thriller *Snatch*. The camera executes rapid partial revolutions, twisting characters beyond 90 degrees from the horizontal. High- and low-canted angles are used elsewhere in the film to underpin its 'hip' off-centre mixture of comedy and violence, and to suggest that the latter should not be taken too seriously. Hyper-rapidly whip-cut elliptical sequences mark, comi-cally, the movements of an American Mafia-type back and forth across the Atlantic, a similarly witty telegraphic effect being created by rapid cuts into flashback detail (a style also used in the comedy-action-war film *Three Kings* (1999)).

Silent star/film-makers such as Chaplin and Keaton made use of editing and other cinematic illusions on some occasions. More often, however, they relied on the unfolding of their own performances within the frame provided by the longer take. This was partly an inheritance from the vaudeville or music

Figure 4 Chico and Groucho in *A Day at the Races* (1937) performing a 'scam' routine in shallow space as if in front of a theatrical curtain.

hall stage, performances sometimes being given frontally, towards a fixed camera, as if taking place on stage, even if more than one set-up might be used. In one lengthy sequence in *A Day at the Races*, for example, Tony (Chico Marx) ensnares Dr Hackenbush (Groucho) in a scam involving the purchase of racing tips and an ever-increasing armful of 'essential' code books, guides and other volumes. The routine is presented in a mixture of full-figure long shots, medium-long and medium shots, all taken from frontal or close to frontal angles, the space behind them shallow, as if the act were a piece of comic business performed in front of a theatrical curtain.

For a star such as Keaton, the development of performance intact within the frame was a way to establish the distinctive nature of business based on real acrobatic ability, marking his own distinctive presence in a crowded marketplace. In *Sherlock Jr.*, for example, Keaton's character climbs onto the roof of a train, leaping from one wagon to another to stay in frame as the train moves in the opposite direction. He eventually runs out of train and grabs onto a water spout, which lowers him part of the way to the ground before washing him the rest of the way. The entire sequence is presented in one unbroken shot, emphasising the reality of the pro-filmic event, and Keaton's performance, in front of the camera. A frontal long-shot routine in *One A.M.* in which a drunken Chaplin tussles with a fold-away bed is extended for more than five minutes, broken only by the insertion of three brief mid-shots used for emphasis (as on one of the occasions when the bed falls on top of him). This style of comedy met with the approval of Bazin, who cites Chaplin as an example of what he advocated as the greater realism created by 'straightforward photographic respect for the unity of space' (1967: 46). The effect could also be faked, however, through careful positioning of the camera. Harold Lloyd's ascent of the building in *Safety Last* was performed only a short distance above the security of a protective ledge; careful framing, to conceal the ledge and to keep the street below in shot, 'made it look as though the feat were all stunt and no trick' (Mast 1979: 157).

The unfolding of action within the frame is an important aspect of the films of Jacques Tati, most notably *Playtime*, in which various events often occur simultaneously in different parts of the screen. In one extended sequence, a multiple-frame effect is created as the viewer is presented with two, and at times four, shop-window views into the lives of the occupants of a block of modernist apartments. If a distanced perspective is one key ingredient of the creation of comic modality, as suggested in the Introduction, this can be created by such formal means: the camera, literally, keeping its distance, less 'involved', it seems, in the development of the action on-screen. Off-screen space can also be used to comic effect, another technique used by Tati to increase the deadpan effect of his comedy. In *Les Vacances de Monsieur Hulot*, for example, Hulot trips while carrying a heavy case through the front door of his hotel; he delays his fall, staggering through the building to the back door, the comic impact of the eventual crash heightened by being heard but not seen, off-screen in the garden, a technique often used in cartoon comedy.

Framing designed to showcase performance skills is often broken to some extent by editing, even where the unfolding of performance remains the principal attraction. Slight changes of camera angle or position can be used to provide an optimal perspective, or just an element of variety, without significantly undermining the development of the act, a technique found in the films of comedian stars from the silent era to contemporary Hollywood. The use of a modicum of editing makes industrial/commercial sense even in the most performative turns, enabling sequences to be constructed without the time-consuming (and therefore expensive) achievement of perfect performance of the entire routine on every occasion. Near the start of *One A.M.*, for example, the camera pans and tilts – and a few closer shots are inserted – to follow Chaplin's antics in an extended series of routines performed around an entrance-hall and on a pair of staircases leading to an upstairs landing. When Jim Carrey does an impression of a sportsman caught in a television slow-motion replay/rewind in *Ace Ventura, Pet Detective* (1994), the sequence (facial distortion, moaning, exaggerated body actions) is presented in a few medium-long and medium shots, with one reaction-shot cut-away. Pro-filmic performance is foregrounded in each case. Longer takes and montage-type effects can also be combined in a single sequence. In *The Patsy*, Stanley Belt is let loose in the antique-filled home of an eminent singing tutor. One encounter, with an awkward sloping-seated chair, is presented primarily in a single shot, highlighting the antics of Jerry Lewis (with the exception of the insertion of a brief reaction shot). Belt gives up on the impossible-seeming chair, moving to one that appears more accommodating and a cut is used, to a closer side-angle, to emphasise the punch-line that comes when, as he sits, the seat breaks.

The framing of comic moments or gags also entails elements of narrative structure, if sometimes rudimentary, as we saw in the case of *L'Arroseur arrosé*. A classic gag in Chaplin's *The Immigrant* is based on one key element of narrative strategy: the distribution of knowledge between on-screen characters or between film-maker and viewer.[13] The film opens with shots of a ship at sea and the rolling swell being experienced by those on deck. We see Chaplin's figure from behind, leaning far out over the rail, his body convulsing with what we assume to be sea-sickness. He then turns smiling to face the camera, revealing that he had been straining to haul up his catch of fish. The gag is based on the initial denial of knowledge to the spectator, the on-screen reality being concealed by the position of the figure within the frame.

Many film (or other) narratives use differential hierarchies of knowledge to construct their dramatic effects. The same goes for comedy. The concealment of information from the viewer can result in a moment of comic surprise when the truth is revealed, as in *The Immigrant* and the 'prison bar' illusions cited above. Comic surprise, or a fresh turn in a gag sequence, might also result from the denial of knowledge to both characters and viewers. The comedy-of-frustration that constitutes the first half of *The Music Box* (1932), in which deliverymen Laurel and Hardy eventually succeed in hauling a piano up a long series of flights of stairs, is topped by the belated revelation to all concerned that they could have driven around by road instead (according to their own eccentric logic, the pair then proceed to carry the piano back down again in order to make use of the road). The order in which the full consequence of narrative action is revealed to the viewer is manipulated to comic effect in *Snatch*. In one incident the film plays on conventional expectations that parallel narrative events in the same sequence will occur simultaneously unless otherwise indicated in advance. The film cuts between scenes involving three different carloads of rival protagonists. A milk carton is casually tossed from the window of one vehicle. We hear, off screen, the resulting crash of another car. Cut back to the scene in one of the other cars, where a delay of some moments follows before *their* windscreen is shown to be the one hit by the milk (just for good measure, and to increase comic implausibility, a hooded figure who escapes from the boot of the second car is promptly hit by the third).[14] Trick framing can also be used to create comedy through sudden changes of perspective or scale. A scene in *The Last Remake of Beau Geste* (1977) opens with what appears to be a shot of a fort in the desert; the camera pulls back, however, revealing that it is really a sandcastle, smashed by a passing troop of soldiers (Harries 2000: 62).

Concealment from characters within the narrative is often used to create comic suspense. Comedy results here from providing the viewer with more knowledge than the character(s). It comes from the sense of anticipation as much as consummation. A limited form of suspense is created in the mischief gags that comprise early films such as *L'Arroseur arrosé*, located in the brief delay between the child stepping on the hosepipe and the 'punchline' in which the gardener is soaked. Gags such as these are developed in two clearly defined phases, as Tom Gunning suggests (1995a: 91–2). The first is a stage of preparation, which sets up the gag (stepping on the hosepipe or, in numerous other early mischief comedies, setting up some other kind of booby-trap, such as an object filled with flour or water); the second is the action that results, the soaking or other indignity enacted on the victim, usually an adult or authority character. A similar kind of structure contributes to the effect of gags found in many subsequent comedies.

In *American Pie* (1999), for example, the preparatory stage of a gag is established when a character ejaculates into a glass of beer. He and his girlfriend then vacate the scene, the bedroom of the house in which a teenager party is being held, leaving the glass behind. Another couple enter. We know what has happened, and we can be pretty sure what is going to happen next (this being a 'gross-out' comedy, a variety to which we will return later), but the characters entering the room are oblivious, like the gardener in *L'Arroseur*. It is in the gap between our and their knowledge that the comic effect is established, a gap that is extended for some minutes in this case to increase the audience's sense of appalled comic anticipation. This is also a feature of the films of Laurel and Hardy, including *The Music Box*. An almost unbearable sense of anticipation is generated by *our* knowledge – intertextual in this case, if we are familiar with the act – that their Sisyphian efforts will repeatedly be thwarted. This is in many respects a defining characteristic of the distinctive slow-burning brand of comedy developed by Laurel and Hardy at the Hal Roach studio.

A similar approach is used in the Warner Bros. Road Runner cartoons, the repeated formula of which assures the viewer that Wile E. Coyote's efforts to catch the Road Runner will *always* fail. About that, there is no surprise; comic suspense and tension is created, however, in the gap between this knowledge and delayed revelation of what *exactly* will go wrong in any particular case.[15] In *Zipping Along* (1953), a series of reversals includes a sequence in which Coyote cuts the rope securing a bridge between two cliffs ... and it is the ground on which he is standing that falls, rather than the crossing. Numerous examples of drawn-out, suspense/tension-inducing comedy are found in the imbecilic routines enacted by Rowan Atkinson's title character in *Bean* (1997), especially in the sequence in which, predictably but agonisingly, he first marks and then, by stages, entirely destroys the face on the priceless original painting of Whistler's Mother. Comedy of this variety can easily become frustrating or irritating, for some if not all viewers, playing on a combination of audience desire for and pleasure in the spectacle of mayhem and a measure of investment in the character and, hence, a desire for such situations to be recovered. What *Bean* offers, typically, is some satisfaction of each: the painting is wrecked, irretrievably, but Bean's comic invention is able to save the day by evading security measures to replace the original with a poster.

Romantic comedy: the comedy of integration?

Romance figures in the background or on the margins of many of the comedies discussed so far. Romance is present often as the excuse or as an initial motivator for comic action. The antics of the Buster Keaton character in films such as *College* and *Steamboat Bill Jr.* (1928) are driven by his desire to achieve union with the girl, as are those of the Harold Lloyd figure in *Safety Last*. Many of Chaplin's films include romantic dimensions, developed to varying extents. Romance usually remains secondary in these examples. It is a device, primarily, rather than something explored or greatly developed in its own terms or as a source of comedy in its own right. Little sense of the interiority of the romantic relationship is established, beyond the protagonist's generally taken-as-read love-for and difference-from, or difficulty-of-access-to, the source of love interest. The latter, often characterised simply as 'the girl', and often played by the same performers (Edna Purviance in many Chaplin films, for example), is developed little more than as a rather abstract and often idealised figure, strictly secondary to the performance of the male comic star. The term 'romantic comedy' implies a much more central and sustained focus on the detail and texture of romance, romantic relationships and character, as both plot material and source of comedy. It also entails a substantial integration of comedy and narrative.

David Huxley (Cary Grant) slips on an olive playfully dropped by Susan Vance (Katherine Hepburn), landing heavily on his posterior. She damages his car. She (accidentally) tears his dinner coat. He (accidentally) tears her dress. She throws gravel at a bedroom window to gain the attention of the occupant, an important lawyer: nothing happens; she throws a larger stone: the lawyer chooses that moment to open the window and gets hit sharply on the head. Huxley and Vance walk into what she declares to be a 'shallow' stream – and disappear up to their necks. The stuff of classic slapstick routines and pratfalls in *Bringing Up Baby* (1938), a film full of madcap schemes, mistaken identities and farce. And yet ... this is all more or less to a purpose: romance.

Huxley and Vance start off as enemies, from his perspective at least, as she sets off a trail of catastrophes that threaten both his life's work (the restoration of a brontosaurus skeleton) and his forthcoming marriage. She falls in love and contrives a series of situations to keep him close. Hers is a zany world of freedom and play, seemingly oblivious to the usual conventions of truth or property. His is dull, imprisoning, work-bound and as ossified as the dinosaur bones with which he works. Slapstick and farce is presented as an intrinsic part of the daffy universe of Susan Vance, into which David Huxley has to be inducted in order to escape from the prim and proper confines of his bride-to-be Alice Swallow (Virginia Walker). The gags are motivated in terms of the overall narrative enterprise. Huxley is distracted by Vance. 'We're not getting anywhere like this,' he complains at one point, echoing the frustration of Trentino in *Duck Soup*. But we are, in this case. Huxley might not yet have realised it, but, unlike the lunacy of the Marx Brothers in *Duck Soup*, that of *Bringing Up Baby* has direction, leading to a kind of transformation-through-love typically asserted by romantic comedy.

Narrative in romantic comedy is a function primarily of character and character relationships. The romantic narrative of *Bringing Up Baby* is played out by the principal comic characters, rather than being an adjunct to the comedy, as is the case in the relatively more narrative-inclined of the Marx Brothers films such as *A Night at the Opera*, in which the romantic narrative forms a background to the clowning of the main attractions. Much of the comedy, including the slapstick elements, emerges from, is integrated into, and shapes, the developing narrative situation. One narrative thread is constantly disrupted by Vance: Huxley's effort to secure a $1 million bequest from the wealthy widow Mrs Carlton Random (May Robson), who turns out to be Vance's aunt. This occurs not in the interests of chaos, however, but in the construction of a romantic narrative that achieves successful resolution (and with it, it turns out, the original narrative aim: Vance inherits the money but offers it to Huxley as part of their eventual union). The larger narrative arc of comedy is created largely through mistaken or unrevealed identities and the pairing of two contrasting central figures, characteristics typical of many romantic comedies. Comedy is based to a significant extent on narrative situation, as opposed to just gag or performances, although this remains a relative rather than an absolute distinction and subject to varying degrees of emphasis.

Defining romantic comedy as a clear-cut genre is difficult, because of the prevalence of both of its constituent terms in popular film. Comedy is widespread and takes many forms. Romance is an obligatory feature of most popular genres, if only at the level of sub-plot (there are exceptions, notably in 'male-oriented' genres such as the war film). Many films include elements of both. Romantic comedy might broadly be defined according to two main features. First, it is a format in which romance is the main and foregrounded element of the narrative, rather than occupying a secondary position. Second, the romance is generally treated lightly, as a matter of comedy rather than of more 'seriously' dramatic or melodramatic relationships. One key defining ingredient, helping to mark the boundary between romantic comedy and romantic melodrama, is the happy ending, a convention of much comedy in film and elsewhere and an essential component of the classical Hollywood romantic comedy.[16]

The madcap, fast-paced, nutty and slapstick elements of *Bringing Up Baby* earned it and some of its contemporaries the label 'screwball comedy', which might be distinguished from calmer and more smoothly integrated romantic

Figure 5 Slapstick play and initial hostility: the screwball Susan Vance (Katherine Hepburn) rips into staid David Huxley (Cary Grant) in *Bringing Up Baby* (1938)

comedies such as *You've Got Mail* (1998). The screwball tradition is associated primarily with the particular context of the 1930s, its zany and slapstick elements an inheritance of vaudeville combined with the rapid-fire smart talk characteristic of films scripted to showcase the recent development of sound. The style of *You've Got Mail* is rather different. The balance of modalities is between romance, comedy and emotional melodrama, rather than between romance and slapstick. But the two films share a number of common features, including the promise of a happy ending.

You've Got Mail, like *Bringing Up Baby*, is structured around the contrasting characteristics of the two principals and issues of mistaken/unrevealed identity. Kathleen Kelly (Meg Ryan) and Joe Fox (Tom Hanks) are drawn into an anonymous and increasingly romantic relationship by e-mail. Their idle musings, abstracted from real face-to-face contact, lead them to what the film presents as a 'genuine' communion of souls. Back in the 'real' world, however, with all its practical baggage, any potential relationship is marred by fundamental conflicts of interest. She is gentle, uncertain about some aspects of her life and unassertive, running a small but much-loved children's book-shop in New York. He is the confident head of a new Fox Books superstore, the opening of which threatens to put her out of business. They meet in her shop, on unequal terms: he knows her identity but she does not know his. A spark occurs which, given the genre, has clearly romantic potential. Fox's identity is subsequently revealed to Kelly, but he gains the advantage again in their increasingly complex relationship when he discovers that she is his anony-mous e-mail correspondent. The comedy is located primarily in the situation created by the multi-layered and conflicting nature of the relationship estab-lished through these unequal distributions of knowledge.

The viewer stands at the top of the knowledge hierarchy. Even when Fox appears to know everything, and takes advantage of Kelly on that basis, the viewer is still in a superior position. Familiarity with the genre, with Ryan and Hanks as romantic comedy protagonists (previously combined in *Sleepless in Seattle* (1993)), and with popular Hollywood-style conventions more gener-ally, enables the viewer to map an expected trajectory of outcomes at a level beyond the compass of those situated within the fictional world. We know, with some certainty, that Fox and Kelly are likely to end up in each other's arms, and so can safely enjoy the accumulation of intervening obstacles and complications typical of romantic comedy. It is this near-certainty of outcome that helps to sustain the comic nature of the film even in the moments of sadness and despair, located particularly in the closure of Kelly's shop.

Narrative and comedy are integrated to a large extent in romantic comedy, although this does not prevent the outbreak of more performative routines, a notable case being the sequence in which Sally (Meg Ryan) simulates orgasm in a crowded restaurant in *When Harry Met Sally* (1989). Other dynamics also push towards an integration or reconciliation of opposing qualities. The protagonists of romantic comedies are often established at the start as adversaries – either directly in conflict or as embodiments of different qualities, or both – whose differences are eventually reconciled. The screwball Susan Vance and the sober David Huxley; the 'nice' but slightly daffy Kathleen Kelly and the more ruthless and ambitious Joe Fox; the cynical and streetwise newspaperman Peter Warne (Clark Gable) and the cosseted heiress Ellie Andrews (Claudette Colbert) in *It Happened One Night* (1934); the smooth and decadent romantic Leon (Melvyn Douglas) and the rationally humourless Soviet bureaucrat (Greta Garbo) in *Ninotchka* (1939); Conservative and Labour by-election candidates Robert Wilcot (Ian Carmichael) and Stella Stoker (Patricia Breedin), asserting mutual attraction in the face of politics and the manipulations of their agents, in *Left, Right and Centre* (1959); New York journalist and Australian backwoodsman in *Crocodile Dundee*; free-spirited prostitute Vivian (Julia Roberts) and closed-down, vertigo-suffering corporate raider Edward (Richard Gere) in *Pretty Woman* (1990); country boy UK (Dominic Makuvachuma) and gangster's moll Sofia (Sibongile Nene) in the Zimbabwean *Jit* (1993); and so on.

Most romantic comedies are centred around the establishment of heterosexual relationships, but not all; a mark of the popular and flexible nature of the format. A broadly similar dynamic towards the bringing together of characters from very different backgrounds – the white working-class tomboy, Randy (Laurel Holloman), and the rich, 'sophisticated' and educated black teenager, Evie (Nicole Parker) – is established, for example, in *The*

Incredibly True Adventure of 2 Girls in Love (1995). One character often learns from the other. Sue Charlton uses the openness to contact with ordinary people that characterises Mick 'Crocodile' Dundee to declare her love, at the last minute, employing a relay of passengers on a crowded subway platform to convey her message to him. Huxley learns the value of foolishness, fun and play. Kelly learns to remove the gloves in her fight with Fox, a lesson taught by Fox himself in his anonymous e-mail guise. The principal lesson of *You've Got Mail*, however, is supplied by Kelly: that the spheres of 'business' and of the 'personal' cannot be separated, that emotion and feeling are more important than reason. The same is asserted in *Pretty Woman*. Edward confronts and overcomes the source of repression in his life (his relationship with his recently deceased father) by converting a rapacious take-over deal into a productive partnership with a new father figure, a conversion of more substance, perhaps, than Vivian's transformation from the world of the brash hooker to that of 'sophisticated' society.

Reconciliations or transformations such as these are another potential source of the pleasure offered by romantic comedies. Real-world issues are addressed but essentially wished away by the supposedly 'universal' solvent of romantic love. The romance of *It Happened One Night*, set in the Depression, can be read as offering a reconciliation of the class division between Andrews and Warne. *You've Got Mail* is a particularly blatant example of the ideological potential of this kind of manoeuvre. The opposition between the small, family-run store and the large discount chain is one that touches upon very real political-economic issues. A fundamental conflict exists between the values represented by the two: those of small-scale operations, whose traditional valorisation in American mythology is underlined in *You've Got Mail* by an only partly tongue-in-cheek reference to the 'Jeffersonian purity' of Kelly's shop, and those of larger and more 'cut-throat' capitalist business enterprises. *You've Got Mail* appears, on one level, to avoid sidestepping these issues. The neighbourhood bookstore is forced to close, when we might have expected the romantic-comic luxury of a last-minute reprieve. The consequences of its closure are mitigated, however. Kelly is offered a job as head of the children's books section of a publisher and, more significantly, gains the time to write a children's book of her own (and the film's emphasis on her highly attuned sensibility on the question of what kinds of books children enjoy implies quite strongly that she will be a success). And, of course, she finds 'true love' with Fox, the realisation of a potential clearly built into the structure of the film from the start.

In both *You've Got Mail* and *Bringing Up Baby*, the initial opposition established between the romantic protagonists is somewhat fake and shallow, brimming with potential to be overcome. David Huxley's early scene with Alice Swallow makes clear to the viewer that, really, he is just waiting to be freed; Joe Fox, as played by Tom Hanks, is just too *nice*, really, to be taken as a representative of 'evil' big business. The opposition is never taken too seriously, in other words. *You've Got Mail* goes just far enough to create a *frisson*, to put something at stake, to create some emotional investment for the viewer. But it maintains the essentially comic dimension of the not-to-be-taken-seriously, of the whimsical fantasy. What is the significance of the use of this kind of approach when dealing with potentially real social, political or economic issues?

A reconcilation of oppositions of some kind is offered by many popular films. In terms suggested by the social anthropologist Claude Lévi-Strauss (1968), popular cultural products can provide an imaginary way of dealing with real issues, often by the imaginary reconciliation of real and/or intractable oppositions faced by a particular culture or society. The specific variety of reconciliation offered by romantic comedy can be linked to a longer dramatic tradition, that of the classical 'New Comedy' traced by Northrop Frye from Menander in ancient Greece to English Restoration comedy. New Comedy – as opposed to the ironic 'Old Comedy' of Aristophanes – is characterised by scenarios in which society is led to a new form of integration through the union of younger couples, forged against the obstruction represented by inflexible members of the older generation. 'In all good New Comedy,' Frye argues, 'there is a social as well as an individual theme which must be sought in the general atmosphere of reconciliation that makes the final marriage possible' (1984: 75). Reconciliation is expressed in the form of a festival ('whether a marriage, a dance or a feast' (76)), suggesting that the dramatic-fictional variety might have deeper roots in social rites of integration. What is offered in the Hollywood version in many cases is the utopian possibility of 'having it all ways' rather than facing up to difficult decisions. This is often asserted through the romantic pairing of the central characters: reconciliation at the individual level implies, or sidesteps, the reconciliation of broader thematic issues. The implication is that social differences of class, power and the like are essentially secondary factors that can be stripped away to reveal an essential common humanity underneath. A powerful individualist ideology lies at the heart of this romantic mythology, denying the role of social or economic determinations. Comedy has something specific to offer in this dimension. The imaginary reconciliation of real oppositions is a magical process, achieved though narrative and other sleights of hand that might seem implausible, illusory or ridiculous. This is true of both the love fantasies of romantic comedies and the magically absurd triumphs of some of the comedian protagonists of service comedies discussed above. A substantial margin for acceptance of this kind of fluff is generally allowed in 'escapist entertainment' films such as those produced in Hollywood or other forms of production based on the Hollywood fantasy model.

In comedy, however, qualities such as these are more positively encouraged or highlighted, sometimes as the defining characteristics of comedy itself, with its license to break even the relatively flexible rules of popular narrative logic. This might make lighter brands of comedy such as romantic comedy particularly effective vehicles for ideology. Their implicit 'don't take it too seriously' helps, potentially, to inoculate them against close interrogation: those who subject comedies to ideological analysis are more likely than most to be criticised for making too much of works of 'mere' entertainment (not that it is possible to predict in advance exactly how such films are received by particular audiences or what their ideological 'effects' might be). If romantic comedy can have ideological implications, in its imaginary reconciliation of both characters and thematic oppositions, these need to be located in the specific social-historical contexts in which it has been produced, particularly in terms of prevailing notions of gender relationships.

The roots of romantic comedy are traced by Charles Musser to a number of 'sophisticated' comedies produced in the 1920s which in turn 'grew out of the long-standing comedy of errors and of manners that played with infidelity among married couples' (1995: 311). The latter included some of the Keystone productions of the mid-1910s, although the lower-middle-class location of the characters and a more slapstick acting style led to the identification of such films as 'marital farces'. Genre categories remained fluid and dynamic, however, 'with sophisticated comedy not always as easily distinguished as one might think' (311). A distinct sub-genre of sophisticated comedy known as 'the comedy of remarriage' emerged by the mid-1920s, Musser suggests, with films such as the silent versions of *Bluebeard's Eighth Wife* (1923, remade in 1938) and *The Awful Truth* (1925, remade in 1937) 'very clearly understood to be comedies with significant romantic aspects' (311). This is the background against which Musser sets the better-known and more celebrated 'comedies of remarriage' and/or 'screwball comedies' of the 1930s.

One of the key historical explanations for the appearance of these films in the 1920s and 1930s is a broader cultural negotiation of changing attitudes towards gender relationships, love and marriage. The divorce rate in the United States rose steadily in the latter part of the nineteenth century before doubling in the decade from 1910 to 1920. This prompted a number of responses: an initial conservative reaction followed by the shaping of new conceptions of marriage based on loving companionship. Divorce and/or remarriage became a structuring element of a substantial number of films from the late 1910s. These and the 'screwball' romances of the 1930s existed in the context of a wide-ranging exploration of the ideal basis for relationships between men and women (see Lent 1995).

Feminist calls for equality appear to have fed into screwball comedy to some extent, although shorn of more radical demands at the political and economic levels. Screwball heroines are physically active, vital, often participating in the paid labour force and enjoying a more equal relationship with men than that found in earlier generations of film comedy, the latter being an important source of the lively and combative style of screwball (Lent 1995: 317). Their relationships with men can be understood in the context of a broader cultural redefinition of marriage during the 1920s: 'Marriage became less a social and economic institution based upon spiritual love and more a sexual and emotional union based on sexual attraction' (320). Play was defined as an important basis for the development of loving companionship, a quality emphasised in many romantic/screwball comedies of the 1930s, including *Bringing Up Baby, The Awful Truth, Holiday* (1938), *You Can't Take It With You* (1938) and *Ninotchka*. The institution of marriage is questioned where it is seen as leading to formal and lifeless relationships, but not when it has the potential to be enlivened by spontaneity, play and foolery. The specific role of the comic dimension is to offer liberation from, and within, social institutions or structures shown to have grown rigid and unyielding to the point at which their continued viability might otherwise be under threat (Rowe 1995: 46).

If the romantic comedies of the 1920s and 1930s can be understood in the context of a wider contemporary process of negotiation around issues of love, marriage and gender relationships, the same might be said of other manifestations of the format, including those of more recent years. Glossy romantic comedies of the 1950s and early 1960s such as *Pillow Talk* (1959) and *Sex and the Single Girl* (1964) are more overtly focused on sex and seduction than their predecessors, products of an era influenced by more open and mechanistic discourses on sexuality (Neale & Krutnik 1990: 169). The romantic comedy of the 1980s, 1990s and early 2000s can be viewed in the light of various responses to renewed assertions of feminism, along with gay rights and other gender-related discourses, from the late 1960s onwards. The conventions of romantic comedy have been questioned or qualified to take some account of challenges to the patriarchal and heterosexist ideologies underpinning the fantasy of romantic love upon which the form usually depends. Brian Henderson (1986) goes as far as to declare the form 'impossible' in this context, a judgement shown by subsequent history to have been precipitate. Frank Krutnik identifies the 'nervous romance' – a term used in the advertising of Woody Allen's *Annie Hall* (1977) – as a new strain developed in the 1970s that exhibits a 'wistful nostalgia' for traditional romantic comedy while acknowledging the impossibility of many of its conventions in a changed social climate (1998: 19). Key examples include *Annie Hall* and *Manhattan* (1979), male-centred films in which romance is presented as complex, frustrating and elusive. In neither case does the central character, played by Allen, end up neatly partnered with the object of his desire. In the former, significantly, it is only in the world of the fiction – a play written by Allen's character, Alvy Singer – that a satisfactory romantic conclusion is reached for the male lead.

Other films have distanced themselves to varying extents from the marriage-based closure implied by the conventional form. *Four Weddings and a Funeral* (1994) eventually cements its promised, central (but, in terms of screen-time, relatively marginal) relationship between Charles (Hugh Grant) and Carrie (Andie MacDowell). But this occurs in the form of a *disavowal* of marriage, a version of the marriage vows based on agreement *not* to marry, to be *not married* together for the rest of their lives. The institution of marriage is questioned, as might be appropriate for a film that includes among its central secondary characters a gay couple. *Four Weddings* maintains the romantic comedy investment in the notion of perfect love-at-first-sight, however, and the ending is coded in familiar terms. The final encounter, commitment and kiss occur in the rain, the central couple becoming soaked: a highly conventional signifier of openness to 'nature' and the kind of disregard for institutionalised social restraint that has been a central ingredient of the sub-genre.

One of the most likely and central expectations established in *My Best Friend's Wedding* (1997) is pointedly not realised. Julianne Potter (Julia Roberts) fails to achieve union with the old best-friend-she-has-really-always-loved (Dermot Mulroney), her feelings having been crystallised by the revelation of his impending marriage to another woman (Cameron Diaz), with whom he appears to have far less in common. This goes against the usual conventions of the form, one of which is that 'wrong' or less appropriate marriage partnerships should be overturned (as happens towards the end of *Four Weddings*), and against the fact that Julianne is the character with whom we are encouraged to be most closely allied, through access to her thoughts, feelings and actions. In both *My Best Friend's Wedding* and *Four Weddings*, friendship, outside the binary relationship of the heterosexual couple, is offered as a rival source of emotional bonding (see Evans & Deleyto 1998). In emphasising the departures offered by films such as this, however, we should not overlook the more prickly aspects of many earlier examples, especially the 'screwball' films of the 1930s. Part of their questioning of what are presented as older and ossified conventions entails a denial of the use of romantic clichés including talk about 'love', kissing and cinematic rhetoric such as emphatic close-ups and lushly romantic scores (Babbington & Evans 1989).

Forget Paris (1995), another ambivalent example, opens with the quintessential comic romantic fantasy as the protagonists Mickey (Billy Crystal) and Ellen (Debra Winger) meet and fall in love in Paris after a mix-up over the location of his father's coffin. The bulk of the film, however, focuses on the real problems they have sustaining the relationship in the face of their incompatible lifestyle desires. *Forget Paris* ends with the kind of exquisitely balanced equivocation made available by the serious-but-not-serious potential of comedy. The couple separate and come together a number of times during the film. At the end they are together, but with a sense of provisionality. 'Are we going to make it?' she asks. 'Piece of cake,' he replies, precisely the phrase he has previously warned against in other contexts as a dangerous tempting of fate. Their togetherness is asserted, but its longevity is undercut, but at the same time, it is not *really* undercut – or is it? – because the undercutting device is a gag. The uncertainty introduced in *Forget Paris* is underlined by the style of narration employed. The story of Mickey and Ellen is related in turn by a group of friends gathering for dinner. One woman, herself about to be married, is offered implicitly as the representative of the romantic comedy

audience. She is the one to whom the story is told and who becomes emotionally involved in its ups and downs. The placing of both the act of narration and
what might be assumed to be the 'typical' fan/viewer within the diegesis is
another questioning or distancing strategy.

The strength and familiarity of romantic comedy convention is such
that much scope is provided for the working of variations on the theme,
without seriously destabilising the format. *Bridget Jones's Diary* (2001) plays
throughout with audience expectations, setting up a proposed match that
is immediately rejected between the title character (Renée Zellweger) and a
dull-and-annoying lawyer, Mark Darcy (Colin Firth), and offering an initially
more likely, although seemingly doomed, romance with her rich, playful and
flirtatious employer Daniel Cleaver (Hugh Grant). Which way the romantic plot
will be resolved is subject to a series of reversals in the latter stages. Bridget's
eventual union with Darcy confounds at least two conventional expectations
(the 'dull', work-obsessed character triumphing over the playful and,
intertextually, the rejection of the character played by the romantic comedy
star, Grant) while confirming others (that 'unlikely' relationships are possible
between seemingly opposite characters who clash throughout the film and
another intertextual reference, supplied by the casting of Firth in a role that
reprises his high-profile performance as the similarly redeemed 'arrogant
bad guy' Darcy in the 1995 BBC television adaptation of Jane Austen's *Pride
and Prejudice*, a novel that forms the template for aspects of the structure of
Bridget Jones's Diary).

You've Got Mail is part of a more substantial embrace of the wish-fulfillment qualities of the romantic myth in the late 1980s and early 1990s. If *Annie
Hall* 'dislocates and disassembles the signifiers and structures of heterosexual romance and romantic comedy', as Krutnik suggests, *When Harry Met
Sally* 'strives to realign and rearticulate them' (1998: 24). The romantic song 'It
Had to be You', for example, is subjected to distancing strategies in *Annie Hall*,
sung tremulously by the title character against a distraction of background
noises; in *When Harry Met Sally*, it becomes part of the romantic armature of
the narrative, played both at the start and in a key sequence leading up to,
and helping to establish, eventual union. The distinctive characteristic of 'new
romances' such as *When Harry Met Sally*, for Krutnik, is the self-consciousness of their attempts to revalidate the characteristics and conventions of the
form. Overt references are made to earlier romantic fictions, including *Casablanca* (1942) in *When Harry Met Sally* and *An Affair to Remember* (1957), the
romantic climax of which (at the top of the Empire State Building) is re-enacted
in *Sleepless in Seattle*. Both films also make extensive use of 'old-fashioned'
love ballads such as 'It Had to be You' on the soundtrack. At one level, the
dream of ideal romantic love is recognised explicitly for what it is: a myth, the
product of fantasy, specifically that produced in the Hollywood of a past age
and consumed, as an emotional indulgence, primarily by women. A procession
of women characters (and a young girl) in *Sleepless in Seattle* are reduced to

tears by scenes from *An Affair to Remember*, a phenomenon that is parodied in a scene in which Sam (Tom Hanks) and a friend come over all emotional about the ending of *The Dirty Dozen* (1967), a properly 'male' source of fantasy-identification. 'You don't want to be in love, you want to be in love in a movie,' suggests a confident of the female protagonist, Annie (Meg Ryan), spelling out the balancing act performed more generally by the film. Annie *is* in a movie, of course, from our point of view, but a degree of distance is established between her world – contemporary with that of its audience, 'up to date' – and that of classical Hollywood. From this point of relative difference, however, films such as these go on to enact the essentials of the myth.

In *Sleepless in Seattle*, for example, the widowed Sam gains his first glimpse of Annie just as he is giving his young son a pragmatic version of what single people do when they get together. 'They try other people on and see how they fit,' he explains. 'But everybody's an adjustment. Nobody's perfect. There's no such thing as perfect...' His words trail off – he is struck dumb – as Annie walks past, a vision accompanied by a magically tinkling piano theme in the soundtrack. Words say one thing, but they are clearly shallow, a gesture, belied by the extra-diegetic rhetoric of romantic comedy convention, other elements of which include the framing of the film's events by romantic/ 'magical' calendar dates such as Christmas, New Year and Valentine's Day and, more generally, the glossy professional lifestyles enjoyed by the protagonists. Sam and Annie meet properly only at the end of the film. Nothing very specific or substantial is offered to suggest any reason for a special affinity; this is expected to be taken entirely on trust, by the sheer weight (and pleasure of giving way to) conventional expectation. The romantic-comedy myth is asserted not through a naïve belief in its illusions by the characters, Krutnik suggests, but out of fear of the alternative, a terror of isolation: 'Even though the old certainties have been tarnished, these films propose that it is better to believe in a myth, a fabrication, than have nothing' (1998: 30).

This is another form of 'having it both ways': addressing some of the shortcomings of the myth and taking into account some of the less tidy and irreconcilable aspects of 'real-life' relationships, while at the same time retaining basic conventions such as a belief in the eventual realisation of something like ideal romantic union. Romantic comedies such as these make an appeal to audiences through a combination of these qualities. They offer pleasurable feel-good fantasy expectations and securities, legitimated by a degree of apparent complexity and cultural verisimilitude. The 'knowingness' of central characters such as Harry and Sally can be shared, implicitly, by the viewer; each can be distanced just far enough to continue to act out, enjoy or desire elements of the fantasy. Another example is found in *Sliding Doors* (1998). Helen (Gwyneth Paltrow) and James (John Hannah) share a special moment alone in small boat at night on the Thames. The time seems right, and James moves in for a kiss. She pulls away, saying: 'I know this is an ideal sort of kissing moment, you know: night, moon, boat, water lapping.

You know, um, it's perfect, and I'm not *not* feeling that it would be nice.' But she does not really know anything about him and is still on the rebound from another relationship ... The conversation continues, James bantering about his childhood love – and then she does kiss him, after all. It is a clichéd romantic comedy moment but, again, one that seeks to distance itself from the cliché to some extent, through the self-conscious awareness of one of the principals, before proceeding to enact the cliché more or less intact. The viewer is flattered by the acknowledgment of the status of the cliché, a way of reviving it just sufficiently to sustain its viability. A less subtle, more perfunctory disavowal occurs at the close of *Pretty Woman*, set in Los Angeles, after the expected union of Edward and Vivian has been supplied, following the conventional narrative tease in scenes towards the end, when the pair appear to separate, not capable of bridging the gulf between them: 'Welcome to Hollywood,' calls an off-screen huckster-figure, introduced earlier in the film: 'This is Hollywood, land of dreams ... keep on dreaming.'

Elsewhere, the wish-fulfillment ending of romantic comedy is sometimes combined with other comic dimensions, to similar effect. *There's Something About Mary* (1998) blends romantic comedy with elements of the gross-out tendency to be examined in the next chapter. It eventually delivers last-minute union between Mary (Cameron Diaz) and Ted (Ben Stiller). The pair go into the characteristic romantic comedy clinch, accompanied by song. But, as else-where in the film, the fictional frame is broken. The camera wheels around to reveal to us the presence of the singer, who is promptly hit by a gunshot aimed at Ted by one of his crazier rivals for Mary's love. Soppy romantic ending, yes, but also undercut in a demonstration of the film's commitment to comic silliness.

Strategies such as these have proved successful at the box office, as were many of the classic romantic comedies of the 1930s. *It Happened One Night* broke box office records and helped to cement the original formula. The revived version established since the 1980s has proved a consistent source of solid returns in Hollywood and elsewhere, including the British hits *Four Weddings and a Funeral* and *Notting Hill*. A number of options have been explored in recent romantic comedy, some more hesitant and questioning than others. While Hollywood examples tend to seek the best of all worlds – a degree of critical self-consciousness, blended with a reenactment of the essentials of the form – some films produced further from the commercial mainstream offer a more questioning and uncertain approach. The smoothly reassuring and ultimately reconciliatory dynamic of the Hollywood model is less likely to be found, or to be assumed to underlie narrative development, in films associated with the American independent sector, for example. A film such as *Trust* (1991), written and directed by Hal Hartley, offers what might appear to be the basis of a conventional, if quirky, romantic comedy relationship between two seemingly very different central characters: the pregnant teenager Maria (Adrienne Shelly) and the older, more educated, idealistic-with-a-tendency-towards-violence Matthew (Martin Donovan). The film proposes some kind of 'rightness' about their fragile relationship, amid oppressive family backgrounds and a world of dishonesty, but where exactly it is likely to lead is seriously in doubt throughout the film, the status of which as romance, comedy or romantic comedy is also very much in question. Kevin Smith's *Chasing Amy* (1997) has a texture sometimes closer to that of conventional romantic comedy – including the standard music-accompanied montage sequence charting the burgeoning of the central relationship – but with the twist that the woman (Joey Lauren Adams) with whom the central character Holden (Ben Affleck) falls in love is gay – and the fact that, for this and associated reasons, the pair are not united at the end.

Within Hollywood, the balance of elements shifts across a fairly wide range, from the romantic-comedy-with-gross-out-and-silliness of *There's Something About Mary* to examples such as *You've Got Mail* that verge closer to a blend of romantic comedy and romantic melodrama. Much of the core of romantic comedy remains intact, which is unsurprising given its potential for the provision of the kind of feel-good entertainment that tends to succeed at the box office. What it offers, primarily, might be a measure of warm and comfortable reassurance – located to a large extent in the tone of gentle comedy – a quality more often found in the maintenance (even if on some occasions subtle and nuanced) than the undercutting of dominant ideological formulations.

two

transgressions and regressions

From grotesque to gross-out

Farting cowboys. Faces grotesquely stuffed with food. Projectile vomiting. Explosive shitting. More explosive shitting. Semen dangling from ear; semen in hair. Semen in beer glass. Copulation with apple pie. Who knows what next...

Some film comedies are subtle, nuanced and 'respectable'. Others are decidedly not. 'Gross-out' has become one of the most lucrative elements in contemporary film comedy: comedy based on crude and deliberate transgressions of the bounds of 'normal' everyday taste. What is the appeal of this kind of comedy and how should it be understood or taken seriously? One option is to consider the examples listed above from the perspective of the previous section: the relationship between comic moments such as these and the narrative structures in which they occur. Gross-out comedy is often sold in publicity material, and discussed in media coverage and more informal discourses, on the basis of these sometimes isolated moments of transgression; it can also be located narratively, as will be seen below. But what about the specific appeal or effect of gross or otherwise crude comedy such as this? Why, for example, the repeated focus on lower regions of the body and the emission of bodily products?

Gross-out comedy can be approached from a broader social-cultural perspective. It can be examined alongside other instances in which the usual bounds of social convention are transgressed, often in similar manners, in a wide range of historical and cultural contexts. A useful starting point is Mikhail Bakhtin's influential study of European popular folk culture in the Middle Ages.[1] The world of the Middle Ages, Bakhtin suggests, was hierarchical, based on strict ideas of order and rank. In certain privileged moments of carnival and festival, however, the usual hierarchies and restrictions were suspended. All that was usually fixed and established was open to change, renewal and a constant state of becoming. The high could be rendered low and the low high; a world turned comically upside-down and inside-out.

Bakhtin's description of carnival is based in a specific social and historical context, but similar phenomena have been found more widely. Many cultures allow for this kind of indulgence in normally unacceptable behaviour on special occasions or by specially qualified individuals such as the 'fool' or the court jester. Social anthropologists have documented numerous instances in cultures across the world (see Apte 1985). Comedy is often found in or alongside religious rituals, for example, and includes various kinds of 'obscene' behaviour such as that permitted by the spirit of carnival. Particularly interesting cases from the point of view of film comedy are the various 'trickster' figures found in the myths and stories told by some cultures, especially those of Native Americans. The trickster, generally, is an unruly male figure who breaks the rules, is governed by uncontrollable biological urges for food and sex and who often lacks a sense of unity and control of his own body parts. As such, the trickster might be seen as a forerunner of some of the stars of comedian comedy, figures whose unruliness often extends to a plasticity of identity marked by internal transformations and impersonations, prominent examples including the performances of Jerry Lewis and Eddie Murphy in the two versions of *The Nutty Professor* (1963, 1996). A more literal connection exists in some cases, including African comedian comics such as Jagua and the animated characters Bugs Bunny and Wile E. Coyote, the latter pair taking their names directly from those of Native American tricksters. The Zimbabwean romantic comedy *Jit* (1993) includes the disruptive presence of the central character's ancestral spirit, Jukwa (Winnie Ndemera), a source of slapstick obstruction until tamed by offerings of alcohol.

How can we make connections between these very wide-ranging cultural examples and the specific case of gross-out comedy? The two occupy very different dimensions. The traditional carnivalesque and comic ritual figures such as the trickster are rooted in the fundamental belief structures and institutions of particular cultures. Gross-out comedy is a secular and commercial entertainment enterprise. Important distinctions can be made between the two realms. The reversals and inversions of the former tend to be compulsory and central to the cultural life; those of the latter offer more marginal and optional experiences (see Turner 1982). A complex process of transition has to be negotiated if we are to understand, historically and culturally, the processes through which elements of revel and ritual found their way into products designed to provide secular-fictional entertainment in dramatic form (see Caputi 1978). There are striking similarities, however, in some of the qualities emphasised by the carnivalesque and gross-out. One of the key aspects of carnivalesque humour for Bakhtin is the representation of the human body as a source of the grotesque. The essential principle of carnival is degradation, 'that is, the lowering of all that is high, spiritual, ideal, abstract; it is a transfer to the material level, to the sphere of earth and body in their indissoluble unity' (1984: 19–20). As far as the body is concerned, this involves a concern 'with the lower stratum of the body, the life of the belly and the reproductive organs; it therefore relates to acts of defecation and copulation, conception and pregnancy and birth' (21). The point about this idea of the body is that 'it is not separated from the rest of the world. It is not a closed, completed unit; it is unfinished, outgrows itself, transgresses its own limits' (26).

A stress in Bakhtin's idea of carnival is put on the parts of the body through which it engages with the world, including the bodily fluids and excretions by which that engagement is often manifested. A similar emphasis is found in Julia Kristeva's psychoanalytically-oriented notion of the abject, that which exists on the border of the existence of the subject: 'The in-between, the ambiguous [that] disturbs identity, system, order' (1982: 4). In both kinds of reading, a confrontation with that which lies on the boundaries, especially those of the body, can play an important part in both questioning and constructing that which lies within: social convention in the former, the psychic formation of the subject in the latter. The activities of tricksters and other ritually-transgressive figures often involve scatological elements such as the simulated or actual use of urine and faeces (Apte 1985: 158). There is an obvious connection here with the favoured terrain of the contemporary Hollywood gross-out movie and the examples listed at the start of this section. Crude comedy in film has long included a focus on matters of the lower regions. The backside is a constant object of violent or otherwise undignified attention in the silent slapstick tradition. Even the more august features of Charlie Chaplin, such as *City Lights* (1931), include a strong dimension of anal humour, as documented by William Paul (1991; 1994). An inability to control anal excretions – to master one of the key boundaries of the body – is a key source of gross-out set-piece gag sequences of more recent years, from the group farting by heavily bean-consuming cowboys in *Blazing Saddles* to the laxative-induced toilet explosions of films such as *Dumb and Dumber* (1994) and *American Pie* (1999). The major *frissons* and talking-point moments in *There's Something About Mary* (1998) and *American Pie* concern the insufficiently controlled or inappropriate emission of semen and, especially, an inversion of the high and low regions of the body. In the former, the semen of Ted ends up dangling from his ear after masturbation and is mistaken by Mary (Cameron Diaz) for, and used as, hair gel. In the latter, as we saw in the previous section, semen ejaculated into a glass of beer is consumed by another male character, Stiffler (Sean W. Scott), producing a gag the reaction to which might include an element

Figure 6   Matter out of place: the semen-in-the-hair gag on the title character in *There's Something About Mary* (1998)

of 'gagging'. In both cases, a fluid associated both with the lower regions and with procreation is brought up to the top of the body, the head, in an act the explicitness of which in *There's Something About Mary* is transgressive of representational norms for anything other than explicit sex films.

In their narrative locations, gross-out moments such as these often manifest the carnivalesque dynamic of bringing low that which has pretensions to 'higher' things, or that which is variously scheming, manipulative or dishonest. Finch (Eddie Kaye Thomas), the victim of the laxative in *American Pie*, sees himself as more sophisticated than his peers. He drinks mochachino from his flask, he insists in tones of superiority, not just ordinary coffee. 'That guy is, like, so refined,' coos one of a group of girls chatting in the toilet (Finch has been tricked into going into the girls' toilet for relief), moments before the noise and smell of his excessive bowel movement suggest otherwise. His reputation is destroyed, temporarily at least, the laxative having been delivered, appropriately, into the beverage through which he has staked one of his claims to greater sophistication. Stiffler is also cast as a deserving victim, a generally less than sympathetic figure in the film. In the semen-in-the-beer scene, it is the girl with whom he enters the bedroom who initially picks up the drink. Stiffler takes it from her as he moves in precipitately for a kiss; he drinks it (as punishment?) immediately after spinning her an unlikely and deceptive line to quell her worries that he will brag to his friends about any sexual activity in which they indulge. The administration of laxative in *Dumb and Dumber* also has a narrative logic; Lloyd (Jim Carrey) gaining revenge on Harry (Jeff Daniels) for betraying him in pursuit of the girl (Lauren Holly).

Gross-out films – or gross-out sequences in films that otherwise conform more generally to formats such as romantic comedy or college/high-school comedy – seek to evoke a response based on transgression of what is usually allowed in 'normal' or 'polite' society. They test how far they can go, William Paul suggests; 'how much they can show without making us turn away, how far they can push the boundaries to provoke a cry of "Oh, gross!" as a sign of approval, an expression of disgust that is pleasurable to call out' (1994: 20). What is involved here, from a sociological perspective, can be seen as a testing of cultural boundaries and restrictions. Cultural worlds are demarcated by all sorts of limitations, the precise nature of which vary from one culture to another. These boundaries are usually policed in some manner. Particular activities are restricted to their 'proper' (culturally sanctioned) time and place. An important division in modern secular societies is established between the 'public' and 'private' realms. Activities deemed suitable to one may not be considered acceptable in the other, a division of particular relevance to the sources of gross-out effects considered above.

What happens when these boundaries are breached, transgressed, in the production of the carnival grotesque, the abject or the gross-out comedy sequence? This has been an area of much general debate, particularly in terms of the political implications of transgression. Is this type of transgression radical or conservative in effect? Are cultural boundaries put into question and undermined, or confirmed and reinforced? For Bakhtin, and many of those influenced by his conception of carnival, it has a radical and liberating potential, breaking through the limitations of dominant cultural norms. Others have questioned this, in the context of the Middle Ages or more generally.[2] If the usual constraints are *permitted* to be breached, in particular circumstances only, the effect might be that of a 'safety valve', a means of letting off steam without really challenging the norm. No single answer can usefully be given to this question. The dialectical exchange between subversion and reconfirmation can be subtle and complex, as is the case with many comic forms, and needs to be considered in specific social and historical context, rather than through sweeping generalisation or the essentialising of categories such as the carnivalesque (Stallybrass & White 1986: 14–16).

What might be the specific function or effect of the kinds of transgressions offered in film comedy? What is the significance of the fact that the gross-out effect, for example, is designed to provoke laughter? Does this reduce or increase any potentially subversive implications, any substantial questioning of the cultural norms that are breached? The joke, for the social anthropologist Mary Douglas, is an 'anti-rite', the opposite of social rituals that serve to reaffirm dominant cultural norms. The joke 'affords opportunity for realising that an accepted pattern has no necessity. Its excitement lies in the suggestion that any particular ordering of experience may be arbitrary and subjective' (1968: 365). The comic effect, however, is based on familiarity with the norm. It is the departure from the norm, and our awareness of the precise extent of that departure, that generates the comic *frisson*. Semen used as hair gel is comic because it is absolutely not meant to be found in such a place, or in a glass of beer. To find transgressions comic, then, presumes a knowledge of the norm. The act of transgression draws attention to the norm and might reinforce it. As Douglas puts it in the context of the joke: 'The strength of its attack is entirely restricted by the consensus on which it depends for recognition' (372). The fact that we *laugh* at the transgression might increase this effect of reinforcement. Laughter has often been seen as a means of enforcing conformity through ridicule of that which does not conform to dominant expectations.[3]

An analysis of the *experience* of a particular form of transgression, whether first-hand or in representation, might help to explain its potential effect. Transgressions of the kinds found in gross-out comedies can provoke a number of reactions. For some viewers, they might be offensive rather than comical. Disgust is a reaction found in most, if not all, cultures to the transgression of the most strongly-policed cultural boundaries, particularly those around bodily borders, orifices and excretions (see W. Miller 1997). A feeling of disgust in these circumstances is a good indication of the extent to which cultural norms have been internalised by the individual. To be disgusted is to reject, viscerally, often violently, that which transgresses against the ordering structures of a particular culture. In the classic anthropological account by Douglas, that which causes offence is defined culturally and relatively, according to 'the old definition of dirt as matter out of place', rather than as a result of any intrinsic qualities: 'Dirt, then, is never a unique, isolated event. Where there is dirt there is a system. Dirt is the by-product of a systematic ordering and classifying of matter, so far as ordering involves rejecting inappropriate elements' (Douglas 1984: 35). William Miller argues that more general or even universal tendencies might exist, particularly in cases such as prohibitions regarding the treatment of excrement, upon which cultural inhibitions might be constructed at a secondary level. The effect is a powerful one, either way.

The gross-out comedy aims to achieve a balance between disgust and comic pleasure, however, rather than unalloyed disgust. The fact that *pleasure* is taken in the representation of transgression opens up the possibility of a more ambiguous cultural meaning. A play is offered between elements of the disgusting, the gross or abject and the comic. And not all laughter takes the form of ridicule. To ridicule the transgressive might be to reinforce the dominant cultural norm, a widespread feature of much comedy. But the laughter provoked by the gross-out moment, when it succeeds in its comic aim, does not always take this form. It is often complicit in the act of transgression.

Gross-out as a distinctive format – in the mainstream Hollywood films of Peter and Bobby Farrelly, for example, or the more marginal works of John Waters – is based largely on the *promise* of gross-out *frissons* offered to, and sought out by, the audience.

The pleasure on offer might be one of vicarious transgression, from which we can maintain a certain safety of distance.[4] The grosser acts are in some cases performed by secondary figures rather than the principals. Bluto (John Belushi) in *National Lampoon's Animal House* (1978) is a good example of this tendency, an unkempt trickster of seemingly unquenchable appetite for food, drink, sex and general mayhem. Bluto offers a grotesque *spectacle* of transgression, rather than being a character with whom we are invited particularly to identify. The same might be said to a lesser extent of Stiffler in *American Pie*: not a grotesque in the same manner but a relatively marginal player in the overall narrative scheme. Gross-out activities also affect more central characters in many of the films considered so far, but they tend to be relatively isolated moments within broadly conventional narrative structures. Films such as *Dumb and Dumber, There's Something About Mary* and *Me, Myself and Irene* (2000) revolve around familiar tales about losers or no-hopers who eventually achieve success, of one kind or another, even if they do not always get the girl in the end (as in the former): very familiar Hollywood narrative stuff.

An ultimately 'safer', more contained and commodified process of comic gross-out transgression might be expected in the works of the Farrelly Brothers and their imitators than in those at the extreme represented by Waters. A truly carnivalesque world of thoroughly inverted values is offered throughout films such as *Pink Flamingos* (1972) and *Female Trouble* (1975). The protagonists are outcasts from 'normal' society, living by their own willfully 'perverse' values. The rival camps represented in *Pink Flamingos* compete furiously for the title of 'filthiest person in the world'. The central character, played in each case by Divine, is not recuperated by any conventionally cosy or romantic ending: a gleeful and unreconstructed killer-on-the-loose at the end of *Pink Flamingos* and executed by electric chair in *Female Trouble*.

Divine (playing Divine/Babs Johnson) eats shit in *Pink Flamingos*, one of the ultimate gross transgressions available within our culture. An interesting comparison can be made between this moment and one of the gross-out gags offered by *Me, Myself and Irene*. The staging in *Pink Flamingos* challenges the viewer with the assertion that 'what you are about to see is the real thing'; a voice-over declares Divine 'the filthiest actress in the world', a move that promises grossness beyond the world of the fiction. The sequence is framed to create a convincing sense of the reality of the pro-filmic act: shit comes out of a dog, is scooped up by Divine and masticated, all in a single unbroken shot. In *Me, Myself and Irene*, Charlie Baileygates (Jim Carrey) squats to shit on the lawn of his neighbour, the darker and more assertive half of his split personality (known as Hank) emerging to take vengeance for the mess made on his own lawn by the neighbour's dog. Cut to a close-up of the extrusion of what appears for a moment to be his shit, its texture a little odd, 'squishy' and particularly gross. The 'shit' is framed in isolation, removed from its context. The camera then pulls back and moves slightly upwards as a bowl is brought into shot to reveal the gag, another example of comedy created through specifically cinematic processes of framing: it is not Baileygates' shit at all, of course, but an ice cream-type desert being dispensed.

The result is a more graded and complex effect – and more unambiguously in the realm of comedy – than that achieved by the direct representation of shit-eating in *Pink Flamingos*. *Me, Myself and Irene* appears to step back from so great an act of transgression, in its transition into the mainstream. The cut from Baileygates squatting to the emerging 'shit' is designed to be comically 'shocking' and transgressive, to meet the expectations aroused by the contemporary gross-out feature. Human excrement is rarely represented in mainstream cinema, especially in its 'live' form; that is to say, while it has not entirely separated from the body. We are led, just for a moment, to believe we are being shown this transgressive act. That particular transgression is then rapidly withdrawn. But there is an effect of 'contamination', very much like that suggested in Bakhtin's notion of the carnivalesque transposition of the matter of higher and lower bodily regions, in the shift from our identification of the substance as shit to ice cream.

Live shit is not really shown in close-up, nor is it actually represented as being eaten. Either would be beyond the bounds of the permissible in a mass-audience comedy. But a substance linked to shit is transformed, in our perception, into one designed to be eaten; and not just eaten, but enjoyed as a special treat. Gross associations are carried into the arena of normally highly consumable products, an effect more subtle but potentially stronger than the more immediate representation of the consumption of the ultimate forbidden material. A similar cross-over effect is found in a sequence in *Caddyshack* (1980) in which a chocolate bar causes comic mayhem after being dropped into a swimming pool and mistaken for a turd. The pool is subsequently emptied and scrubbed clean by a figure dressed in full body-suit-and-helmet protective overalls; he then finds the offending item and proceeds to eat it (presumably having identified its real nature), to the horror of onlookers.

The shit/ice cream gag in *Me, Myself and Irene* is ambiguous, both transgressive and non-transgressive. An image of grotesque transgression is offered, then almost immediately removed, but the gross-out effect lingers. It can be enjoyed either way. Ambiguity such as this may characterise the implications of the gross-out gag-moment more generally, a transgression that can be enjoyed both *as* transgression and as a source of comedy that reinforces the norm transgressed. Comedy is a form in which film-makers can get away with grotesque transgressions that would not be permitted elsewhere in the mainstream (another softened parallel between *Pink Flamingos* and *Me, Myself and Irene* is the grotesque use of a chicken: stuffed comically up a characters ass in the latter, where we only see the result, not the action itself; used more disturbingly as an instrument of what appears to be the sexual penetration of a woman in the former). As such, it has a radical or subversive potential. But the fact that such transgressions occur in broad and often farcical comedy – by definition, not meant to be taken seriously – is liable to reduce their impact. Comedy can provide a thrill of transgression offered in an environment that renders it largely safe and unthreatening; it can have its cake, ice cream (or its shit!) and eat it.

A contradiction is found in some cases between what is stated by the narrative and the basis of the gross-out or related comedy effects. The Farrelly Brothers' *Shallow Hal* (2001) sets out an 'enlightened' narrative-based case against judging people – specifically, men judging women – according to superficial criteria of physical appearance. This is developed in a sustained fashion, the case being made that contemporary Western culture 'hypnotises' males into obsession with particular and restrictive facial and bodily images. The whole point of most of the laughs solicited by the film, however, is to draw on precisely the extent to which the audience has been hypnotised in the same way. It is the internalisation of assumptions about bodily images – primarily, about very large women – that is the basis of its central comic thrust (the main protagonist, Hal, having been counter-hypnotised to see 'ugly' women as 'beautiful', to project their 'inner beauty' onto outer appearances, a source of numerous gags throughout the film). One of the biggest 'gross-out' laugh/groans in the crowded screening I attended came at the moment when Hal (Jack Black) gives a prolonged kiss to a large women he mistakes for the women he has come to love, Rosemary (Gwyneth Paltrow), after his hypnotism has been reversed. At the level of 'gut' emotional reaction, the film is playing on the assumption that there is something essentially grotesque and out-of-the-ordinary about such contact with a large woman (the same does not seem to apply to the climactic kisses between Hal and Rosemary, because they are underpinned by audience knowledge that Paltrow is only *playing* large, thanks to make-up and prosthetic body extension). If *Shallow Hal* also offers a critique of such assumptions, in which the viewer might be implicated, it seems very much the weaker ingredient in the mixture. Some investment is put into the narrative dimension – implication in the moral and emotional journey undertaken by Hal – but it seems likely to be a good deal less, for the target audience of the film, than that which banks on the mobilization of stereotype. Narrative remains a significant aspect of the film, but comic *frisson* – which has a different story to tell – is likely to be in the foreground.

Whether it is taken to be subversive, conformist or an unstable mixture of the two, comedy that presents a transgression of dominant cultural norms can tell us a great deal about the conventions of the society in which it is produced. The emphasis in contemporary gross-out comedy on matters of the lower bodily regions (their functions, excretions and shifts of the latter from low to high) suggests the existence of a broader cultural environment in which the functions of the body are to a large extent repressed, or at least confined to the realms of the private and hidden. A culture less repressive of such material would be unlikely to find it so potent a source of comedy; less would be at stake. This is a question of differences within particular cultures or historical periods as well as between one and another. Attitudes towards forms of comedy defined as grotesque, crude, or gross involve judgements of 'taste' that are closely associated with the cultural politics through which different social groups mark their distinctions from one another.

Taste, as Pierre Bourdieu (1984) argues, is not something neutral and free-standing. It is intimately connected with matters such as social status and class. A taste for subtlety and refinement tends to be cultivated by those of greater wealth and 'higher' social class. It is a way of demonstrating their acquisition of 'cultural capital', resources of knowledge and discrimination acquired through education and a particular kind of upbringing. 'Refined' taste is important less in itself than as a way of distinguishing the members of some groups from others. Those wishing to define themselves as of 'superior' social standing are likely to reject forms such as gross-out comedy, with its emphasis on corporeality and on the transgression of bodily boundaries, in favour of supposedly more 'subtle' and cerebral comic formats (this is a very generalised account, of course; the reality of taste preferences is likely to be a good deal more complex, with more overlapping between consumption categories, than Bourdieu's account and its use in the wider study of culture sometimes implies). 'Lower' forms of comedy, defined as 'crude' and lacking subtlety, have usually been seen as the preserve of either the young or groups of lower class or social standing. Their enjoyment generally requires fewer reserves of expensively acquired cultural capital, and so is accessible to those of lesser means; they also offer more intense and immediate returns of pleasure, qualities seen by Bourdieu as appropriate to the needs of lower-class audiences seeking short-term release from the rigours of their existence. Less culturally 'respectable' forms, along with offbeat or 'cult' material such as the comedy of Waters, can also generate their own special competences and investments, however, a form of subcultural capital that can be equally discriminating on its own terrain (see Thornton 1995).

Comedy, including the rapid growth in film comedy, played a significant part in the negotiation of the taste and class hierarchies of American society in the early twentieth century, an issue bound up with the relationship between gag and narrative discussed in the previous chapter (see Jenkins 1992). A new brand of humour developed, a combination of factors such as the rapid pace and harsh quality of urban American life, the contribution of new immigrant groups, an increase in the commercial production of popular cultural materials and a longer tradition of vulgar native comedy. This represented a challenge to the 'genteel' comic tradition advocated by the guardians of middle-class proprieties. The issue was not so much the existence of the crude and more direct 'New Humour', Henry Jenkins suggests, but its expansion, a process that threatened to blur taste categories that had served to naturalise social and economic inequalities: 'Materials previously restricted to the masculine culture of the saloons and the oral discourse of the ghetto were now gaining national prominence through the industrialization of amusements' (38). A whole range of broader social anxieties – 'about industrialization, urbanization, immigration, unionization, women's suffrage, and generational conflicts' – were translated into anxiety about the New Humour (41). A desire to satisfy such anxieties, to appeal to middle-class demands for decorum, and at the same time to provide the emotional intensity sought by the 'masses', is seen by Jenkins as the driving force behind the compromise mixture of narrative and crude slapstick characteristic of many of the film comedies of the early decades of the twentieth century.

A similar compromise is found in the contemporary Hollywood gross-out comedy, the grotesque elements usually taking the form of 'crude' gags located within generally more 'respectable' narrative frames. Gross-out has its own specific historical and industrial context, however. It is important to attend to these specifics, as Jenkins does in great detail in the case of early sound comedy, if we are to avoid the tendency to essentialise or universalise forms such the carnivalesque or grotesque comedy. The mix offered by the gross-out comedy in Hollywood might be explained by factors of gender more than social class, for example. The gross-out and/or sex-chasing elements of films such as *There's Something About Mary* and *American Pie* appear to be designed to appeal principally to relatively young male audiences. Elements of romantic comedy are more likely to be targeted at a female audience. A combination of the two offers the prospect of the industrially attractive 'date-movie', aimed at a teenage and young adult audience and with something to satisfy the expectations of both genders.

Hollywood-style gross-out, in its current form, is usually traced back to films of the late 1970s and early 1980s, notably *Animal House*, *Porky's* (1981) and their many imitators and sequels. *M*A*S*H* (1970) and *American Graffiti* (1973) are identified by William Paul as key predecessors and points of reference. Gross-out marked a resurgence of an episodic and slapstick style of comedy, Paul suggests, displacing romantic comedy from the position of dominance it had occupied in Hollywood comedy from the 1920s to the 1970s. Romantic comedy went into something of a decline in the 1970s and early 1980s, before returning with a vengeance in the later 1980s and 1990s. Gross-out underwent a decline of its own from the end of the 1980s, according to Paul. It, too, has since launched a major recovery, however, rivaling romantic comedy once again as the most lucrative form of comedy, and not only in Hollywood. It is not surprising, therefore, that many recent successes have offered a blend of elements of the two forms, seeking to play simultaneously on the commercial strengths of each.

The social and historical roots of gross-out are traced by Paul to wider cultural movements in the second half of the twentieth century, from the 1960s especially, involving a shift in the boundaries between what was considered acceptable in public rather than private discourses. This shift was institution-alised in the cinema by the development of the ratings system in America in 1968. A situation in which all films faced censorship or problems of distribu-tion unless deemed suitable for a general audience, of any age group, was replaced by one in which the bounds of the permissible were loosened. This provided an important marketing device for Hollywood, encouraging the pro-duction of more explicit sexual, violent and otherwise potentially 'offensive' material to differentiate its product from that of broadcast television.

Another factor helping to promote the production of gross-out-style comedy was the post-war baby-boom, an increase in the birth rate from the late 1940s that created a large teenage population in subsequent years. Teenagers and younger adults gained a greater centrality in the culture at large and became a key target market for Hollywood, especially from the 1970s. The teenage audience of today includes many second-generation products of the baby-boom, the offspring of the original boomers. Gross-out or 'vulgar' comedy, often revolving around sex, was also subject to a more general tendency in Hollywood from the 1970s in which previously 'minor', 'exploitation' or low-budget forms or genres, such as those aimed at a teenage audience, were elevated to glossier and bigger-budget treatment. As William Paul suggests: 'What is most striking about *Animal House* in the history of Hollywood comedy is not its vulgarity but rather the vulgarity within the wrappings of slick and seemingly high production values' (1994: 92). The same can be said of the gross-out movies of today, which include a number of relatively high-profile and mainstream features. They occupy an industrial and social location very different from that of the marginal position of the extreme carnivalesque films of John Waters, for example, the products of an 'underground' and counter-cultural milieu (that is, before Waters moved into the Hollywood mainstream with films such as *Polyester* (1981) and *Hairspray* (1988)).

Similarly specific social, historical and industrial explanations can be offered for the appearance of gross or carnivalesque comedy elsewhere. In Britain, 'vulgar' film comedy from the long-running *Carry On* series to an example such as *Guest House Paradiso* (1999), featuring Rik Mayall and Adrian Edmonson, can be located within a long tradition of working-class Brit-ish humour (see Medhurst 1986). In the case of *Carry On*, the more immediate sources might be the comedy of the musical hall skit or the 'saucy' seaside postcard, forms associated particularly with the north of England. Imperatives deriving from bodily functions, needs or desires – sexuality, excretion, a pref-erence for idleness – are asserted, as source of comedy, in the face of repres-sive or bureaucratic institutions (Jordan 1983). For performers such as Mayall and Edmonson, it is a not entirely 'alternative' form of comedy, developed in standup comedy clubs and on minority television channels such as BBC2 and Channel 4 in the 1980s before being translated onto film. *Kevin and Perry Go Large* (2000) is another example of movement from small screen to big and a clear case of aping the Hollywood gross-out cycle of the period; formula set pieces include a cut from a joke about 'spunk' to the splatting of white liquid (which turns out to be shampoo being squirted onto a car) and a pus-laden sequence of spot squeezing. Further afield, carnivalesque features of the films of Dusan Makavejev, such as *Nevinost bez saštite* ('Innocence Unprotected', 1968) and *W.R. – Misterije organizma* ('W.R. – Mysteries of the Organism', 1971), have been attributed to a mixture of traditional Serbian folk parody and humour and the particular upsurge of irreverence found in the more specific context of the Yugoslavian 'New Wave' in the state-communist era of the late 1960s (Horton 1991b). The use of a Bakhtinian perspective in this context returns us full circle to the context in which Bakhtin himself was writing, his work having been taken at least partially as disguised commentary on the repressive culture of Stalinism in the 1930s.

The grotesque or gross-out sometimes pushes towards the boundaries of film comedy. At what point does it cease to be comic? Is it a question of moving too close to reality? Does the climactic gross-out effect of *Pink Flamingos* cross the line by apparently depicting a real act of shit-eating? It is hard to say. Films such as *Female Trouble* and *Pink Flamingos* may be hysterically comic to some but offensive (or merely irritating) to others, occupying a space close to the uncertain and variable boundary between the comic and the non-comic. An element of offence is often intended in gross-out, as part of its transgression of the norm, whether in the context of the Hollywood mainstream or more marginal or avowedly subversive films. A deliberate strategy in some examples of the contemporary Hollywood variety is to be politically 'incorrect', up to a point, to flout what are seen to be 'orthodoxies' dictating subjects that should not be the subject of comedy. Physical disability, for example, is a major source of the gags in the Farrelly Brothers' film *Kingpin* (1996), many of which play mercilessly on the cheap prosthetic hand owned by the central character, Roy Munson (Woody Harrelson). Varying degrees of mental limitation, incapacity or illness are major elements of Farrelly Brothers productions.

'Political correctness', where it is deemed to have become a repressive institution, is more grist to the gross-out mill (although, it should be said, the notion of political correctness has been used primarily as a means to undermine attacks on deeply entrenched sexism, racism and other discriminatory discourses, rather than being such an established orthodoxy in its own right; it is hardly as if mainstream comedy is lacking in racist and/or sexist dimensions, as we will see in Chapter Four). Films such as those of the Farrellys hedge their bets on issues such as this, however, a typical characteristic of mainstream productions that do not want to give too much offense to potential viewers. A key measure of virtue in *There's Something About Mary*, for example, is a positive attitude towards Mary's brother Warren (W. Earl Brown), a character with learning difficulties. *Me, Myself and Irene* presents us with a black midget character who launches a tirade at Baileygates, unfairly accusing him of a variety of discriminations, a scene that appears to want to have it both ways: to provoke its own potential 'PC' critics while also to some extent inoculating itself against their attack.

Are there any subjects inappropriate to comedy? Almost certainly not, in any general or absolute sense, although comedies that touch on sensitive issues often generate controversy, an issue to which we will return in the final chapter. In particular contexts, the realm of the gross or grotesque deemed to be 'acceptable' does have limits, or occurs in distinct cycles. In the short term, at least, a degree of upping the ante is built into the gross-out phenomenon: that which seems particularly gross at one moment can appear tame in the light of subsequent indignities, as *Animal House* might seem to an audience twenty years on. Farting, shitting and other aspects of anality have been around in the mainstream for some time. Explicit semen-out-of-place gags are a relatively recent phenomenon in Hollywood, becoming common currency in the late 1990s. Hollywood, being innately conservative for commercial reasons, in the sense of being keenly aware of the dangers of alienating audiences, tends to go through periods of consolidation after such breakthroughs in what is allowed to reach the screen, however, rather than continually pushing back the boundaries, a process evidenced by the rather forced and less visceral gross-out highlights of successors to *American Pie* such as *Road Trip* (2000) and *American Pie 2* (2001). Some bodily process and excretions remain largely subject to taboo, most notably menstruation, a source of prohibitions in many cultures. Brief comic mention of a woman's

Figure 7 The grotesque Bakhtinian body: Mr Creosote (Terry Jones) prior to explosion in *Monty Python's The Meaning of Life* (1983)

unusually heavy period occurs in *Monty Python's The Meaning of Life* (1983). It is located, significantly, in the midst of a major gross-out sequence: a classic manifestation of the Bakhtinian grotesque body in which the hugely obese Mr Creosote (Terry Jones, plus prosthetic body extension) projectile vomits his way through an obscenely enormous dinner before exploding over his fellow diners in a posh restaurant. The passing reference to menstruation – specifically, to the possibility of 'bleeding all over the seat', a comment that causes discomfort to the woman's male accompaniment – is perhaps more transgressive of the representational norms of male-dominated culture than the main gross-out attraction. It is hard to imagine a mainstream gross-out comedy of the near future including projectile menstrual bleeding among its comic attractions, for example. Menstruation jokes may have become staples of the stand-up routines of some women performers, such as Jo Brand on British stage and television, but these are restricted to the domain of abstract verbal accounts. The depiction of menstruation is more likely to be associated in film with horror, the classic example being *Carrie* (1976), a fact that speaks volumes about male fears of supposedly 'monstrous' aspects of female bodily processes.[5]

A space outside: childishness, play and the 'pre-Oedipal'

Childishness and play. Blissful freedom from the responsibilities of 'adult' behaviour. A magical realm outside the confining spaces of the dominant cultural universe. If comedy sometimes engages in a *trans*gression of social boundaries, with a variety of possible or likely effects, it can also provide images of *re*gression to a world that appears almost pre-social, from the immature foolery of slapstick and the antics of the comedian star to the gross-out moments examined above. This may be one of the key pleasures and indulgences (or irritations, for the non-enthusiast) provided by some forms of film comedy. It can be understood from a number of perspectives, including a foray into the world of psychoanalytic theory.

A strong component of the childish is characteristic of many of the stars of comedian comedy, from the baby face of Harry Langdon to the drooling antics of Jim Carrey. Langdon is the most childlike of the silent stars, although con-temporaries such as Chaplin and Keaton are also diminutive and often cast as naïve or innocents. Other figures often presented as particularly childish in appearance and/or behaviour include Laurel (especially) and Hardy, the Marx Brothers (especially Harpo), the Three Stooges, George Formby, Bob Hope, Lou Costello, Jerry Lewis, Norman Wisdom, Pee-Wee Herman and Jim Carrey, along with many others, including some of the more widely ranging interna-tional examples cited in Chapter One. Freudian psychoanalytic theory offers one way of examining exactly how such performers are situated, although this can also be translated into more sociological or political/ideological terms.

The realm of comic play might be understood in terms of the Freudian concept of the pre-Oedipal, the stage in early childhood before we are said to begin to take up what will become our relatively fixed positions (especially sexually) within the grown-up social arena, a process described by Freud in terms of the resolution of the Oedipus complex.

The pre-Oedipal has been characterised in various accounts – drawing on and extrapolating from Freud – as a world of fluid, unstructured and unstable possibilities, before the erection of social prohibitions. This is seen as potentially liberating, although less in terms of what it might actually be like to inhabit a pre-Oedipal realm (should such a thing be possible for anyone other than the young child) than through the contrast it appears to offer to the constraints of the adult and/or social arena. The pre-Oedipal might be seen in this way, metaphorically, as a world of freedom and play, of unfixed identity and polymorphous perversity, whether or not we accept the specific psychic mechanisms described by Freud. In the universe of the Marx Brothers, for example, we find a fluidity of relationship between language and reality. There is a tendency to literalise the metaphorical (Groucho's character looking for the official university seal in *Horse Feathers* (1932), for instance, and being presented by Harpo with a real live sea mammal) and to slide in gag routines from one meaning of a word to another, suggesting an imperfectly anchored entry into the symbolic arena of culture.[6] Jokes, according to Freud, provide pleasure by allowing a prolongation of the playful state of early childhood, in which there is no requirement to make sense in behaviour such as the use of language, in the face of adult critical reason (1976: 179). (At a later stage in the development of his theories of the mechanisms of the psyche, Freud locates humour in the realm of the pleasure principle. It is here, he speculates, that the super-ego, a component of the ego, offers comfort to the hard-pressed ego by asserting that the apparently dangerous world 'is nothing but a game for children – just worth making a jest about' (1990: 433).) Something like the pre-Oedipal might be used from a sociological perspective, to signify a stage before the young child is entirely socialised or inducted into a particular set of cultural beliefs, practices and behaviours. The specifics of Freud's account of Oedipal dynamics may have some purchase within the particular context of the Western/patriarchal society in which it was developed, even if it might be less applicable elsewhere.

Comedian comedy can be read in terms of a dialectical exchange between something like the pre-Oedipal and the Oedipal. This is another way of approaching the tension between disruption and integration considered in the previous chapter. The pre-Oedipal, in a psychoanalytically-informed account, is the arena of disruption, play and fluidity, including the unmotivated or excessively extended gag or comic performance. The Oedipal is the movement towards integration, into both narrative structure and the world of adult social relationships. The comic character/performer, figured as disruptive, playful and childlike, might be required to undergo an Oedipal process of

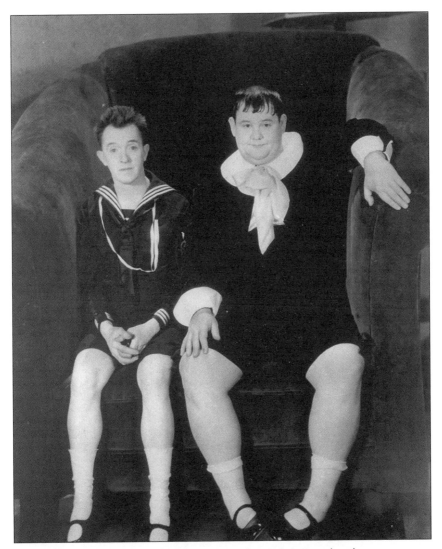

Figure 8   Stan Laurel and Oliver Hardy in full regressive mode in *Brats* (1930)

growth, signified by developments such as the establishment of a 'grown-up' relationship with a member of the opposite sex or the assumption of an authoritative, prestigious or otherwise successful and 'well-adjusted' social role. Alternatively, the character might remain wedded to the imaginary world of the pre-Oedipal. Or, as so often, we might find a compromise between the two: a movement towards adult/social integration combined with a continued celebration of the world of playful comedy.

The Strong Man (1926) introduces us to a typically childlike Harry Langdon character, Paul Bergot, a Belgian soldier caught up in the First World War and stranded, appropriately, in No Man's Land. A bean tin is set up on a mound as a target for his machine gun, but he keeps missing. Cue blankly puzzled look on the pale and rounded babyish features. He gets out a catapult, a child's weapon more to his measure, and immediately hits the target, using the same device to see off a German solider armed with a pistol. Setting off later on an odyssey across America, Bergot passes blithely through the main plot contrivances of the film, curling up and shrinking from the perceived amorous threat of a woman at one moment, placing his fingers in his mouth in another childlike gesture in the face of a later puzzlement. At the end he is united with the woman of his dreams. He is also appointed as a police officer in the American border community to which he has inadvertently helped bring order against the forces of crime and corruption.

The trajectory of these events has clear scope to be read in Oedipal terms. Bergot's integration is established at the levels of both heterosexual relationship and assumption of (male, legal) authority. The presence of the distinctive Langdon persona goes a long way to undermine this resolution, however. He cuts an absurd and unlikely figure as a cop, the uniform seeming a touch too large, its formal lines only heightening the juvenile appearance of its occupant's features. One of his first actions in uniform is to fall off a kerb. Exactly what kind of 'adult' relationship he might be able to sustain with the

Figure 9   Blank-faced babyish incomprehension: Harry Langdon out of his league in *The Strong Man* (1926)

girl (Priscilla Bonner) remains open to question; her blindness, and the fact that she is the daughter of a clergyman, establishes her as a kindred spirit of innocence.

The films of Jerry Lewis figure prominently in considerations of the pre-Oedipal or Oedipal dynamics of comedian comedy.[7] Lewis is one of the most crazily infantile of comedian stars, his performances built to a large extent out of childish mannerisms and incapacities. The speech of his characters lapses frequently into screeches, screams or incoherent and childlike stammering and burbling. A sense of clearly established identity is sometimes lacking, especially in the numerous films in which he plays more than one character: from the Jekyll and Hyde split personality of *The Nutty Professor* to five roles in *Three on a Couch* (1966) and seven in *The Family Jewels* (1965). Scott Bukatman interprets these qualities using Jacques Lacan's reformulation of Freudian theory, particularly his conception of the mirror stage of development. In the mirror stage, the young child is said to gain a ('misrecognised') sense of its individual coherence through the recognition of its image in the mirror (Lacan 1977). In Lacanian theory, a major influence on film theory in recent decades, the movie screen is seen as playing a role akin to that of the mirror, reflecting back to the viewer and reinforcing an ideal image of the unified ego (a theoretical assumption that has been questioned from a number of directions, as have psychoanalytical interpretations of cinema more generally). The films of Lewis offer something different, Bukatman suggests, an 'image of motor incapacity, sexual ambiguity, and unfixed identity', a perspective 'more closely aligned with the image of the infant, as Lacan puts it, "still sunk in his motor incapacity and nursling dependence"' (1991: 203, quoting Lacan 1977: 2).

A similar perspective is taken by Steven Shaviro (1993) in an attempt to explain the particularly *embarrassing* potential of Lewis's comedy, a quality largely responsible for its ability to generate irritation as much as pleasure for many viewers. Unlike most forms of slapstick, Shaviro suggests, the Lewis variety does not offer carnivalesque release from usual standards of responsibility. It is based instead on exaggerated respect for dominant social values. Excessive respect for authority can be a source of subversive humour, as Shaviro argues, citing the work of Gilles Deleuze on masochism. 'By scrupulously applying the law,' Deleuze suggests, 'we are able to demonstrate its absurdity and provoke the very disorder that it is intended to prevent or to conjure' (1991: 88). The masochist, for Deleuze, is a rebel, a humorist who seeks to reduce the law to its logical consequences. This reading might be applied to Lewis, Shaviro suggests, 'but his comic personas never possess the *will* to twist and pervert the law that characterises the true masochist. Lewis is an anarchist not in spite of, but because of, his hyperconformism: he disseminates chaos in the course of earnestly trying to do exactly what bosses, psychoanalysts, media specialists, and other technicians of normalising power want him to do' (1993: 110). His characters are not asserted as individuals in opposition to social institutions, in the manner found in much comedian comedy; they give way, instead, to 'an embarrassing orgy of humiliation and abjection' (112). Any degree of identification with such characters 'opens the door not to a solidification, but to a schizophrenic fragmentation and disintegration of the personality' (121).

The power of cinema significantly to shape or construct its spectator has been greatly exaggerated in psychoanalytically-influenced film theory; to suggest that the *offering* of so humiliating a source of identification might prove a source of comedy that entails elements of irritation or embarrassment, however, requires a far smaller leap of faith. But it is important to remember that Lewis was phenomenally popular during his heyday, however much he has since fallen from favour. As Ed Sikov argues, this suggests some more specific resonance between the figures played by Lewis and the particular cultural complexes of the immediate postwar decades in America, a period characterised by Sikov as one in which film comedy provided a liberating outlet in a time of extraordinary repression. Lewis, in this account, 'is the hysterical manifestation of his culture's failed repression – imminent sexual criticism incarnate. To look at Lewis today is to remind ourselves too uncomfortably of who we were and what made us hysterical. His current reputation is not at all surprising' (1994: 190). In more abstract psychoanalytical terms, Gaylyn Studlar (1988) argues that one of the central pleasures offered by cinema in general – not just the kinds of comedy considered in this section – is the opportunity it provides for regression to something closer to the fluidity of identity associated with the pre-Oedipal.[8]

A more conventional Oedipal dynamic exists on the narrative surface of *The Disorderly Orderly* (1964), in which Lewis plays the hospital orderly Jerome Littlefield, who has been kept from following his father into a brilliant medical career by a syndrome defined as 'neurotic identification empathy'. Jerome's problem is that he is overly sensitive to the suffering of others. Patients only have to describe their ailments for Jerome to go into comic paroxysms of empathetic pain. He is unable entirely to separate himself from others, it seems, to establish the boundaries of his own individuality. A cure is effected when a plot device enables him to escape an obsession with a previously unattainable woman that he has been carrying for years. The film ends with a proposal to marry a more suitable girlfriend and the prospect of a renewed medical career, following in the footsteps of his father: a classic Oedipal resolution. It is not clear that we should expect Jerome-as-manifested-by-Lewis to be converted so easily or entirely into a grown-up, however, especially as the resolution is secured partly through an extended and extremely madcap slapstick chase sequence the lunacy of which is primarily his responsibility.

A movement towards something like an Oedipal resolution is disrupted at the end of *The Patsy* (1964). The Lewis character, the hapless and childlike imbecile Stanley Belt, becomes an 'unlikely' success after being plucked from his job as a hotel bellboy to be moulded into the replacement for a dead comedian. After achieving success, through his own inventiveness, Belt suddenly becomes a more capable and assertive figure, ordering around the team who had sought to manipulate him in order to maintain their own careers. At this point, however, when a dynamic of growth appears to have come to fruition, play is taken onto another level. Belt falls from the hotel balcony, repeating the gag cited in Chapter One, but in this case the unreal status of the event is made more explicitly manifest: the fictional frame is broken as Belt reappears saying 'it's a movie, see, I'm fine', addressing his co-star by her real name and calling the crew for a lunch break. A metafictional level of play is asserted although, in this case, the figure of Lewis occupies the position of 'adult' controlling authority that he gained in his real career as director of this and many of the films in which he appears (Krutnik 1994: 21–2).

A compromise solution, combining elements of the Oedipal and pre-Oedipal, is perhaps the most common option in this kind of comedy, articulated in a number of ways, from childlike adult to adult-like child. Pee-Wee Herman, in *Pee-Wee's Big Adventure* (1985), offers another image of the childlike adult, a bizarre example of arrested (mental? social?) development, reminiscent of Langdon with his whitened face and lipstick-emphasised mouth; the nasal- and lispy-voiced, chuckling and mincing occupant of an eccentric play-world of toys and bright primary colours. Pee-Wee certainly appears to lack sexual maturity and much in the way of adult perspective. He resists the efforts of Dotty (Elizabeth Daily) to get him on a date to the local drive-in, investing instead in a fetishistic over-attachment to his bicycle, the theft of which drives the main narrative line of the film. A series of adventures on the road does lead the otherwise overbearing Pee-Wee to develop, to learn some humility and to acknowledge his attraction to Dotty; she does, in the end, get her desired date at the drive-in. It remains very much Pee-Wee's show, however, the movie playing at the drive-in being based on his own adventures. The extent of the romantic integration is, again, questionable; it is unclear how much romancing Dotty is likely to achieve at a drive-in attended not in a car but with the hero's eccentric two-wheeled object of desire.

The figure of the childlike adult is also a major feature of the Robin Williams vehicle *Mrs Doubtfire*, in which Daniel Hillard is painted as lacking in adult/parental responsibility. Not only does he get sacked at the start of the film, but he allows a birthday party for one of his children to descend into anarchy. His masquerade as Doubtfire, however, enables him to have it both ways: to combine his playful side with that of the strict-but-loveable adult. At the end of the film, reconciliation of the opposition between the two is institutionalised in the form of Hillard's openly-acknowledged *performance* of Doubtfire in a children's television show. The performative skills of Williams have also been used elsewhere to explore the interface between adult and childhood: *Hook* (1991) and *Jack* (1996) present the spectacle of the middle-aged star as, respectively, an over-worked and neglectful adult rediscovering his inner child and a prodigiously-developed child in adult-sized body.

The behaviour of the principals of *Dumb and Dumber* is irrepressibly child-like and irresponsible, a source of much of the comedy of the film. Sent out to buy 'just the bare essentials' with the last of the principals' limited cash, Lloyd emerges from a shop wearing a ludicrous giant stetson and carrying two cases of beer and a bunch of plastic windmills. Stumbling later across a fortune they intend to restore to its owner, the pair blow it recklessly on a flashy hotel room, a Ferrari and absurdly loud clothes. Playing in the snow in a would-be lyrical interlude, Harry demonstrates an infantile lack of perspective, hurling snowballs with excessive force and generally demonstrating an lack of understanding of the acceptable boundaries of play. Like Pee-Wee and his neighbour Francis (Mark Holton) in *Pee-Wee's Big Adventure*, Lloyd and Harry engage in childish verbal battles. They play 'tag' in their van, seated each side of a hit-man with serious designs on their lives. The dialogue is reduced to a series of rapid interchanges that goes something like this : 'You're it – you're it – you're it – quitsies – anti-quitsies – you're it – quitsies – no anti-quitsies, no startsies – you can't do that – can too – cannot, stamped it – can too, double stamped it, no erasies – cannot, tripled stamped it, no erasies, touched-boo-make-it-true – you can't triple stamp a double stamp, you can't triple stamp a double stamp...' at which point Lloyd sticks his fingers in his ears and lah-lah's loudly, with his tongue, to block out his partner's continuing complaints. The hit-man despairs.

Carrey's Lloyd reverts to babyhood, in a manner reminiscent of Langdon, especially when under sexual threat, curling into a foetal position and sucking his thumb when approached by a homosexual bully in a toilet. In typical Hollywood comedy style, and more by accident than intent, they help to foil the villains and win the day, as far as the underlying plot device goes, eventually contributing to the capture of the kidnappers whose ransom loot Lloyd inadvertently picks up at the start of the film. They end up a success in part of the plot, but not in the romantic dimension. Mary's husband is released from kidnap and returns to secure the girl. Lloyd shoots him, but only in his daydreams. The pair are left on the road in their realm of childlike simplicity, too dim even to realise that a passing coach-load of fantasy women on a 'national bikini tour', seeking two 'oil boys' to grease them up before each competition, could possible be referring to them. Their tag squabble resumes as the credits roll...

Images of the adult-like child are found less frequently than the childlike adult, perhaps because they offer a less obvious route towards the comic pleasures of regression. A similar effect can be achieved, however. In *Big* (1988) a 12-year-old boy gets his wish to be 'big', waking up the next morning as a man of 30. The result, for the viewer, is something close to the spectacle of the childlike adult. The physically adult Scott (Tom Hanks) achieves success working for a toy company, initially in a lowly computing post. His child's instinct for the toys that will prove most popular with his contemporaries earns rapid promotion and wealth that is converted into a large apartment equipped with indulgences such as a trampoline, an indoor basketball hoop and a *Coca-Cola* machine. The image is of an apparently adult figure (although given adolescent mannerisms in Hanks' understated performance) granted the freedom, resources and licence to live a life of play. Complications intrude, however. Scott begins to lose some of his childish qualities. He swaps casual attire for a suit and tie and neglects his childhood best friend. Realising what is happening, he opts for a return home, managing to undo the spell and return to his proper place. He grows, but paradoxically, learning the value of his real childhood, a process that in this case entails the abandonment of a burgeoning relationship with an adult woman.

Another variation on this theme is found in *Vice Versa* (from the same year, 1988; a remake of the 1948 British original), where a magical wish-fulfillment allows an adult and child to swap bodies (each thinking the other has an easier life). The obsessively tidy workaholic Marshall Seymour (Judge Reinhold) is loosened up and rendered more 'human' after occupying the body of his 11-year-old son Charlie (Fred Savage) and having his place taken by the son. Charlie-in-the-body-of-Marshall is, again, the comic figure of the adult freed from most of the weight of mature responsibility and, as a result, opened to new insights. It is through his incarnation by his son that Marshall's romantic relationship with his colleague Sam (Corrine Bohrer) is not only saved but develops to the point of a proposal of marriage; the son also manages, through recourse to blunt honesty, to save the father's career. The fully-realised adult, the film suggests, requires a combination of the virtues of maturity and childlike innocence.

An apparently magical wish-fulfilment (in fact, simply a catalogue of parental errors) is also responsible the plight of Kevin (Macaulay Culkin), left to fend for himself in *Home Alone* (1990). This, again, seems in part to be the achievement of a child's dream of freedom to indulge, to sit in front of the television watching junk movies and eating junk food without any parental intervention. But Kevin, characterised by other members of the family as incompetent, learns to manage for himself in more adult ways. His trip to the supermarket is primarily in search of sensible products such as bread, milk, toilet rolls and washing liquid rather than more indulgences, a source of comedy based on incongruity resulting from the play between adult and child imperatives. The former seem to be to the fore in the climactic scenes of the film, in which Kevin takes on the role of protector of the family home against an onslaught from two burglars. But here again the resonances are mixed, largely as a result of the mode in which the more adult and responsible role is performed: the series of defences erected by Kevin – ice on the stairways, a red-hot door handle and a range of other booby-traps – result in a feast of cartoon slapstick silliness of a more playful and pre-Oedipal cast.

A rare female version of the role-reversal scenario is found in *Freaky Friday* (1977), the immediate forerunner of the 1980s and 1990s cycle of age-swap comedies, in which mother Ellen (Ruth Buzzi) and daughter Annabel (Jodie

Foster) are granted their simultaneous Friday the 13th wishes to switch places for a day. Each generates slapstick chaos in the body and world of the other – mother facing the rigours of the school day, daughter the demands of domesticity – and each is presented as coming through the experience with new enlightenment and growth. Over-regulating mother becomes loosened up while sloppy, rebellious and underachieving tomboy makes a move in the direction of prescribed feminine development (in terms of appearance, combing her newly-curled hair in front of a mirror, for example, and burgeoning romance). The film ends with the imminent prospect of a similar transfer between younger brother and father, prefiguring the coupling that was to be favoured by its successors. The fact that the scenario has been enacted far more often in this arena suggests a greater cultural investment, as a potential 'problem' capable of imaginary reconciliation within a patriarchal context, in the issue of adult-male gender formation. Adult/child role-reversal comedies offer a version of the spectacle of regression that is more narrative-led, and more narratively-legitimated, than that usually found in the infantile antics of a performer such as Jerry Lewis. They may, as a result, have less potential to unsettle and/or embarrass the viewer, a clear rationale being given for instances of incongruously regressive behaviour.

From a social-cultural perspective, films such as these can be read as attempting a negotiation between the rival demands of the pre-Oedipal and the Oedipal, the comic pleasures and freedoms of the former and the necessary social responsibilities of the latter. Where exactly does the balance lie? For Steve Seidman, it is usually in favour of social conformity and integration, the Oedipal half of the equation. He acknowledges the difficulty with which this is sometimes achieved in comedian-centred comedy, a difficulty marked by the frequent recurrence of performative elements that go well beyond the requirements of any Oedipal narrative frame, 'since these performances showcase the comic figure's penchant toward the imaginary, instinctual, and subjective, and earn him applause' (1979: 78). Transformation is the resolution of most comedian comedy films, Seidman suggests, providing 'a reaffirmation of culture's belief in social conformity' (78). The social or mythic function of comedian comedy, in this account, is to work through and reconcile competing dynamics such as those of the pre-Oedipal and the Oedipal, to indulge some of the pleasures of the one while asserting the ultimate necessity of the latter. Comedian comedy is thus located in the broader process of socialisation necessary to all cultures, offering 'a narrative model for how to evolve into a coherent individual, for taking one's place in the social order, and for regulating difference in order to be an accepted member of collective life' (146).

The balance of Seidman's conclusion might be contested, however, in favour of a less clear-cut distinction between the merits of the two components of the pre-Oedipal/Oedipal dynamic. Arguments can be made on more than one level. Seidman's focus on the mythic role of this brand of comedy might be challenged in part from an industrial perspective. The films considered above continue to celebrate the world of playful fantasy and slap-stick, despite the inclusion of a variety of Oedipal dynamics, because these are to a large extent the qualities according to which the films themselves are sold. To offer an entirely Oedipal resolution would be to deny some of the key pleasures of this kind of film comedy. That is exactly what Seidman claims ultimately to be the case. The comic figure 'must be made to conform to cul-tural values by divesting himself of his creativity, or else face rejection. The generic problems of individual evolution and cultural initiation are resolved *at the expense of what makes the genre entertaining*' (141; emphasis added). This does not seem to be the case in the examples considered above, in which a significant investment in the world of comic nonconformity and play is main-tained even in the midst of movements towards integration, or more generally. A consistent tendency in Hollywood and many other mainstream productions is to valorise the very qualities of 'entertainment' enshrined in popular cinema itself.[9] One of the key pleasures offered to the viewer is the space to enjoy the spectacle of childish regression, safely bounded by its fictional and – further, its specifically comic, avowedly non-serious – location.

A celebration of the childish and playful realm, figured in terms of the pre-Oedipal or otherwise, is also an important part of the social, cultural or ideological location of the comedy considered in this section. There is a politics of play. What is asserted by many of these films is the existence and value of an essentially primary and 'natural' realm of human existence. Social roles and structures may be seen as necessary or unavoidable, but they are often viewed as essentially secondary and prone to corruption. The childish comic figure is celebrated as one capable of seeing or breaking through what is characterised as a veneer of social conventions based on dishonesty and hypocrisy. Thus, the naïve Stanley Belt in *The Patsy* is the only character honest enough to laugh at the absurdly enormous umbrella hat worn by the columnist Hedda Hopper at his press launch party, to the horror of his minders ('You've come across somebody who hasn't yet learned to be phoney', as Hopper acknowledges), while the under-socialised Scott in *Big* can openly spit out a mouthful of caviar, accepting the immediate evidence of his own taste rather than the conventionally-established high status of an elite foodstuff. The figure of the innocent simpleton is widely used as a device to create distance from normally taken-for-granted social conventions, other examples including the unworldly Amish Ishmael Boorg (Randy Quaid) thrust into the arena of competitive bowling in *Kingpin*.

The supposedly pre-social or natural qualities of the domain occupied by comic performers are implied in some cases by references to animals or animal-like behaviour, both verbal and in the antics of performance. Monkeys and dogs figure especially frequently, examples of the former including Buster Keaton's replacement of an ape in a vaudeville act in *The Playhouse* (1921) and the transformation of Oliver Hardy into a chimpanzee in *Dirty Work* (1933) (Seidman 1979: 65–8). The monkey stands as a symbol of regression or an absence of satisfactory evolution, overtly so in *Monkey Business* (1952), in which a chimpanzee accidentally hits upon the rejuvenation formula sought by the scientist Barnaby Fulton (Cary Grant). An explicit connection is made here between regression and the world of slapstick. Youth, Fulton expostulates after a number of embarrassing encounters, entails 'maladjustment, near-idiocy and a series of low-comedy disasters'; a world that in this case, unusually, is open to male and female, a significant proportion of the comic spectacle being provided by the childlike behaviour under the influence of Fulton's wife, Edwina (Ginger Rogers). The dog is one of the few animals widely kept in close proximity to the 'normal' domestic scene (in contemporary urban western society, at least), figured as a sniffer-out of undesirable qualities in characters in films ranging historically from *The Awful Truth* (1937) to *There's Something About Mary*.

Unsocialised, uncontrolled and apparently instinctual drives to gratify desires for food, drink and sex sometimes characterise the childlike comic figure, another point of similarity with the trickster figures of myth. Harpo Marx is a good example of such appetite, devouring a range of unsuitable items including ink, a button from a bellboy's jacket, a flower and part of a telephone in *The Cocoanuts* (1929), Groucho's lit cigar and part of Chico's tie in *A Night at the Opera*, a thermometer and poison in *A Day at the Races* and tending, throughout, to grab without restraint at any passing female figure. Unfettered bodily response is also found in some animated figures, especially those of Tex Avery, the crazed distortions of which suggest a direct expression of emotions and desires, often related to sex and consumption: 'Avery derives humour from illustrating how the body would react if it did have the capacity to properly express the intensity of its feelings' (Wells 1998: 148). In *Swing Shift Cinderella*, for example, the wolf's reaction on first sight of the curvy female star is to pant, cough, leap up into the air, somersault, spin around the branch of a tree, clap his hands and feet and kick himself in the head before falling smitten to the ground. The mask that brings about cartoon-like transformation in *The Mask*, including explicit homage to *Swing Shift Cinderella*, brings the wearer's innermost unsocialised desires to life, we are told.

It was precisely a fear of the kind of loss of bodily control manifested in these and many other examples that was a driving force behind the denigration of laughter-creating forms of comedy in neoclassical debate in the sixteenth century, a tradition dating back to the writings of Plato and Aristotle (Neale & Krutnik 1990: 62–3). The physiological act of laughter itself constitutes an upsurge of bodily response. Its causes might be socially grounded, and actual laughter-responses are subject to control and/or repression – the level and extent of laughter tends to be regulated, upwards or downwards, according to viewing context; for writers such as Ben Johnson, however, the generation of laughter is unseemly, a sign of moral turpitude, especially for those of the 'higher' classes. This is one reason, Neale and Krutnik suggest, for the development of so many plot-based approaches to comedy in the period. A

Figure 10   Unlimited appetite: Harpo Marx making a meal of Chico's tie in *A Night at the Opera* (1935)

similar dynamic appears to drive later critical discomfort with 'lower' forms of film comedy, from the 1910s to date.

Animalistic qualities are also foregrounded in the gross-out format considered in the previous section, a variety labelled 'animal comedy' by William Paul. The protagonists often exhibit characteristics of immaturity or stupidity, as we have seen in the case of *Dumb and Dumber*, and are sometimes set as childlike figures against those in adult/authority roles such as college principals, police or army officers. The focus of many gross-out moments on activities such as farting and shitting, or on substances such as faeces, urine and semen displaced to the upper regions, suggests an indulgence of the anal and oral drives described in the Freudian account of pre-Oedipal sexuality. The fact that these activities are experienced *as* gross within the fictional world, however, suggests some movement towards the internalisation of adult/cultural norms. The specific pleasure of this kind of comedy, from a Freudian perspective, lies in the opportunity it offers for a vicarious release from the usual adult requirement to repress any delight in the anally or orally fixated world of the pre-Oedipal. Whether repression, here, is understood as a matter of innate psychic process or social proscription (or a combination of the two) is a subject of much debate.

The varying balance between elements of gross-out and of romantic comedy is another dynamic that might also be read from a pre-Oedipal/

Oedipal perspective. The protagonists develop, in some cases, to the point at which they are able to engage in grown-up – or at least, relatively grown-up – romantic or sexual relationships, leaving behind the arena of anal/oral gross-out effects (examples might include *There's Something About Mary* and *American Pie*). In others, including *Dumb and Dumber*, any such development remains limited or retarded. Gross-out films often feature, and are primarily targeted at, groups or individuals located at the border between adolescence and adulthood. This may be one reason why many of these films express an ambivalence about the relative merits of the two, as Paul suggests. The principal focus of Hollywood 'animal' comedy is on the gratification of individual sexual desire (usually male). It might seem contradictory for this act of sexual initiation to be taken as a benchmark of maturity, yet 'this is an act that specifically defines connection to another person' (1994: 172). It is also a more grown-up activity than the sexually-related behaviour with which some characters have to make do in the meantime.

In Seidman's account, the animalistic state usually has to be left behind or overcome in a narrative of individual evolution that mirrors broader cultural requirements of socialisation. Gross-out or animal comedy retains a greater investment in the celebration of the animalistic, however, if only as a guard against what are seen as the excesses of over-civilised or over-socialised rigidity. The same goes for some romantic comedies. The classic example is *Bringing Up Baby*, which establishes a series of parallels and oppositions between certain characters, characteristics and its own principal representative of the animal kingdom, the eponymous leopard. Both the madcap Susan and the repressed David are associated with the leopard, at different moments in the film, through devices such as verbal references and clothes (her spotted negligee and a spotted veil; his spotted tie) (Babbington & Evans 1989: 32). The leopard is a representative of the animal/natural forces from which David appears to have become alienated and to which, the film suggests, he needs to be restored. The leopard stands for nature and, by extension, sexuality, the precise nature of which are rendered somewhat ambiguous by the film's inclusion of *two* leopards, the more-or-less tame Baby and a dangerous man-killer inadvertently released by David (a representative of the darker forces unleashed from his unconsciousness, as it might be read from a Freudian perspective). The name 'Baby' suggests a parallel between the animalistic and the infantile and seemingly consequence-free world of play occupied by the wealthy Susan (who never seems to have to worry much about the scrapes into which she gets) and into which David is led, through a series of playfully absurd actions designed to break down the armour of dull respectability.

The key sequences leading towards the eventual union of David and Susan take place in a Connecticut forest in which they attempt to catch Baby, a classic instance of the 'magical' realm, a liminal place outside normal cultural constraints, in which play, regression and comic transformation can occur in various combinations. Different versions of this pastoral or utopian sphere are found in romantic comedies dating back to Shakespeare's *As You Like It* and *A Midsummer Night's Dream*.[10] Romantic attachments are often initiated, forged or consummated on this kind of terrain or its modern equivalents. The privileged space in *Holiday* (1938) is explicitly labelled the 'playroom', the one zone of informality, freedom and fun in a vast, stuffy and museum-like Fifth Avenue mansion. It is here, amid a clutter of childhood toys and musical instruments, that Johnny (Cary Grant) first meets Linda (Katherine Hepburn), the sister of the woman with whom he is supposed to be in love, and where the pair realise their 'natural' affinity as rebellious free spirits (Johnny's reaction to worries is to perform handsprings and other improvised acrobatics). A similarly liminal space is provided by the Vanderhof house in *You Can't Take It With You* (1938), a refuge from the world of dull business routine in which assorted oddballs and eccentrics can pursue their unlikely dreams; and, characteristically, an influence that leads to the transformation-through-play (in this case, musical) of the threatening force represented by a manipulative tycoon.

States of physical transit or transition offer one source of space for the romantic revelation, transformation or consummation, a version that in Hollywood comes with resonances of the American frontier and/or road-movie traditions. Examples include the cross-country drives of *It Happened One Night* and *When Harry Met Sally*; and, on water, range from the luxurious surroundings of a liner in mid-ocean in *The Lady Eve* (1941) to the mid-Thames rowboat (complete with full Moon and the twinkling lights of a bridge) in *Sliding Doors*. In *You've Got Mail* the magical dimension takes the late-twentieth-century form of cyberspace, another realm understood by some as a potentially utopian place in which normal social constraints need not apply; in which characters such as Kelly and Fox can discover themselves in their 'true' natures, unencumbered by baggage such as their relative positions in the socio-economic sphere.

The very notion of a place outside the social is itself a social construct, however, and one with deeply ideological implications. Even if non-socialised aspects of life do exist, any discourse about them immediately enters into the socio-cultural arena. To suggest that spheres such as the social, cultural or economic are essentially secondary is to deny the extent to which they in fact structure and call into being many aspects of our lives, including large parts of phenomena such as gender and the enactment of gender-roles (see G. King 1996). The celebration of childlike play found in many film comedies can be seen partly as an expression of the ideology of commercial entertainment institutions such as Hollywood, keen to praise the characteristics of their own products. One of the most blatant, if somewhat ironic, manifestations of this tendency is found in *Sullivan's Travels* (1941), in which a director of popular features engages in research in preparation for a more 'serious' and strait-laced production, only to be taught the value of the foolish nonsense on which his career has been based when he lands up in prison and joins the other inmates in experiencing the release in laughter provided by a show of cartoons.

But the celebration of 'regressive' forms of play also participates in broader social, cultural and ideological discourses that tend to have conservative or reactionary implications. Crazy, anarchic, pre-Oedipal or childlike behaviour might be celebrated in some cases as a way of questioning or attacking *particular* social structures or institutions, of one variety or another. In *Holiday* and *You Can't Take It With You*, for example, it is an obsession with the accumulation of power and riches for their own sake. But it can easily slip into a more general advocation of the primacy of a realm of 'nature' – the 'innocent' pre-social or a-social – that has the effect of presenting as natural or inevitable social structures or relationships that are the outcome of particular (and therefore contingent and potentially changeable) social or historical processes. The potential ideological implications of this are open to examination both generally and in particularly heightened historical contexts: the Depression of 1930s America, the age of the 'classic' Hollywood romantic comedy, for example; or the Reagan era of the 1980s, a period that saw the production of a clutch of comedies that use the figure of the child effectively to naturalise representations of phenomena such as the family and parent-child relationships that were subjects of heated political controversy at the time.

From a Freudian perspective, the pleasure of comedy lies in its potential to release forces that are usually repressed, for one reason or another; a return to 'primal' pleasures, which might include those of the kinds of bodily functions highlighted in gross-out comedy; *un*socialised behaviour that bursts through the restraints of normally acceptable conduct. The kind of repression that might be escaped in the realm of comedy need not be seen as 'primary' or essential, however, a quality that is often problematic in the Freudian account. It might be understood as a product of more specific social and historical factors, including urges to escape from overly constraining frameworks such as those prescribed in dominant practices of gender-role socialisation. In film comedy, repression is also a fictional invention, of course, designed specifically in some cases to create the opportunity for pleasurable entertainment based on that deemed to be transgressive within only these limited confines.

three

satire and parody

Satire: comedy with an edge

American politics is corrupt. The only groups that achieve real representation are those rich enough to make large donations to the major parties. Politicians and governments do not care about anyone else, except when making empty promises in cynical search of votes. Jobs are lost because contributors make more money investing in Mexico. The rich get richer while the poor and racially oppressed die in poverty. American foreign policy, meanwhile, is based on lies. Supposed 'enemies' are conjured up to serve partisan political purposes at home, primarily to keep one administration or interest group or another in power.

These are fairly radical political claims, unlikely to be expressed in mainstream forms such as Hollywood cinema, we might think. Yet they are precisely the arguments voiced, among others, in two late 1990s films featuring major star performers. *Wag the Dog* (1997) and *Bulworth* (1998) are examples of political satire, a form that treads an uneasy line between comedy and more obviously 'serious' and contentious material. Satire is comedy with an edge and a target, usually social or political in some way. It can be relatively light and playful, or in deadly earnest; in some cases it can land its producers in jail, exile or even worse. Satire is sometimes used as a way of voicing criticism of oppressive or totalitarian regimes, such as those of Stalinist rule in the Soviet Union or Eastern Europe, or various administrations in Latin America: a potentially dangerous business. But it is a form of comedy that also widens the scope for social/political criticism in the relatively mainstream film products of more 'liberal' societies such as the United States.

What, though, is the effect of voicing this kind of material through a form of comedy? Does it undermine the impact of what is being said, or might its effect be heightened? The answer depends on the precise manner in which comedy is mobilised to satirical/critical effect in any individual example. Satire is a somewhat unstable quality. It shades at one end into broader and generally 'safer' comic forms. At the other, it reaches into darker realms, beyond that usually considered to be comic. Not all satire is oppositional in relation to its place of production, as a subversive undercurrent. Satire can also be used as a form in which to attack external enemies. In some cases, however, comedy of a satirical variety might be the *only* way in which internal social or political criticism can reach an audience.

Satire with a real, sustained or unmeliorated cutting edge is relatively uncommon in mainstream, mass-audience commercial cinema. This is not surprising. Most forms of comedy tend to pull their punches. Any serious implications are usually insulated or substantially reduced by the assurance that, as comedy, a film is ultimately 'just kidding', even if it does contain the more dramatic undertow identified by Raymond Durgnat (1969: 23). This is one of the great attractions of comedy as a whole: its ability to tread in potentially sensitive areas without the risk that might be associated with a straight or more serious treatment. Satire does not always offer this safety net, although the precise balance between the serious and the comical is variable. Satire may be the primary mode of a film or, perhaps more frequently, just one component among others. It can be harsh and biting, assuming a particular moral or political standpoint. In Northrop Frye's definition of satire: 'Its moral norms are relatively clear, and it assumes standards against which the grotesque and absurd are measured' (1957: 233). Frye distinguishes satire in this way from irony, in which he suggests the attitude of the author is left uncertain. As such, film satire risks causing offence to significant numbers of potential viewers, a quality that makes it less attractive generally for film-makers seeking to reach a mass audience. In Hollywood, for example, satire of a sharply political nature is more likely to be offered as a niche-audience product than as the stuff of enormous box-office expectations. Even here, as we will see, its edge may be blunted in numerous ways.

Satire in literature has a long and distinguished history, dating back at least as far as ancient Greece and Rome, including a flowering in eighteenth-century English writing in the works of major figures such as Jonathan Swift and Alexander Pope. Upsurges in the production of satire are often associated with particular social/historical circumstances: 'The pattern of great eras of satire parallels eras of public excess, hardship, impropriety, and aberration, notably post-Republican Rome, Britain's Restoration Era, and America's Prohibition Era and Great Depression' (Snodgrass 1996: 406–7). Much the same

can be said, in general, of satire in film, although broad social-historical associations such as these need to be balanced by more local, specific and contingent factors. Hollywood satires such as *Bulworth* and *Wag the Dog* can be
seen as products of a period in which American faith in politics and politicians
reached a lower than average ebb as a result of criticism of the role played by
party funding and/or the revelation of sexual indiscretions during the Clinton
era. They also owe their existence to the fact that they were driven or sup-
ported by big 'name' stars with industrial clout: Warren Beatty in *Bulworth* and
Robert De Niro and Dustin Hoffman in *Wag the Dog*. Beatty produced, directed
and performed numerous other duties as well as starring in *Bulworth*, a film
that was made under an open-ended deal between Beatty and Twentieth Century Fox that bypassed the possibility of studio objection to the material (the
political dimension was not added to the project until after the studio commitment had been made). *Wag the Dog* was produced by De Niro and Hoffman's
own production companies on a modest $15 million budget and shot in just 29
days, unusually quick by Hollywood standards.

Elements of satire that might be related in part to the context of Depression
and post-Depression eras are present in some of the Hollywood comedies of
the 1930s and 1940s. *Duck Soup* can be read as madcap satire of government
and war-mongering, even if the crazy antics of the Marx Brothers outweigh
any very serious perspective. Less zany, but ultimately more soft-centred, is
the assault on political corruption launched in Frank Capra's *Mr Smith Goes
to Washington* (1939). A sharper and wittier satirical edge is present in a
number of films from the period directed by Preston Sturges, including *The
Great McGinty* (1940), on political manipulation, and *Hail the Conquering Hero*
(1944), on American hero-worship. Satire continued to exist in the Hollywood
of the 1950s, despite the pressure for conservative conformity imposed by the
McCarthyite gaze. The postwar era produced mainstream comedy of a tone
darker 'and more explicitly unnerving in its implications' than that of the preceding period, according to Ed Sikov (1994: 123). Notable examples are found
in the 1950s films of Billy Wilder, including bleakly satirical treatment of the
press in *Ace in the Hole* (aka *The Big Carnival*, 1951) – in which a down-on-his-
luck reporter (Kirk Douglas) cynically prolongs the ordeal of a man trapped
underground in order to use the story as his route back into the big time; the
victim dies as a result – and of Hollywood itself in *Sunset Boulevard* (1950).
The 1960s and 1970s were marked by the production of a number of prominent
and biting black comedies and satires, usually understood as manifestations
of a period of heightened social conflict and a questioning of established
values and institutions (see McCaffrey 1992). Examples include the dark
political and military satires of *Dr Strangelove* (1964) and *Catch-22* (1970)
and the comedy of youthful generation-gap alienation found in *The Graduate*
(1967). Elsewhere, in British cinema, satire has ranged from the gently satirical
spirit of some of the Ealing comedies, most notably *The Man in the White Suit*
(1951), to the heavier-handed assaults on various aspects of society during

the Thatcher era found in the microcosmic setting of *Britannia Hospital* (1982) and in *How to Get Ahead in Advertising* (1989).

Harsher social-political contexts have given birth to striking examples of satire on film, although an indirect approach might be required in the more extreme circumstances. Direct social satire of the regime was close to an impossibility in the cinema during the Stalinist era in the Soviet Union, for example: 'The atmosphere of ideological intolerance and constant pressure on film-makers excluded any possibility of openly conversing, of showing social shortcomings on screen, or of critically depicting reality that correspond with the nature of satiric view' (Tolstykh 1993: 18). But submerged currents can be detected in some cases. *Neobychainyie prikliucheniia mistera Vesta v strane bol'shevikov* ('The Extraordinary Adventures of Mr West in the Land of the Bolsheviks', 1924), directed by the pioneering montage theorist Lev Kuleshov, is designed as a satire of American anti-Soviet propaganda: an example of state-sanctioned satire of external opposition. The film makes fun of its representative American, John West (Porfiry Podobed), the naïveté with which he is taken in by stories about 'savage Bolsheviks', thus laying himself open to the trickery of a Russian criminal gang, and the slapstick-style antics of his loyal servant, 'Cowboy' Jeddie (Boris Barnet). But the film could also be read in places as satirical critique of the Soviet system itself. Part of the charade enacted by the gang to extort money from Mr West includes putting him on mock autocratic trial, in which he is given no opportunity to mount a defence. It seems plausible, Vlada Petric suggests, 'that the Soviet audience, while laughing at the "absurd" situations of Mr West (who by his looks and behaviour resembles Harold Lloyd), intimately related the kidnappers' "atrocities" to the methods used by the GPU (Stalinist secret police) behind the closed doors of their monstrous enterprise. The Soviet audience probably laughed at Mr West's crazy exploits, while discreetly chuckling at the presentation of an environment that was a parody of what they knew was the practice common to the Bolshevik establishment' (1993: 69). The film ends with Mr West finally being introduced to the official face of the Bolshevik regime by a friendly police officer. He witnesses some of the sights of Moscow, watches a military parade pass by (real footage, with which the fictional figure is intercut) and radiograms home to his wife to 'Burn those New York magazines, hang a portrait of Lenin on the wall, long live the Bolsheviks!' It is hard to tell from a distance how this might have played at the time, but, again, as Petric suggests, it could well be taken ironically.

A similar degree of ambivalence is traced by Peter Christensen in *Postselui Meri Pikford* ('The Kiss of Mary Pickford', 1927). The film is a satirical attack on the desire of some Soviet citizens to consume western products such as Hollywood films and star images, but it also offers success to the hero who acts out a bourgeois romantic myth (P. Christensen 1993: 55). The popular musical comedy *Volga, Volga* (1938), reputedly Stalin's favourite film, depicts the transformation of a backward town into a model of Soviet industrial growth and efficiency, a shift the absurdity of which suggests satirical or parodic intentions even if they might not have been realised by all of those involved in the production, argues Maya Turovskaya (1993). In other cases, allegorical forms are used to avoid the hazards of more direct satire.[1]

Satire was also used where possible by film-makers in Eastern Europe during the years of state communist rule, usually during periods in which particular historical factors led to a relaxation of the normally strict Stalinist restrictions on cultural production. Liberalisation in Czechoslovakia in the mid-to-late 1960s, for example, saw the appearance of films such as *Ostre Sledované Vlaky* ('Closely Observed Trains', 1966) and *Hori, Má Panenko* ('The Fireman's Ball', 1967). The former is set under German occupation during the Second World War but lends itself to a reading in terms of later dominance by the Soviet Union and its representatives. Its satire is relatively gentle (although the end is tragic), poking fun at a German officer, with his talk of assorted 'tactical retreats' in the face of the Allied advance across Europe, and a stationmaster who rails ineffectually against 'decadence' and the sexual activity of the young (and the tears it causes in the fabric of his precious leather-upholstered sofa). The latter traces the collapse into chaos of a celebration mounted by the local fire brigade, a farrago in which the raffle prizes are gradually stolen, the contestants in a beauty contest flee and the firemen prove incapable of saving the burning home of an elderly man. A world of lust, corruption and incompetence is suggested, the specific events taking on broader symbolic or allegorical resonances; they certainly did for the Czech authorities, which banned the film from being shown. These and other films have their roots in a combination of the immediate historical context and a longer tradition of satire in Czech culture (see Daniel 1983).

A significant feature of satire in Eastern Europe in this period is the use of animation as a vehicle in which to raise issues of political sensitivity. Animation can provide an effective forum for satire in difficult circumstances for a reason that otherwise tends to annoy proponents of the medium: the fact that it tends to be taken less seriously than 'live' action, often being associated culturally and historically with works designed for children. This, plus the status of the animated world as one coded more obviously as fantasy, makes it a relatively safe arena for satirical or other comic and allegorical interventions. The Czech puppet animator Jirí Trnka is one of the most notable exponents of the art, satirising Hollywood and American consumer society in *Dárek* ('The Gift', 1946) and aspects of the German occupation of Czechoslovakia in *Pérák SS* ('Springer and the SS-Men', 1946) (see Holloway 1983). In his best known film, *Ruka* ('The Hand', 1965), produced during the beginnings of the thaw in Czechoslovakia but before the 'Prague Spring' of 1968, his attention turns to the internal oppressions associated with state communism. An artisan's effort to make a simple pot in which to keep his flowers is repeatedly interrupted by the appearance of a giant hand that reshapes his work into its own image, an undisguised metaphor for the treatment of the artist by the totalitarian

Figure 11   The artisan oppressed by the symbol of totalitarian force in Jiří Trnka's *Ruka* (1965)

state. The potter is eventually forced to do the bidding of the hand, and several others that join in the oppression, when he is reduced to the status of a puppet, imprisoned in bird cage and manipulated with strings to sculpt the figure of a hand from a block. He escapes briefly but eventually pays the price of his attempted freedom with his life.

Dark satire is mixed with more obviously comic elements in some of the films produced by the distinctive Zagreb school of animation that appeared in Yugoslavia during the 1960s. *Ceremonija* ('The Ceremony', 1965), directed by Bordo Dovnikovic, establishes a light-hearted mood as five figures constantly disrupt the efforts of a sixth to line them up for what appears to be a photograph in front of a wall. One or another is constantly out of position and they all keep falling into jumbled heaps, to the comic frustration of their would-be organiser, from whose perspective a framing image is sometimes imposed on the chaos, encouraging the assumption that he is a photographer. When they do, finally, get into and remain in place, however, his shout and a grin towards the camera leads it to pan to the right to reveal the presence of the firing squad whose attentions they then receive. *Zid* ('The Wall', 1965), directed by Ante Zaninovic, offers a series of cartoon-comedy attempts by a seemingly naked long-haired man to tackle a high brick wall that lies in his path, and that disappears on one side into the distance – suggesting a structure such as the Berlin Wall – while another figure, in suit and tie, watches passively. The naked man eventually charges headlong at the wall and makes a hole but appears to die in the effort;

the other walks through, but only to be confronted by an identical structure on the other side. Pavao Stalter's *Peti* ('The Fifth One', 1964) can be read as a metaphor for persistence capable of leading to social change. The four members of a string quartet play together in harmony and repeatedly reject the contribution of a fifth player equipped, incongruously, with an enormous tuba. After several encounters, the tuba player is taken off screen-right and a shot is heard. The quartet returns and strikes up its tune. More time passes than in the previous cases but, eventually, the tuba player reappears, this time with a bandage on the front of his hat. He starts to play his simple bass notes – and the other join in to his beat, bowing, it seems, to the inevitable.

Animation has also been used to satirical effect in some mainstream western productions, although to varied and often limited critical effect. Dave and Max Fleischer's *Gulliver's Travels* suffers from reduction to children's fare, retaining none of the bite of Swift's original. This is the result not of the use of animation itself but the fact that the film was made at the end of a period in which the Fleischers had been under commercial pressure to 'Disneyfy' their product, to abandon a more amoral freewheeling style in order to compete with the dominant force in the industry (Klein 1993: 85). It is no accident that the film looks and feels closer to Disney's *Snow White and the Seven Dwarfs* (1937). The British animated version of *Animal Farm* (1955) is much more in the spirit of its literary source, George Orwell's fable of betrayed revolution, although an upbeat ending is imposed on the material. More recently, moments of satire are found in *South Park: Bigger, Longer and Uncut* (1999), in which America declares war on Canada after the farting-and-swearing-based humour of a Canadian comic duo beloved by the television series regulars is used as a scapegoat on which to pin the ills of society. Targets for satire, with some edge, among the more general silliness and a spoof-musical structure, include military plans in which all the black troops are allocated to 'Operation Human Shield' while their white counterparts are in 'Operation Get Behind the Darkies'. Animation also has a long history of use in state or privately produced satire of external enemies, examples including crude anti-German propaganda shorts made during the First World War (see Ward 2002).

The later Soviet years – the 'stagnation' period under Brezhnev and his successors and the period of *perestroika* (restructuring) and *glasnost* (openness) reforms under Gorbachev – saw a more open turn towards satire that continued into the post-Soviet era. Satirical dissections of numerous elements of politics and society appeared, with varying frequency, in Czechoslovakia, Yugoslavia, Hungary, Bulgaria and the Soviet Union and/or Russia itself.[2] The Georgian film *Monanieba* ('Repentance', 1986) is a striking late Soviet-era example dealing with the sensitive matter of Stalin's rule of terror in the 1930s, a satirical tragic-comedy that was only allowed into production as a result of the support of the Georgian party secretary (and later Soviet foreign minister) Eduard Shevardnadze and the distance of the republic from the centre of the Soviet Union (Lawton 1989). The central figure, the recently deceased Varlam

Aravidze (Avtandil Makharadze), is presented as a blend of Stalin, Hitler and Mussolini. The crimes of his rule come to light during a court hearing against a woman who keeps digging up his body, refusing to let the man and his past rest in peace. The film mixes an apparently contemporary setting with incongruous archaic features such as horse-drawn carriages and guards clad in armour and carrying pikestaffs. Satirical exaggeration is made of the ludicrous charges on which alleged traitors were arraigned during Stalin's purges: in this case a figure who confesses to attempting, with 2,700 fellow conspirators, to dig a tunnel from Bombay to London. The victim claims to be 'cunning and sly', believing that his confession to such absurdities can only lead higher authorities to intervene to end such lunacy. 'We'll sign anything, reduce it all to nonsense,' he declares: a comment that seems deeply double-edged in the context of the film.

The decrepitude of the late Soviet era is suggested metaphorically by the collapse of buildings in *Tsisperi mtebi anu arachveulebrivi ambavi* ('Blue Mountains', 1983) and *Fontan* ('Fountain', 1988). The former, another product of the Georgian film industry, is a portrait of inertia and meaninglessness, figured formally through the repetition of images in each of four sequences of 'non-events' at a publishing house to which the central figure brings the manuscript of his new novel (J. Christensen 1993: 111). The principal setting of *Fontan* is a disaster-prone Leningrad apartment building that collapses around its inhabitants, despite their efforts to get help from Party and other authorities: 'In one scene as the roof is caving in, for instance, men agree to hold the roof on their own shoulders propped up in part by old Communist signs bearing Party slogans in yet another visual satiric metaphor' (Horton 1993: 142).

If the climate of the Soviet Union and its satellites was more often than not inhospitable to satire, until its period of decline, much greater leeway has often been available under the state-communist regime established by the Cuban revolution in 1959. Notable satires include *La muerte de un burocrata* ('The Death of a Bureaucrat', 1966), a combination of broad slapstick, paying tribute to stars of the Hollywood silent era, and exposure of the absurdities of excessive bureaucratic regulation under socialism. Juanchin (Salvador Wood) wrestles with the system after the work card of his late uncle Paco, an exemplary worker who invented a machine for the mass production of heroic busts, is mistakenly buried along with the body, leaving his widow unable to claim her pension. Madcap farce ensues, as Juanchin enlists the help of cemetery workers to recover the document after being told official exhumation is not allowed within two years of burial without possession of a court order. Once removed from his grave, however, uncle Paco cannot be reburied unless an exhumation order exists to legitimate the fact that he is not already in the ground. A riotous melée breaks out when the undertaker attempts to proceed against the orders of the chief bureaucrat, a classic slapstick escalation from a Laurel and Hardy-style duel involving mutual damage to possessions (undertaker assaults bureaucrat's record book; bureaucrat rips headlights and mudguard from hearse) to all-out funeral-flower fight. Further Kafkaesque bureaucratic procedures and misunderstandings follow before Juanchin eventually strangles the bureaucrat and is hauled off in a straitjacket.

Demasiando miedo a la vida o Plaff ('Too Afraid of Life, or Splatt', 1988) offers further satire of Cuban bureaucratic inertia. The chemical engineer Clarita (Thais Valdés) invents a polymer of greater efficiency than the one currently being imported from Canada at the cost of precious hard currency. A valuable resource, made from pig excrement. It cannot be developed, however, because it does not fit into the existing plan. When the go-ahead is eventually given, it can only be handled by the appropriate bureaucratic body – and, yes, there is an Institute for the Development and Investigation of Excrement ('we have the last word when it comes to excrement'). A filing cabinet, meanwhile, has appeared from nowhere, just inside the office of Clarita's superior, a source of recurrent slapstick humour as he and others keep walking into it. An identical cabinet turns out to have gone missing from the excrement institute: enormous piles of memos, replies-to-memos and answers-to-replies are testament to the bureaucratic absurdity of the procedure required even to attempt its recovery. If official inertia is one side of the coin, the other is the equally absurd revolutionary optimism with which goals are pursued once adopted by the system. Towards the end of the film an official knocks on Clarita's door to tell her that a plant is, finally, to be built to manufacture her polymer – and it is expected to open in a month. To her protests that this is impossible, given that the product has only been developed so far under laboratory conditions, the confident reply is that it has to open on the 12th of the next month as this is Chemist's Day and everyone has been invited to the ceremony.

The satirical gaze is turned here on the institutionalised-revolutionary habit of celebrating the supposed heroic zeal of just about every kind of worker, a device also applied to the film itself. The first images appear upside-down on the screen. A voice-over then informs us that the first reel has been lost. This, and a number of subsequent technical glitches, is explained by the fact that the film has been made in a rush – to be ready in time for Film-maker's Day. Performers step out of role on more than one occasion to complain about missing props or to apologise for forgetting lines. The film includes numerous examples of rough and incomplete-appearing editing and poor-quality sound. One 'missing' scene is described by the voice-over. These self-reflexive devices can be read on more than one level: as satire of the inadequacies of over-hasty revolutionary production generally, within the body of the film, and as a joke at the expense of the influential manifesto 'For an Imperfect Cinema' by the Cuban film-maker Julio García Espinosa, a call for the acceptance of a politically engaged cinema that does not seek to replicate the slick technical 'perfection' associated with Hollywood.[3]

Satire has also been wielded as a weapon of political critique elsewhere in Latin America. *El Viaje* ('The Voyage', 1993), an Argentinian-French-Spanish co-production in which a teenager travels across the continent in search of his father, uses a number of biting satirical images to highlight the kind of economic and political strategies that help to keep much of the continent in a state of underdevelopment. In Brazil, when the Ministry of Finance demands another round of belt-tightening, the population is required to tighten the notches on absurd bondage-type outfits. The metaphor of 'belt tightening' – a typical IMF/World Bank prescription and a euphemism for painful spending cuts in areas such as wages and social services – is taken literally, a satirical device used to reveal its absurdity. Another target is the attitude taken by many regional leaders towards the dominant power, the United States. We witness the annual meeting of the Organization of Countries on their Knees, another literalisation of metaphor: the leaders of various nations are in attendance on their knees. Not just this, but their spokesman, the Argentinian president Dr Frog delivers an apologia for the adoption of this humble position: safer than standing, leaving the head vulnerable to stray bullets, while far from the horizontal posture of indolence and death. Kneeling, he concludes, is the only alternative to ensure an average existence in the continent within the guidelines of the New International Order: a satirical attack on national leaders complicit with the neo-colonial international order dictated by the United States (Dr Frog plays a game of tennis with Mr Wolf, the American president, each on his knees; the latter wins and gets to his feet while the former remains in the submissive position). The satirical portrait contains overt references to Argentinian president Carlos Menem, who instituted neo-liberal programmes of privatisation and cuts in public spending; for his troubles, director Fernando Solanas, co-author of one of the key 1960s political manifestos of third cinema, was shot in the legs during filming (J. King 2000: 264–7).

Striking similarities are found in the targets of many satires produced in very different parts of the world. Politics, politicians and bureaucratic institutions are favourite subjects, from the United States and Britain to the Soviet Union, Latin America and elsewhere. Against these, the favoured characters are often represented as manifestations of a more 'human' (which usually implies 'individual') spirit. A specific political line is often replaced by a general attack on the institutions of all sides. In Britain, *The Man in the White Suit* and *Britannia Hospital* attack the institutionalised bases of power of both right and left, of bosses and trade unions. This can have somewhat conservative implications: both institutions might be capable of absurdity or oppression, but they are hardly equal in their resources. As far as the Hollywood examples go, the tendency to focus the attack on institutions imposes limitations on the extent to which many satires are really to be distinguished – for all their potential for radical critique – from more mainstream films, comedies or otherwise. *Bulworth* voices perhaps the most radical criticism of the broader American political system, but it does so in a voice of a rebellious individualism that fits rather more easily with prevailing and dominant ideologies. A cynical distrust of politics, politicians and government institutions is quite deeply ingrained in many American myths and ideologies, including their Hollywood

Figure 12   Satirising representatives of the ruling and working classes: *Britannia Hospital* (1982)

manifestations. In *Bulworth*, the viewer is invited to identify with the slightly unhinged voice of Senator Jay Billington Bulworth (Beatty), in his last-minute alienation from the dishonest process that is about to see him re-elected to office. The film's object of attack is not Bulworth, despite the comic spectacle he makes of himself, but the corrupt system and its more loyal representatives in the form of the easy targets provided by political advisers, PR consultants and the like. A more incisive satire of political candidature is found in *Bob Roberts* (1992), a pointed documentary spoof charting the senatorial campaign of a smilingly odious 1960s-hating right-wing folk-singer-turned-politician (writer-director Tim Robbins). The film offers an exquisitely understated facsimile of the textures and tones of extreme-religious-right political propaganda, including limpid campaigning music videos that could quite easily be taken for the real thing. The background to the campaign, the events leading up to American-led military action against Iraq in 1991 – some of the real political issues of which are addressed by Roberts' rival, Brickley Paiste (Gore Vidal) – add a more specific contemporary edge, if at the risk of replacing the satirical with more directly political argument.

A mark of the real satirical power of *Dr Strangelove*, Robert Kolker suggests, is the distance maintained throughout between the viewer and any of the crazed principals whose activities propel the world towards nuclear destruction: 'The satirical mode requires observation and judgement rather than identification ... the conventions of psychological realism and character motivation are removed' (1988: 113). This is a quality rarely found in Hollywood or other film comedy in the commercial mainstream. *Wag the Dog* satirises the *process* of falsified and corrupt foreign policy manoeuvres, but not its principal architect, the political fixer Ronnie Brean (De Niro), who is presented as an object for identification and/or admiration (a more distanced and mocking attitude is reserved for the over-the-top Hollywood producer Stan Moss, played by Hoffman, who helps to concoct the fabrication). The conventions of psychological 'realism' and character motivation are crucial building blocks in the Hollywood model and not often surrendered. The power of *Bob Roberts* lies to a large extent in the ironic distance from the central character maintained through the 'documentary' frame and the attack the film makes on the nakedly individualist ideology he promotes. We need to look at the kinds of discursive positions through which satire is mounted in these films if we are to be clear about the precise location and strength of the satire that is on offer.

Both *Bulworth* and *Being There* (1979), for example, draw on aspects of the childish/playful/innocent qualities examined in the previous chapter. But they do so in different ways. The hero of Bulworth is positioned as a figure who rebels against the official party lies through a shift at the level of modes of discourse. He adopts the playful-but-incisive discourse of rap and it is only this, it seems, that enables him to voice his radical critique. By the latter stages of the film he has swapped suit and tie for 'street' clothes: baggy shorts, shades and a baseball cap giving him the appearance of an overgrown child. The transformation might be discomforting for the viewer in some respects – the spectacle of a white superstar actor claiming to access the truth by speaking the language of black street culture, an issue to which we will return – but we are intended broadly to identify with his rejuvenated and awakened position as opposed to that of the political establishment. The appeal of the playful and/or childlike rebellious presence is *mobilised* in *Bulworth* as a key ingredient of its strategy. *Being There* offers something closer to a *critique* of this discourse. When the simpleton gardener Chance (Peter Sellers) comes into accidental contact with the upper echelons of the American political system, his naïve and literal comments about gardening are taken for profound metaphorical observations on the state of the nation. Chance the gardener becomes Chauncey Gardiner, a presidential adviser, chat-show guest and prospective future incumbent of the highest office, in a withering satire on politics, the media *and* the trope of childlike innocence/insight so widely employed in Hollywood comedy. The viewer is kept removed from the characters, including Chance, through distanced and formal compositions within the spaces of the mansion within which most of the action unfolds.

The degree and power of satire varies from one case to another. It is often hedged by other comic (or serious) strategies. *Bulworth*, for instance, also includes a farcical hit-man murder plot (Bulworth having ordered his own assassination at the start) that would be at home in the *Pink Panther* series. *Canadian Bacon* (1995), a film that preceded *Wag the Dog* in satirising foreign policy – a president faring badly in the polls engineers war with Canada

– mixes its satire with much more familiar and lightweight knock-about comedy in which a group of caricature 'little guys', led by John Candy's small-town sheriff, triumph over the machinations of politicians and a renegade arms-industrialist. The film has some real satirical bite, making connections between its comic-fictional antics and real historical events such as the use of alleged incidents in the Tonkin Gulf in 1964 to lever Congress into supporting action against Vietnam. Absurd broad comedy and caricature dilute the satirical impact but also help to enable films such as this to gain finance, distribution and a broader audience than would otherwise be the case. The precise boundary of the substantially satirical is not easy to identify, but it might be suggested by a darker and/or sharper edge in the overall mix.

In the treatment of the military, for example, a comparison might be made between close contemporaries *M*A*S*H* and *Catch-22*. Each offers black comedy with satirical dimensions. *M*A*S*H*, however, provides a much cosier and safer source of allegiance for the viewer. The main protagonists are established unambiguously as our intended point of reference: a classic and ultimately untroubled case of individual comic rebellion against institutional absurdity. *Catch-22* is far more absurd and darkly surreal. The central character Yossarian (Alan Arkin) tries to rebel, in the name of individual sanity. He provides some conventional point of reference in these terms, but is a lonely and ineffectual figure whose eventual escape (in a rubber dinghy, to paddle from the Mediterranean to Sweden) is absurd. The insane world of the film, reflected formally by a non-linear and sometimes nightmarish narrative structure, includes dark satire of capitalist business ethics: essential supplies such as parachutes and morphine are replaced by share certificates in the venture created by the entrepreneur Milo Minderbinder (John Voight), who eventually organises the bombing of his own airfield by the Germans in the interests of business logic ('What's good for M & M Enterprises...').

In representations of the media – another relatively easy and recurring target – the bounds of satire and less edgy comedy-with-some-serious-content might be marked by the difference between *Network* (1976) and *Broadcast News* (1987). The former is a coruscating and uncompromising assault on the implications of cynical corporate takeover and audience-chasing. The latter meliorates its revelation of news hypocrisy and manipulation through the conventions of (not entirely resolved) romantic comedy. Both films address substantial issues quite explicitly and in a sustained manner. The key difference is one of tone. There are moments of farce in *Network* – the leader of a 'revolutionary' Marxist group arguing vehemently, incongruously, for the retention of her share of distribution rights, for example – but they are never divorced from the more 'serious' issues raised by the film. They do not offer comic 'relief', as such, from the satirical thrust. *Broadcast News* allows space for slapstick/farce of a much more 'innocent' and largely incidental variety (a production assistant slamming into or dodging obstacles while running pell-mell to deliver a tape in time for a last-second deadline; an aspiring news anchor suffering a bout of anxiety sweating that is exaggerated to a ludicrous extent, even if it does have more substantial implications for the career of the character). *Broadcast News* offers a close-up focus on individual character and relationships, presented quirkily but essentially from a liberal-humanist perspective. *Network* is more detached and biting, a quality highlighted in Faye Dunaway's performance as a work-obsessed and personal-emotionally blank head of programming.

Varying stances are also found in Hollywood satires that focus on broader areas of American life, especially that of the well-heeled middle-class subur-ban milieu. *The Graduate* (1967) drifts from sharp images of youthful aliena-tion towards more conventional romantic comedy. Some satires do pull their punches in the end, or in their endings, resorting to more familiar and safer comic routines or losing their edge. Others stick it out to the final credits, not letting us (or the protagonists) off the hook. *Bulworth*, along with *Network*, ends with the assassination of the central character (just when it appears that the film is to opt for the ultimate fantasy cop-out, cementing an unlikely relationship between Bulworth and a young black woman). *Wag the Dog* has a softer texture but ends with Moss being taken out by a hit-man because he cannot be trusted to keep quiet about his role in the events, even if the deed is softened by occurring off-screen. *Dr Strangelove* finishes with the end of the world, to the detached and ironic accompaniment of Vera Lynn.

Heathers (1989) mounts a penetrating satire of high school in-group hier-archies and offers a blackly comic series of murders that is sustained through-out and in which our relatively innocent point of identification (Winona Ryder) is implicated, even if she is distanced progressively from the crazy Jason Dean (Christian Slater). The theme of cheery suburban murder is picked up in *Serial Mom* (1994), in which the fresh-faced 'perfect mom' Beverly Sutphin (Kathleen Turner) is also an irretrievably crazed serial murderer *and* remains a principal subject of audience allegiance (an effective translation into the mainstream of the insistence on 'perversion' found in the earlier films of the director, John Waters). The media is again one of the targets of *Serial Mom*, feeding on the case and turning Beverly into a public hero. A noisier and more rhetorical treat-ment of this issue is found in *Natural Born Killers* (1994), a good example of the kind of satire that courts controversy, partly around the very question of its satirical status: *is* it satire, and of what, exactly (the media, clearly, but also the killers?), and are all viewers likely to take it that way, rather than as celebration of its protagonists?[4] In similarly controversial territory is *American Psycho* (2000), a searing depiction of deadening 1980s high 'yuppie' culture (including the mortification of the hero when a colleague produces a more impressive business card) that softens its blows only slightly through the belated suggestion that its murderous events might be the stuff of fantasy. A core of unsullied humanism is left intact in many cases: a rebellion against the institutions that come under attack. This is true of most but not all Hollywood satires (not *American Psycho*), particularly those closer to the mainstream, and of many examples from further afield. *El Viaje*, for example, ends with the achievement of insight and independence by its wandering hero. Films such as *La muerte de un burocrata*, *Plaff* and *Monanieba* also offer central characters of human conscience and sustained moral values, whatever travails they might face. The darker boundaries of satire are inhabited by a number of late Soviet examples, including *Monanieba*, *Merzavets* ('The Villain', 1989) and *Gorod zero* ('Zero City', 1989). As Andrew Horton suggests: 'Satire is, like an unstable electron particle, always in danger of breaking down, becoming something else' (1993: 138). In the transitional phase of the Soviet Union, from 1986 to 1986, he finds a move 'from a liberating joyful carnivalesque form of satire to a darkly troubling formula in which both the carnivalesque and satiric laughter completely break down' (138).

The impact of the comic element on the critical power of satire varies according to the precise blend found in any particular example. In Hollywood, the norm is to dilute the satirical edge or for it to cut, ultimately, in the direction of established comic or social norms. Particular circumstances usually need to intervene if this is not to be the case. This might be a matter of broad social and industrial context that widens the bounds of the permissible. Prominent examples would be the 'Hollywood Renaissance' of the later 1960s to the mid-to-late 1970s (see G. King 2002) and the *glasnost* era in the Soviet Union. Or, as in the case of *Bulworth*, the crucial factor might be the industrial clout and commitment of particular film-makers. Satire has its own specific effect as a way of representing sources of absurdity or oppression. Its comic dimension offers a considerable degree of latitude – or protection – for the representation of aspects of life that might otherwise be prevented from reaching the screen by industrial or political factors. That is one undoubted strength and appeal of the form. The comic/satiric edge also has intrinsic merits, beyond the practicalities of whether or not particular types of films can be brought to the screen in one context or another. It offers a way of tackling serious social-political material without slipping into over-insistent or 'preachy' realms of melodrama or straight propaganda. Satiric comedy, like many other forms, remains potentially double-edged, capable of cutting more than one way at a time.

From satire to parody; from deconstruction to reaffirmation?

The line drawn between satire and parody is usually marked by a shift of target. The target of satire is social or political. Some kind of reference is implied, more or less explicitly, to institutions of the real world, a fact that is responsible for its potentially more serious modality. The target of parody tends to be formal or aesthetic. Familiar conventions, representational devices or modes of discourse are the subject of humorous assault or exposure. In film, a range of different kinds of targets are available. Parody may be aimed at individual films, such as *Repossessed* (1990), a parody-sequel to *The Exorcist* (1973), the Brazilian *Bacalhau* ('Codfish', 1976), a parody of *Jaws* (1975), and *Silence of the Hams* (1994), spoofing *Silence of the Lambs* (1991). Film genres or shorter-term cycles are major sources of parody: the western, in numerous examples to be considered below, the *Airport* series (1970, 1974, 1977, 1979) in *Airplane!* (1980), the prison camp movie (especially *The Great Escape* (1963)) in *Chicken Run* (2000), a clutch of horror films in *Scary Movie* (2000). A popular form of recent parody takes one individual film or genre as its principle target while scattering references more randomly to other recent or classic films. Particular film directors or film styles offer another range of targets: Hitchcock in *High Anxiety* (1977), the classical Hollywood adventure in *Road to Utopia* (1945), the European 'art' movie in *Love and Death* (1975), documentary conventions in *Zelig* (1983) and *This Is Spinal Tap* (1984). The contemporary Hollywood system of production, including the 'pitching' of film projects – 'so, it's kind of a psychic-political-thriller-comedy with a heart … not unlike *Ghost* meets *Manchurian Candidate*' – is subjected to satirical parody in *The Player* (1992), while the vicissitudes of shooting in the low-budget independent scene get the treatment in *Living in Oblivion* (1995).

More basic or fundamental conventions of the fiction film might also be subjected to parodic exposure, as in the sequence of comic transformations of location through editing in *Sherlock Jr.* discussed in Chapter One. *Road to Utopia* makes fun of the narrative weakness associated with the comedian-centered format. A figure appears at the start to warn the viewer that the film is 'not very clear in spots'. He has been sent by the studio front office, he says, to offer periodic guidance in the hope that 'an occasional word from me might help to clarify the plot and other vague portions of the film. Personally I doubt it'. Animated comedy includes many such self-referential gags, including Tex Avery's *Lucky Ducky* (1948) in which a typical cartoon chase takes the characters into the realm of black and white; retracing their steps, they find a sign reading 'Technicolor Ends Here', and run back into their usual terrain. Constant self-reference to its drawn status – a frequent source of animation gags – is made in *Comicalamities* (1928), in which Felix the Cat enlists the help of the animator to provide eraser and pen to improve the features of a female feline; he goes to great lengths to impress her but, when she remains aloof, he tears her from the paper in exasperation and rips it to shreds. Parody might also be offered of an unlimited range of non-film-specific items, such as Leslie Nielsen's lampoon of singers including Elton John and Michael Jackson as part of the final assault on the devil in *Repossessed*.

The terms satire and parody are often used rather loosely and imprecisely, as if interchangeable. This can be a source of confusion. The two are not always entirely separate, however; they can overlap to a significant extent. Satire can be achieved through parody, as in *Bob Roberts*, the political satire of which is mounted through parody of both documentary conventions and music video/propaganda. Parody, aimed at formal or aesthetic conventions,

Figure 13 Smilingly odious: Tim Robbins as the right-wing folk-singing candidate in *Bob Roberts* (1992)

can have satirical impact. At one extreme, parody can be seen as a form of attack, debunking and undermining familiar conventions in a manner that has potential social or political implications. At the other, it might ultimately be a form of celebration or reaffirmation of the object of its apparent mockery.

Consider, for example, some different approaches to the conventions of the western, a genre that has been the subject of numerous parodic treatments. At the satirical end of the scale we find films such as *Little Big Man* (1970) and *Buffalo Bill and the Indians, or Sitting Bull's History Lesson* (1976), productions associated with the critical discourses found in some films of the Hollywood Renaissance. In the area of broader and less obviously critical parody, many examples are available, from comedians Laurel and Hardy in *Way Out West* and Bob Hope in *The Paleface* (1948) and *Son of Paleface* (1952) to Jirí Trnka's puppet short *Arie prerie* ('The Song of the Prairie', 1949) and, in more recent decades, from *Carry On Cowboy* (1965) to *Blazing Saddles* (1974) and *!Three Amigos!* (1986). *Little Big Man* and *Buffalo Bill and the Indians* set out to deconstruct some of the key mythologies of the western. The principal satirical effect of *Little Big Man* lies in its treatment of one of the main underlying oppositions around which many westerns revolve: the opposition between the world of the white settlers and that of the Native American inhabitants, coded in many cases as an opposition between 'civilisation' and 'savagery'.

One of the key discursive manoeuvres of many 'classic' westerns is to offer a negotiation of this opposition, a way of having the best of both worlds: a measure of 'civilisation' kept in tune with 'nature' and 'authenticity' through its contact with 'wilderness' virtues. The classic western hero is one who

109

straddles the two worlds, the frontiersman who is at home in the wilderness without being 'savage' and who makes a limited commitment to the potentially decadent and 'fallen' universe of white civilisation. *Little Big Man* subjects the conventional movement of the hero between the two worlds to a process of parodic exaggeration. Its hero Jack Crabb/Little Big Man (Dustin Hoffman) undergoes a absurd series of transformations across the cultural divide, moving backward and forwards between upbringings in the white and Native American worlds. He tries on almost every male western role in the book: white boy, Native American initiate, pious white youth, con artist, married-and-settled storekeeper, gunfighter, frontiersman/searcher-after-wife-taken-by-Indians, mule-skinner to General Custer, mad hermit and scout. The film highlights the extent to which many of these are merely acted roles. Each is shown to be absurd, although the Native American identity, in the shape of the Cheyenne, is privileged by the film, presented as somewhat daffy but essentially more noble and civilised than that of hypocritical, marauding and invading white society. *Little Big Man* and *Buffalo Bill and the Indians* each offer deconstructive parodies of legendary heroes of the west. The former debunks the heroic status of General Custer, depicted as stupidly vain and arrogant. The latter figures its Buffalo Bill as petty, selfish and manipulative. *Little Big Man* and *Buffalo Bill and the Indians* are parodic to the extent that they undo, expose or undermine some of the fictional conventions associated with the western genre. What makes them satirical is the fact that these conventions have substantial significance beyond the bounds of the text, as components of a frontier myth or ideology that has played an important part in American self-conceptions. The critique crosses over from one realm to another, from conventions of representation to those of political/ideological discourses in the real world.

Undermining conventions at a formal/fictional level can have broader implications; this can be true, at some level, of all parody. In some cases, however, this aspect seems more clearly to the fore. A serious satirical intent, with targets beyond those of a 'mere' film genre, is signalled in *Little Big Man* and *Buffalo Bill and the Indians* by departures from the mode of comedy. *Little Big Man* celebrates and mourns Native American culture, in a late 1960s/early 1970s counter-cultural guise, drawing implicit parallels between the massacre of Native Americans and contemporary events in Vietnam. *Buffalo Bill and the Indians* offers much less in the way of broad comedy, more closely approximating the distanced variety of satire examined above. The viewer is given little grounds for identification with the central character Buffalo Bill (Paul Newman), unlike *Little Big Man* which has a much more sentimental core rooted the experiences of its main protagonist.

What about more broadly comic parodies, without the avowedly 'serious' dimensions of *Little Big Man* and *Buffalo Bill and the Indians*? Elements of satire can also be detected in some cases, although they may be more isolated or less clear-cut. *Blazing Saddles*, for example, is an unpretentious comic romp through a number of western roles and conventions. Most critics read some serious and more satirical edge, however, in the characterisation of the central figure, Bart (Cleavon Little), an African-American worker on a railroad gang who becomes inadvertently elevated to the role of town sheriff. A substantial part of the comedy of the film is rooted in the characterisation of most of the townspeople as spectacularly stupid as well as racist. Racist assumptions are parodied in the unconventional revelation of Bart's character as a 'dazzling urbanite' who rides on a Gucci saddle and sings sophisticated lines such as 'I get no kick from champagne' rather than the 'nigger work-songs' expected by the bosses of the rail gang. The film also mocks architects of the theft of Native American land, such as the grasping attorney general Hedley Lamarr (Harvey Korman) and infantile governor (Mel Brooks).

One measure of a satirical dimension is the ability for parodic comedy to cause offence – in broadly social-political terms – a measure on which *Blazing Saddles* might score for some viewers, given the prevalence of implicit or explicit racist views in America and elsewhere. Another (non-western) parody in which this might be a defining factor is *Monty Python's Life of Brian* (1979), a distinctly non-serious parody of the Biblical/Roman epic that was banned in some places for alleged offences of blasphemy. If the content of parody includes material of an overtly political or religious nature, it seems, it is potentially liable to be taken more seriously by some viewers: either as desirable – a good satirical critique or exposure – or offensive, depending on the perspective of the viewer.

Many film parodies remain the stuff of lightweight knockabout comedy, however, with little likelihood of being taken too seriously. *Carry On Cowboy,* for example, is very much the familiar *Carry On* formula of gently salacious humour applied to the western genre, one of a number of genre parodies produced in the *Carry On* canon. Light parody is also a favoured terrain for many comedian comics, the disruptive nature of their characters often being defined in terms of their lack of fit with genre conventions: the cowardly dentist Painless Potter (Bob Hope) in *The Paleface*, Stan Laurel and Oliver Hardy stumbling as themselves through the western landscape of *Way Out West*, or Steve Martin as Lucky Day in *!Three Amigos!* Even Jirí Trnka's treatment of the western in *Arie prerie* seems to be an affectionate parody, including a struggle between slick singing cowboy and evil gambler figures, without the more obviously satirical edge of some of his other works. Comic undercutting is often used in parody to defuse potential for the material to slide into more serious or contentious realms, although the results can never be guaranteed.

How, for example, might different viewers take some of the skits in *Don't Be a Menace to South Central While Drinking Your Juice in the Hood* (1995), a broad and unsubtle parody of the black ghetto/gang male-initiation sub-genre? The two central characters are arrested 'for being black on a Friday night', a gag that could be construed as part of a satirical revelation of the racist policing of black communities in Los Angeles. To find it comic is, presumably, to recognise the element of truth contained in the joke: that young black males *are*, on balance, likely to be arrested in part simply for being young black males in particular places at particular times, as well as the fact that this might be the typical narrative stuff of the Hollywood ghetto/gang movie format. The exaggerated and ludicrous context in which the incident occurs – the ridiculous appearance and behaviour of the characters, Ashtray (Shawn Wayans) and Loc Dog (Marlon Wayans) along with other absurdities and self-reflexive devices – tends to undercut any serious implications, but this does not mean that they are guaranteed to disappear entirely. Much depends on the orientation of the viewer, but even this is not likely to be easily reducible to a single perspective on such material.

Parodies mock their targets, but in doing so they pay an effective form of tribute to the originals. To become a target for parody is to have achieved a certain status, even if the parody is of a less affectionate variety. If the western is the genre that has come in for the largest number of parodic treatments, as seems likely, this is because the western has been one of the most popular and enduring genres, even if it has receded from this position in recent decades. Individual film targets are usually titles that are particularly well known, as a result of significant box-office success and/or broader cultural prominence. Parodies that aspire to mainstream commercial success have to be based on targets familiar to a sufficiently large audience for the parodic effect to work, for the relationship to the original to be detectable by a reasonably large proportion of viewers. The experience of parody, for the viewer, requires engagement on at least two levels: that of the parody itself and that of its object, a duality that has to be recognised by the viewer for the film to be understood *as* parody rather than any other form of comedy (Harries 2000: 24).

Parodies of Hollywood films or genres produced outside the United States can take on a range of other implications, sometimes but not always involving more critical and satirical elements. A strong tradition of parodying Hollywood exists in the Brazilian film industry, for example. Parody can be 'well suited to the needs of oppositional culture', suggest Robert Stam, João Luiz Vieira and Ismail Xavier, 'precisely because it deploys the force of the dominant discourse against itself' (1995: 405). In some cases, Brazilian parody has a satirical edge. *Nem Sansão Nem Dalila* ('Neither Samson Nor Delilah', 1954) uses a parody of Cecil B. De Mille's *Samson and Delilah* (1949) to mount an allegorical critique of military takeover (Vieira 1995). The existence of many parodies of Hollywood films indicates the extent to which American cinema has penetrated Brazilian culture, as Vieira suggests: if familiarity with the originals could not be taken for granted, the parodies would not work. The target of the parodies is not so much the originals, however, or the unequal economic relationship between the American and domestic film industries, Vieira argues, as the limitations of Brazilian cinema when measured against the standards set by its stronger rival. Vieira is critical of films such as *Bacalhau* and *Matar ou Morrer* ('To Kill or

Figure 14   The western held up to ridicule in *!Three Amigos!* (1986)

Die', 1954), based on *High Noon* (1952), for missing potential opportunities to expose the ideological frameworks of the Hollywood originals: 'In the case of *Jaws*, for example, showing the victory of the police and the technocrat, who is the oceanographer, over the people, represented grotesquely by the fisherman Quint, or the victory of technical and bureaucratic knowledge, allied to the police apparatus, over the empiricism of the fisherman' (266). What Vieira advocates would be a move in the direction from parody to satire, a much more distanced and critical attitude to the material, instead of a film such as *Bacalhau* that 'closely follows the linear narrative structure of *Jaws*, keeping only the superficial and external aspects that might trigger the spectator's memory of the original' (266).

Parody of some aspects of a genre or film type can serve a process of renewal, clearing away elements considered to the stuff of cliché and myth in favour of others presented as more 'authentic'. An example of this process is found in *Unforgiven* (1992), one of the few relatively 'straight' westerns to have earned significant box-office success in recent decades. One figure of the 'legendary' gun-fighter, English Bob (Richard Harris), is subjected to merciless lampoon, the character shown up as a cowardly fake whose heroic deeds exist only in the pages of fictionalised biography. Against this charlatan, implicitly, the film develops the central character William Munny (Clint Eastwood), a figure with a darker but equally legendary gun-fighting past who is treated as more grittily authentic. The impression for which the film appears to strive is to renew some of the conventions of the western, to restore the genre to commercial viability, by separating itself from and discarding one variety of (fake) mythic hero while reconstructing another. How far this is successful remains open to question, especially during the climax in which Munny becomes an avenging angel figure who – while played straight – comes close to a parody of a persona for which Eastwood has become famous. How exactly does parody work, though, in general? What kinds of relationships exist between parodic texts and their sources?

A range of different relationships have been suggested by theorists of parody in film, literature and the arts more generally. Parody is sometimes seen as maintaining an attitude of critical distance from its object. In other cases, it might appear to be more closely implicated in the characteristics of the original. The term parody, derived from the Greek *parodia*, contains mixed resonances. The prefix *para* has connotations of 'contra' or 'against', suggesting an attitude of mockery or ridicule, but it can also mean 'besides', suggesting a more intimate relationship (Hutcheon 1985: 32). For Dan Harries the key characteristic of film parody is a mixture of the two rather than an overriding emphasis on one or the other: 'Parodic texts simultaneously generate similarity to and difference from their targets in a regulated fashion – privileging neither' (2000: 8). As Margaret Rose (1993) suggests, parody is generally a more ambivalent form than satire because it uses some of the materials of its target as part of its own structure, a requirement not necessary to satire. At the satirical end of parody, the element of difference between text and target might be more pronounced than usual. At the opposite extreme are what Wes Gehring (1999) terms parodies of reaffirmation, in which similarity plays a large part: parodies that reconstitute as they deflate their targets. Most parodies, however, offer a more even balance between the two.

Harries outlines a productive model in which the similarities and differences within film parodies can be charted along three principal axes (drawn in part from the genre theory developed by Rick Altman (1986)). The first of these is comprised of the individual elements of the source material, the *semantic* or *lexical* units (in a western, for example, these might include the geographical and historical setting, particular locations within this broad setting such as the sheriff's office or saloon, and particular characters associated with the genre such as the gunfighter, the 'Indian' or the scheming Eastern politician). The second axis is the *syntax* of the original, the narrative-based structures into which these individual elements are composed in any particular film or genre (for example, the broad opposition between representatives of frontier 'authenticity' and Eastern 'decadence', or more localised plot developments). The final element is film *style*, the particular mobilisation of film conventions associated with a particular film, genre or a broader mode such as documentary, expressionism or the 'classical' Hollywood style.

One of the most basic means of creating parody, Harries suggests, is by faithfully replicating some semantic/lexical, syntactic or stylistic aspects of the original while altering others. Parody, like much comedy, is often a matter of incongruity. It requires some anchorage in the original, which means all aspects of the target are unlikely to be altered at the same time: 'In other words, parody operates in terms of a system of "logical absurdity", with one dimension needed to ensure a logic and another for difference-creating absurdity. This is the necessary oscillation between similarity to and difference from a target that allows parody to maintain either the lexicon, syntax or style while manipulating the others' (2000: 9). Harries identifies six primary methods of combining similarity and difference across the three axes that can fruitfully be applied to a wide range of film parody: reiteration, inversion, misdirection, literalisation, extraneous inclusion and exaggeration.

Reiteration provides anchorage in the original, the point of departure on which the comic effects of various forms of disruption and absurdity are based. A major source of reiteration, especially in genre parodies, is the use of settings and props resembling or identical to those of the target objects. *Young Frankenstein* is an oft-cited example, a film that reused many of the distinctive props from the original 1930s Universal films to create an 'authentic' base from which to mount its comic assaults. The western townscapes of films such as *Carry On Cowboy* and *Blazing Saddles* have much the same solidity as those found in non-comic treatments; the set of the real starship created by an alien race in *Galaxy Quest* (1999) strongly resembles that of the *Star Trek* television series, the main subject of the film's parodic dimension. The use of performers associated with the original versions of particular films or genres is another recurrent strategy: Linda Blair from *The Exorcist* in *Repossessed*; classical horror performers such as Lon Chaney, Bela Lugosi and Boris Karloff in the comedian-centred spoofs *Abbott and Costello Meet Frankenstein* (1948) and *Abbott and Costello Meet Dr Jekyll and Mr Hyde* (1953); Roy Rogers and Trigger as themselves in *Son of Paleface*; John Hurt in an *Alien*-related cameo in *Spaceballs* (1987). Titles that play on those of the originals are another obvious source of reiteration, helping to make very clear the target of the comedy, examples including *The Three Must-Get-Theres*, (1922), *Porklips Now* (1980), and the portmanteau style in the likes of *Don't Be a Menace to South Central While Drinking Your Juice in the Hood*. Narrative elements are also reiterated in many cases, as in *Spaceballs*, which raids its principal target, *Star Wars*, at the level of both individual scenes and broader plot dynamics. Stylistic elements are another source of reiteration: the black and white footage of *Young Frankenstein*, for example, and the grainy hand-held verité-style cinematography used in the dark spoof documentary *C' Est Arrivé Près de Chez Vous* ('Man Bites Dog', 1992).

Inversion is one way parody can move away from the conventions or more specific details of their target objects, 'a parodic method to modify either the lexicon, syntax or style by way of creating a signifier which ironically suggests an opposite meaning from its employment in the target text' (Harries 2000: 55). A good example offered by Harries is the inversion of singing styles presented in the chain-gang sequence in *Blazing Saddles*: after the gang launch into their jazzy Cole Porter number, the foreman and his men, in their efforts to encourage the kind of singing they expect to hear, end up giving their own lively rendition of the 'Camptown Lady'. Inversion is also provided by figures who fail to match up to those on whom they are clearly based, as is the case with the bumbling and diminutive Dark Helmet (Rick Moranis) in *Spaceballs* and the not-so 'irresistible to women' seeming figure of Austin Powers (Mike Myers) in *Austin Powers: International Man of Mystery* (1997). In *Repossessed*, inversion is found in the use of pea soup: prepared by the Linda Blair character, Nancy, in its normal role as a foodstuff to be eaten rather than the substance associated with the green vomit in *The Exorcist*; further inversion is offered when the exorcist figure Father Jedediah Mayii (Leslie Nielsen) green-vomits on the possessed Nancy ('so, how do you like it?').

A second form of departure suggested by Harries is misdirection, an effect that occurs 'when specific elements are evoked, and initially played out in a manner similar to the target text, but then are transformed to deliver an unexpected turn in the eventual parodic presentation' (38). *Don't be a Menace to South Central* is a source of a number of examples. In one sequence we are presented, to a rap accompaniment, with a montage of kitchen activities including the measuring out of quantities of white power. A shot follows of one of the central characters, Loc Dog, putting his finger in his mouth and rubbing it around on his gums before nodding to the camera, a convention of the familiar 'cutting-cocaine' routine that is undercut when the following longer shot reveals that he has really just been icing a cake. An earlier scene uses a similar strategy to parody the obligatory gang-initiation scene. Menacing comments to a 'new kid', including 'if you fall you better pick your punk ass up' and, to others, 'don't cut him no slack', are followed by the revelation that what is involved is a skipping routine, entirely incongruous in the context. At the level of style, titles supplying narrative information or time and place are a favourite source of numerous forms of parodic play, including misdirection, as in *Monty Python's Life of Brian* (1979), in which the opening post-credit title moves from the standard-enough 'Judea A.D. 33' to the increasingly incongruous, in both detail and imprecision, 'Saturday Afternoon' and 'About Tea Time'.

Literalisation is another frequently-exploited source of parodic humour, a device identified above in the satire of *El Viaje*, with its world of literal belt-tightening and peoples-on-their-knees. The taking literally of figures of speech or other conventions is common currency in recent parody. The jamming of the radar of the enemy ship in *Spaceballs* (1987) involves, inevitably, the use of a giant pot of jam to clog up the system. 'Give me the strongest thing you've got,' demands a depressed detective Frank Drebin (Leslie Nielsen) in a bar in *The Naked Gun 2½: The Smell of Fear* (1991): a muscled body-builder is presented. 'On second thought, how about a Black Russian?' tries Drebin. 'Very well, sir,' replies the barman, glancing towards the camera as he departs with a quick shake of the head to quell audience expectations that this, too, will be given the literal treatment used as a recurrent source of gags in this and other spoofs from the David and Jerry Zucker and Jim Abrahams stable. When Dr Evil (Mike Myers) plans the death of Austin Powers and Vanessa Kensington (Elizabeth Hurley) in *Austin Powers: International Man of Mystery* (1997), he spells out literally the standard absurdity of the equivalent sequence in the James Bond films: 'I'm going to place him in an easily escapable situation involving an overly elaborate and exotic death ... begin the unnecessarily slow-moving dipping mechanism ... I'm going to leave them alone and not actually witness them dying; I'm just going to assume it all went to plan – what?' The Tex Avery cartoon *A Symphony in Slang* (1951) is comprised of an extended sequence of literalisations of language: 'I carried on' (figure carries the letters 'o' and 'n'); 'I went to pieces' (body parts fall off), his girl has 'little ones' (figure '1's running around on legs); and so on.

Literalisation can also be used at the level of film style, a major source of the self-reflexive strategies employed by many film parodies. The location of sound, usually a taken-for-granted convention to which explicit attention is not drawn, is brought into question through its literalisation within the scene in a number of examples. A classic instance in *Blazing Saddles* has Bart riding through the desert to the accompaniment of a big sound soundtrack, only for the camera to reveal the presence of Count Basie in the scene, conducting his players in the middle of nowhere. What appears to be non-diegetic sound – imposed from outside, rather than being created inside the fictional or diegetic world on screen – turns out to be diegetic. A similar effect is created in *Repossessed* when Father Mayii enters Nancy's room, equipped with camera and tape-recorder. The image of Nancy on the bed is strongly evocative of the equivalent scene in *The Exorcist*. Music builds to a crescendo until Mayii presses a switch on his tape-recorder and it stops, abruptly, in the moment of relocation to literalised diegetic status. Another style-literalisation gag in the film has Mayii in a room in which venetian blinds appear to have created the striped-shadow effect associated with film noir; until, that is, we see that Mayii himself has black stripes painted onto his face and shirt. In *Scary Movie*, the central character Cindy (Anna Faris) is being terrorised *Scream*-style by a maniac on the telephone. The phone rings again, the camera enacting a conventionally emphatic swirling movement in towards the phone; cut to another shot, again a conventional device, in which the camera looms in closer to Cindy. But the second shot goes too far, intruding into the fictional space and hitting her on the head, shattering the illusion. In *Austin Powers*, the status of one minor character is literalised: the function of Basil Exposition (Michael York) is largely one of providing background plot exposition.

The fifth category is extraneous inclusion, a strategy that works 'by inserting "foreign" lexical units into a conventionalised syntax or through the inclusion of narrative scenes that fall outside of the target text's general conventions' (Harries 2000: 77). The scattershot variety of parody is liable to include numerous examples of this kind, the result of its opportunistic attempt to include a wide range of references that might have little if anything to do with the conventions of the primary target. *Scary Movie*, for example, operates primarily through an extended parody of a combination of the *Scream* films (1996, 1997, 2000) and *I Know What You Did Last Summer* (1997), with references to some other horror films thrown in for good measure. But it also includes a climactic fight sequence shot in the stylised slow-motion martial-arts style used in *The Matrix* (1999), an extraneous inclusion that includes a further extraneous dimension of its own as a sequence of flying-though-the-air-standing-kicking segues into a Riverdance step. Other examples include the toll booth that suddenly appears in the middle of nowhere and absurdly delays an angry mob in *Blazing Saddles* and a moment of incongruity in *Robin Hood: Men in Tights* (1993) in which the evil Prince John (Richard Lewis) closes the portcullis on his castle gate with an electronic remote control. Extraneous inclusion is found in *Austin Powers* in the shape of two cutaway scenes that show the reactions of family and friends to the deaths of two of the villain's henchmen, details that are usually passed over without pause ('people never think how things affect the family of a henchman'). Stylistic examples include the use of the *Jaws* theme out of context in *Airplane* and *Spaceballs*.

The dividing line between extraneous inclusion and exaggeration, the final category suggested by Harries, is not always entirely clear. Exaggeration, one of the most favoured strategies of film parody, can lead towards extraneous inclusion through a process of extrapolation from what might be considered normal, according to the conventions at issue, to the entirely ludicrous. A logical escalation is offered in some cases, however, rather than an arbitrary leap to the extraneous. A classic example is the sequence in *Airplane* in which a 'hysterical' passenger is slapped by a doctor – normal-conventional enough – followed by a procession of passengers equipped with weapons ranging from a baseball bat to a handgun. A similar logic of escalation is offered in a rival gun-pulling sequence in *Don't Be a Menace to South Central*: from guns to grenade launcher to nuclear missile. Frank Drebin's love-interest in *The Naked Gun 2½* goes home to feed her cat, then a pair of chickens, two small pigs and an enormous fat one. The forensic expert at a crime scene finds a footprint, from which a cast is made, in appro-priate police-story style, but follows this with the production of a dinosaur footprint and, digging further, timber that might be from Noah's Ark. Escala-tion of this kind is a useful device for the parodist, offering a bridge from the world of the relatively normal and conventional to that of the comically ludi-crous. Exaggeration generally is one of the easiest and most obvious parodic strategies, demonstrating the arbitrariness of familiar conventions through their extension to the point of absurdity. The implausible feats of shooting skill central to the creation of many a western hero are parodied, through exaggeration, for example, in cases ranging from the Rumpo Kid (Sid James) beating three others in a walk-down shoot-out in *Carry On Cowboy* to the antics of the central figure of *Arie prerie*, who spells out a heart in bullet holes to impress the girl.

The history of film parody dates back to the birth of the medium. The experience of early cinema spectatorship itself was parodied in *Uncle Josh at the Moving Picture Show* (1900) and *The Countryman and the Cinematograph* (1901), depictions of 'hick' figures who take the image on the screen for reality. Many comedies of the 1910s and 1920 are parodies of other films of the period. The melodramas of D. W. Griffith were a particularly popular target, from parody of the last-minute rescue, which does not quite go according to plan in Mack Sennett's *Help! Help!* (1912), to a feature-length parody of the epic three-part structure of *Intolerance* (1916) in Buster Keaton's *Three Ages* (1923).[5] Genre parodies remained popular in Hollywood through the 1930s, especially in animated short films, a format in which parody continued to thrive after its relative decline elsewhere. *A Corny Concerto* (1943) parodied the Disney epic *Fantasia* (1940), reducing its elevated pretensions to the familiar craziness of the typical Warner Bros. chase cartoon, even if set to classical strains. *Bacall to Arms* (1946) contains a film-within-a-film spoof of a sexually charged encounter between Lauren Bacall and Humphrey Bogart in *To Have and Have Not* (1944), while *Daffy Duck Goes to Hollywood* (1938) features a chicken performer with the voice of Katherine Hepburn; just two of many films of the period that parody stars from Hollywood and other forms of popular entertainment. The output of live-action parody in Hollywood declined during the 1940s and 1950s, Harries suggests, for three main reasons. The studio system went into a period of economic instability in which genre films were generally seen as something of a 'security blanket', a reliable source of profits rather than a suitable target for anything more than the occasional burlesque. Elements of self-reflexivity and critical evaluation appeared in some genre films, none more so than the 'revisionist' western of the 1950s, but these stopped short of full-blown parody. The production of parody was also hit by the demise of non-feature-length supporting films, the shorter format of which had provided an ideal forum for wide-ranging parodic forays. This quality was found, instead, on television, in the form of skit-based comedy shows, as the new medium began to take over some of Hollywood's role as mass-media parodist (Harries 2000: 20).

But parody has made a remarkable comeback in film since the 1960s and 1970s, becoming ubiquitous in Hollywood by the 1980s, 1990s and in the early 2000s. No genre, sub-genre or prominent feature is safe from its assaults, with parodies often following closely on the heels of – and sometimes seeming to merge with – their targets. Comic points of reference in *Scary Movie*, for example, include films such as *The Blair Witch Project* (1999) and *The Sixth Sense* (1999) that appeared only a year earlier, while the *Scream* series combines self-referential parody with continued mobilisation of the strategies used by the kinds of films to which it refers. Why should parody have become so prevalent? A number of different answers are available, ranging in scope from sweeping theories of cultural change to more specific developments within Hollywood.

For some commentators, the prevalence of parody in film, and elsewhere, is a manifestation of a 'postmodern' state of culture and society. The concept of the postmodern has been defined in many differing ways, in different disciplines, a full account of which is beyond the scope of this book. One recurring feature, however, is a sense of the postmodern as a condition in which culture turns in on itself, recycling and reworking the products of the past, rather than moving forward. Existing forms are recombined and played around with, originality taking the form of new juxtapositions of old materials. Contemporary parody films might be included in this process, along with sequels and remakes, as re-visitations of familiar cultural products, especially perhaps in the scattershot brand of parody that mixes reference to a wide range of texts beyond the principal target film or genre.

Postmodern parody is sometimes taken to indicate a state of cultural exhaustion, a wearing out of existing forms and their lack of replacement by anything radically new. Some approaches to film genre might fit this perspective. Thomas Schatz (1981), an influential theorist, suggests an evolutionary process of development in which any particular genre is likely to go through a series of stages that culminate in a state of over-familiarity, cliché or decadence ripe for the genre parody. Some of the genres developed during the Hollywood 'studio era', from the 1920s to the 1950s, might be said to have reached this stage in more recent decades, the western being one of the most obvious potential examples. Theorists who consider parody in a postmodern context have been as split as elsewhere on the question of whether parody has radical/critical deconstructive or uncritical/reactionary affirmative implications.[6]

Many questions are raised by these and other versions of the postmodern, both generally and in more specific relation to film and film parody. At the level of genre, evolutionary stages such as those suggested by Schatz might not adequately account for the varied uses for which genre frameworks might be available at any particular moment. Parodic instances might be found before a genre reaches what is defined as the 'classical' period that is meant to precede any more general decline into cliché and decadence, for example, while apparently 'classical' genre films might also contain parodic references of which today's audience is unaware.[7] More generally, it is unclear that any popular cultural products develop in ways other than through the recombination of existing elements, which might rob this conception of the postmodern of any great claims to be a specific condition affecting particular cultures in a particular epoch. At the very least, any claims about parody and the postmodern need to be rooted in some specific historical or social ground.

One such claim that might be grounded in developments of recent decades is that a growth in parody on film has been encouraged by a greater level of film literacy among the viewing public, a result of the release since the mid-1950s of growing numbers of films to television and, subsequently, to home video. A vast repertoire of earlier films became available to new audiences, taken out of their original contexts, as a ground against which parodies could play. The development of Film Studies in the 1960s, as a formal university discipline, contributed further to self-conscious awareness of conventions such as those of genre or of the styles associated with particular film-makers. In this respect parody in film appears to follow a wider pattern: 'Historians of parody agree that parody prospers in periods of cultural sophistication that enable paro-dists to rely on the competence of the reader (viewer, listener) of the parody' (Hutcheon 1985: 19). The late 1960s saw the emergence to prominence of a new generation of Hollywood film-makers brought up in this climate, including frequent parodists Woody Allen and Mel Brooks, both of whom wrote in the 1950s for *Your Show of Shows* (1950–54), a television comedy-variety format that included film parody sketches (Gehring 1999: 19).

The general (more radical than usual) cultural climate of the 1960s and early 1970s might also be a factor in the renewed growth of parody, at both its satirical and less satirical ends. Even where it is not put to clearly satirical effect, parody can have broader political-ideological implications, merely through the act of rendering visible and exposing to ridicule and question the dominant con-ventions of major genres, films or the film-making process: making apparent the fact that these are discursive constructs, fabrications; 'a demonstration of the constructed nature of any cultural product' (Harries 2000: 125). Parody in film can create what Russian formalist theories of literature see as a radical effect of 'defamiliarisation', in which self-conscious attention is drawn to conventions that are usually naturalised and rendered relatively invisible by the text.[8] It is questionable, however, whether the context of reception of Hollywood-style parody is generally likely to encourage any substantial questioning more than a comic reaffirmation of the conventions involved.

Numerous parodies were produced in Hollywood in the 1960s, a notable batch grouping around the James Bond films, themselves increasingly prone to self-parody, a cycle that has offered irresistible ground for parody ranging from *Our Man Flint* (1966) and *Casino Royale* (1967) to *Spy Hard* (1996) and *Austin Powers: The Spy Who Shagged Me* (1999). The 1970s saw further growth in the production of parody, boosted by the box-office success of prominent examples such as *Blazing Saddles* and *Airplane!* The industrial appeal of parody in this era is not hard to identify. The climate of Hollywood from the mid-1970s has been dominated by a search for commercial safety and stability, following the partial deconstruction of the old studio system in the 1950s and the financial crisis and period of relative experimentation in the later 1960s and early 1970s. Parodies, like sequels – and the distinction is sometimes blurred, as in the case of some of the Bond films – offer a blend of repetitive familiarity-with-difference that is especially attractive to Hollywood in this context.

Based on previously successful films, genres and sub-genres, parodies have a potentially pre-established audience. All comedy is founded on assumptions of existing in-group knowledge: the background against which comedy works its disruptions, inversions or exaggerations. The same goes for parody. Much of the parody of an example such as *Scary Movie* would be lost on anyone who had not seen or was otherwise unaware of a reasonable proportion of its sources. This can be risky. Parodies might want to avoid limiting their appeal only to viewers who can catch most if not all of the references. They do this, in varying degrees, by including narrative dynamics of their own, that stand to some extent independent of the network of intertextual points of reference. But parodies of recent films or cycles have one in-built advantage: their target audience is likely to be substantially the same as that of the originals, as is the case with *Scary Movie*, which offers appeals of its own (including some gross-out moments, such as a penis penetrating through a head!) that are aimed at the same relatively youthful (and probably male-led) audience as most of the targets of its parody. The fact that source texts are likely to be familiar to the potential audience gives parody an in-built pre-sold quality, another characteristic central to the contemporary Hollywood economy of risk-aversion. This is also attractive to other, more exploitative forms of parody such as those produced for the soft- and hard-core sex film markets. Parodic reference to well-known Hollywood films offers a form of product-recognition in a crowded and uncertain market, one in which buyers might be more likely than usual to seize upon the identification offered by such markers, examples ranging from the soft-core *The Erotic Witch Project* (1999) to hard-core films such as *The Sperminator* (1985) and *Edward Penishands* (1991). Inventive parody in such films is usually limited to witty play on the titles of the originals, and in some cases the basic scenario (such as that of the unusual endowment of the central character of the latter), neither of which are likely to extend very far into the main substance offered to the viewer. Parody, here, is primarily a framing device around which to situate conventionalised sequences of sexual activity. In some cases, however, Tanya Krzywinska suggests, the dimension of deliberate, parodic comedy might also play a more significant role in both seeking to transcend 'the clichéd, unintentional comedy' of other sex films and in the various dimensions of anxiety and disavowal that might be involved in the consumption of such material (1998–99: 19).

Not all contemporary Hollywood parodies succeed at the box office (there is no such thing as a guaranteed safe bet, after all), but they offer solid prospects, certainly less risk (although also less prestige) than is usually associated with satire: some of the appeal of the original – exactly how much depending on the mix – combined with the generally reliable and relatively inexpensive performance of comic burlesque or silliness in general. Many parodies have performed very healthily, usually on much lower budgets that their sources (*Hot Shots!* (1991) grossed $176 million worldwide, an impressive figure even when compared with the blockbuster $344 million taken by *Top Gun* (1986)).[9] What might be the appeal for the viewer?

Parody, like other forms of comedy, works on the basis of audience expectations: in this case, expectations at the level of film forms and conventions.

Pleasure, in popular cultural products, is produced to a large extent through the (initial or eventual) satisfaction of expectations. In comedy, some expectations are met but the specifically comic effect often resides in their disruption. As Harries suggests, 'much of the pleasure from parodic discourse is in the transgression of such expectations and the relishing of the disruption of a normative pattern' (2000: 198). Enjoyment lies, often, in the gap opened up between expected norm and disruptive ingredient. This is not a purely disruptive experience, however, as we have seen in other comic forms. Disruption and transgression are themselves expected, when they occur in a context clearly marked as parodic. Most film parodies are marked in this way, though the presence of particular comic performers (ranging from Bob Hope to Leslie Nielsen), outlandish titles (such as *Don't Be a Menace to South Central While Drinking your Juice in the Hood* or *Naked Gun 33 ⅓: The Final Insult* (1994)) or secondary discourses such as posters, advertising, trailers and reviews. A pleasurable sense of expectation-of-disruption is created through the typical parody blend of reiteration with qualities such as inversion, misdirection, literalisation, extraneous inclusion and exaggeration. The opening title crawl of *Spaceballs*, for example, filling in previous plot detail, mirrors the adventure-serial format used in the *Star Wars* films, but the viewer is cued to expect some self-conscious subversion of the device, which eventually comes in the final lines of text reading: 'If you can read this you don't need glasses.'

Parody is another form of comedy that can offer something of the best of all worlds. It offers the pleasure of standing back from familiar conventions, to see them for what they are, as constructs that are often ridiculous when extrapolated or otherwise subjected to closer examination. But it can also play positively on our familiarity with and continued enjoyment of the deployment of the same conventions. Merciless parody can undermine the future viability of particular conventions. *Airplane!* was widely held to have made untenable any future films in the *Airport* series, which may have been the case. But films based on planes in jeopardy have not disappeared. Scary movies are unlikely to be stopped in their tracks by the appearance of *Scary Movie* (or its contemporary, *Shriek If You Know What I Did Last Friday the 13th* (2000)), any more than the action film has substantially been undermined by parodies such as *Hot Shots!* or *Hot Shots: Part Deux* (1993). Parodies can exist quite happily alongside their straight cousins, profitably spoofing the originals without threatening their existence. Too close a relationship between the two can become problematic in some cases, however, especially if it is likely to lead to audience confusion about what exactly to expect.

The balance is not always easy to get right. At one extreme, a measure of reflexive knowingness and self-mockery can be introduced into versions that are otherwise played relatively straight. A good example in Hollywood action cinema is *Die Hard* (1988), a film that combines ironic self-awareness with a none-the-less-effective mobilisation of the dynamics of action-adventure-suspense. At the other extreme is the all-out parody found in examples such as the *Hot Shots!* films, in which little investment is offered in anything other than the dimension of burlesque. The territory in between these poles can be a tricky one to negotiate successfully. *The Last Action Hero* (1993, with the same director as *Die Hard*, John McTiernan), featuring Arnold Schwarzenegger, is a good example of what can go wrong. The film was a major disappointment at the box-office, a consequence, perhaps, of its attempt to have it all ways, in the construction of a product designed to appeal across a range of audience demographics. *The Last Action Hero* combines large doses of action-spectacle with thorough-going parodic deconstruction of its own premises, including the status of the central figure, Jack Slater (Schwarzenegger), a Schwarzenegger-type action star played by an actor identified *as* Schwarzenegger within the fictional world. Slater is made aware of his nature as a purely fictional creation by a young fan of his films who is magically projected into the world on screen. Many of the events of the film are, as a result, undercut by acknowledgement of their action-movie-conventional status. What appeared to the makers to be a clever mix of reiteration and comic deconstruction did not go down well with viewers, perhaps because it tried too hard to have the best of both worlds, rather than favouring one dimension over the other and thus being more clearly located in terms of appropriate audience expectations.[10]

To the extent that it can be read as parody, a film such as *Die Hard* would fall into the category of what Wes Gehring terms the parody of reaffirmation, 'a more subdued approach that manages comic deflation with an eventual reaffirmation of the subject under attack' (1999: 6). The difference between parody and its original is less clear-cut than is the case in the broader variety. Examples cited by Gehring include *Butch Cassidy and the Sundance Kid* (1969), a subtly tongue-in-cheek but also poignant western, and *An American Werewolf in London* (1981), a balance between real horror and comic self-reflexivity ('Have you ever talked to a corpse?' complains a reluctant convert to the ranks of the undead: 'It's boring'). An earlier example is *The Cat and the Canary* (1939), a Bob Hope star-vehicle that sustains much of the atmosphere of the 'old dark house' format despite antics from the comedian that include self-reflexive comments about similarities between the situation and the plots of numerous plays in which his actor-character has appeared. The most prominent, sustained and perhaps the most extreme recent example of this kind of reaffirmative parody is the *Scream* series. The *Scream* films offer a move-by-move deconstruction of the slasher-horror recipe, in which key characters draw explicit and comic attention to the rules of the form. In *Scream 2*, for example, one character elaborates the 'rules for sequels', such as the fact that the body count is always bigger and the death scenes are always more elaborate with more blood and gore: 'Carnage candy; your core audience just expects it.' At the same time, however, the films enact the format itself (there is more 'carnage candy', and a larger body-count, in *Scream 2* than in *Scream*, for example). The conventions of the slasher-horror film are deconstructed and reinstated at the same time, a duality that makes commercial sense by offering a combination of pleasures. The net effect is such that the dimension of comic self-reflection does not override the production of horror-suspense.

The relatively straightforward spoof or lampoon offers pleasure by drawing our attention to the conventional, arbitrary or clichéd nature of various features of the target object. Our recognition of the conventions (usually assumed implicitly) is taken *explicitly* for granted: we are thus positioned as knowing, elevated to a flattering location of superiority to the target, rather than being assumed to be 'taken in' by the usual relatively seamless flow of fictional contrivances. Viewers of *Hot Shots: Part Deux* (1993) can laugh at the absurdities of films such as *Rambo: First Blood Part II* (1985), for example, positioning themselves as superior to an audience that might be imagined passively to consume such 'nonsense'. Actual audience understandings of films are unlikely to reduce to such one-dimensional experiences, however, especially given the extent to which audiences for parodies and their targets are liable to overlap. The pleasure, again, might be that of having it both ways, the precise blend varying according the particular strategies adopted by any individual example or cycle. A sense of recognition and mastery is created, potentially, for the viewer who 'gets' the references. All texts require the active understanding and contribution of the audience; but, as Hutcheon suggests, the role of the viewer or reader of parody is more explicit because 'it is part of the strategy of both parody and irony that their acts of communication cannot be considered completed unless the precise encoding intention is realized in the recognition of the viewer' (1985: 6). An extra *frisson* of pleasure is offered to the viewer who picks up the references and thus contributes more openly than usual to the completion of the circuit of meaning-creation.

The price of this pleasurable mastery, however, may be a reduction in the effectiveness of the conventions involved. Given that these conventions are usually taken on board by the parody itself, as part of its own substance, the effect might be to render the parody film less satisfying in some respects as an entertainment in its own right. Some parodies offer good illustration of the problems associated with heavily gag-centred film comedy. A scattershot collection of gags and parodic routines might be offered at the expense of much in the way of independent narrative development, for example. This can create difficulty in sustaining audience interest once the initial novelty – marked by the difference between the parody and its target – begins to wear off; as the exaggerations and inversions of the parodic world become established as new norms for the duration of the film. It is notable that parodies, like broad and gag-based comedy in general, tend to have relatively short running times, a recognition of the difficulty of sustaining such gag sequences at length.

The *Scream* films manage to avoid this problem by putting a stronger than usual emphasis on the strategy of reiteration. Considerable stretches of the films, especially the high-points of horror-suspense, are barely if at all distinguishable from the 'straight' version. *Scream*, for example, opens with a scene direct from the slasher tradition, played entirely conventionally until the moment when a threatening figure on the telephone comments: 'You should never say "who's there". Don't you watch scary movies? It's a death wish. You might as well just come out here to investigate a *strange noise* or something.' The self-conscious reference, and more, including a quiz in which he demands the names of the killers in *Halloween* (1978) and *Friday the 13th* (1980), acts to some extent to distance us from the dilemma of the young woman who is being terrorised. But the horror-suspense dynamic continues at the same time. Real suspense and narrative tension are generated throughout the sequence, and the rest of the film, despite the recourse to comic self-reflexivity. *Scream 2* adds another layer of reflexivity, opening with the screening of a film based on the events depicted in *Scream*, an event that is itself interrupted by further outbreaks of slasher-killing. *Scream 3* goes the obligatory stage further, located in and around the Hollywood set of the film-second-sequel-within-the-film-second-sequel, *Stab 3*, and juxtaposing its characters with those playing them in the second-level fictional version. 'I'm Candy, the chick who gets killed second, I'm only in two scenes,' complains one of the performers, in her second scene shortly before she is killed. The narrative revisits and destabilises the background scenario established in the first in the series, according, as we are informed, to the rules for concluding parts of trilogies; the originally 'real' events, within the diegesis, turn out to have been set up by a film director. Each entry in the series is a self-standing slasher-horror film *as well as* an increasingly self-conscious and, by implication, parodic reflection on the conventions of the form. To create this effect, the *Scream* films avoid the excesses of inversion, exaggeration and extraneous inclusion found in broader forms, a strategy that locates them at the margins of the parodic.

Scary Movie, in contrast, goes for an unambiguously parodic stance. The opening sequence revisits that of *Scream*, once again, reiterating elements of character, setting and events but combining this with plenty of broad comic departure. A teenage blonde is alone in a palatial suburban home, preparing popcorn on the stove. The phone rings and the croaky-voiced caller begins to play the usual game. But then the girl farts (extraneous inclusion), a sound picked up by the caller. When asked about her favourite scary movie, she cracks a joke (extraneous inclusion, again). The 'creepy' dimension is developed for a few moments, up to the original *frisson* line (following the caller's request for the girl's name): ''Cause I wanna know who I'm looking at.' This is a chilling moment in the original, signifying the nearby presence of the killer, but is deflated here by a cut to the masked-and-robed figure from the *Scream* films sitting on a bench looking at her pictures in a copy of *Playboy* (misdirection). The line 'I want to see what your insides look like', another direct lift from the original, is undercut by her comment: 'Turn to page 54.' As the sequence continues, the popcorn container on the stove, which is neglected and eventually catches fire amid the opening of *Scream*, swells to absurd proportions (exaggeration). When the girl is confronted by the knife-wielding killer in her hallway, a table presents her with a selection of objects from which to choose (banana, hand-grenade, a pair of knives and a gun) of which she selects the banana (exaggeration of the generic assumption of victim-dumbness). As she runs outside (banana in hand), she is presented with two road signs next to the pool: one arrow, labelled 'safety', points to the left, the other, 'death', to the right; needless to say, she goes right (literalisation of the previous convention). And so on. The fictional frame is broken on a regular basis, something that does not happen in the *Scream* films.

The *Scream* series takes reflexivity to extremes of its own. In the first film, for example, a character watches *Halloween* on video, playing the game of shouting warnings to the central character to 'look behind you' when the killer appears. At the same time, *Scream*'s own killer is behind him, inviting us to shout the same warning to him. Two other characters within the narrative also watch him, helplessly, from outside, on a video monitor that has been set up in the room, adding another layer of reflexivity. This is all highly contrived and 'implausible', of course. It invites the viewer to experience the sequence as a multi-layered and parodic game rather than part of a narrative within which to become strongly involved. Attention is drawn to the fictional conventions, but the frame is not broken in the overt manner found in *Scary Movie* and many other parodies; the sequence of events *could* happen, logically, within the self-contained diegetic world, even if it might not seem very likely. On one level, the acknowledgement of slasher conventions within the narrative world offers

Figure 15   Literalisation of slasher conventions in *Scary Movie* (2000)

a form of verisimilitude: they are conventions likely to be familiar to characters such as those who inhabit the films, who, if they did become involved in such events in reality, would be likely to recognise the kinds of parallels highlighted by the films themselves. A notion of 'copycat' killing serves to motivate the merger of fact and fictional dimensions within the series. No such logic exists in *Scary Movie*, which presents itself with no pretension to be other than an all-out spoof.

A similar comparison can be made between the science fiction parody found in *Spaceballs* and *Galaxy Quest* (1999). *Spaceballs* is a typically broad Mel Brooks spoof, aimed principally at *Star Wars* although also including a wider range of parodic reference points including *Lawrence of Arabia* (1962), *Alien* (1979) and *Planet of the Apes* (1968). The narrative is a rather thinly developed play on that of the main target, little more than a hook for the deployment of a variety of broad parodic gags. *Galaxy Quest*, like the *Scream* films, combines parody with more substantial and 'straight' dimensions of its own. Parody here is aimed at the *Star Trek* television series and its convention-going fans, each of which are subjected to lampoon. In addition, however, *Galaxy Quest* offers its own narrative dynamic, a plot in which the fictional cast of a television science-fiction series very like *Star Trek* are contacted by *real* aliens who have tuned into the show and believe them to be the characters they play. The actors are then propelled into what is, for them, a real space drama, a scenario in which continued parody of the television show gains increased dimension and comic effect. The operative modality structure is one that is often found in more affecting varieties of comedy, in which comic distance/insulation is combined with emotional allegiance and implication in the events on screen.

four

comedy and representation

As a social product, comedy is often involved – implicitly or explicitly – in the politics of representation: the way one group or another is identified, distinguished and portrayed. Who and what we laugh at, and why, has implications in terms of both how we see others and how we define ourselves, the two often closely interconnected. Gender, race/ethnicity and nationality are three major sets of grounds (although not the only ones) on which such distinctions and identifications are constructed and articulated; as such, it is not surprising that they should be recurrent sources of comic material in film as elsewhere. Comedy has the ability to both question and reconfirm prevailing definitions, as we have seen, giving it a potent but also ambiguous ideological potential, whether read as a symptom of existing social relationships or as a more active component of the politics of representation. These are large and contentious areas of debate that could easily fill a book-length study on their own. What follows makes no claim to sketch more than an outline of some central issues on the territories of gender, race/ethnicity and nationality.

Comedy, gender and gender-bending

Disruptive, childlike and playful trickster-type characters are usually male, as are most of the stars of comedian comedy. Grotesque and gross-out comedy are also, primarily, the preserves of male performers. Women are often characterised in comedy as sources of repression or oppression, as representatives of dull conformity with the norms of 'civilisation': in effect, in some cases, as opponents of the world of comedy itself, with its freedoms from usual social and formal constraints. Most, if not all, of the comedy considered so far in this book has implications in terms of the representation of gender. Silent slapstick is replete with images of imprisoning women, for example, fierce creatures whose childlike spouses – the stars of the films – risk chastisement as the price for any attempted escape: John Bunny's card game in *A Cure for Pokeritis* (1912), Harry Langdon's unlicensed weekend pleasures in *Saturday Afternoon* (1925), Laurel and Hardy (temporarily) fooling their wives to carouse at an all-male convention in *Sons of the Desert* (1933), to name just three. Gender-specific issues are also close to the fore in the comedy of regression, defined in part through difficulties of accession by male characters to 'proper' masculine behaviour.

Comedy is often created through departures from what are considered to be 'normal' or dominant gender roles: the 'feminised' or childlike male and the 'masculinised' woman, for example, or anything that falls between the binary gender poles. Carnivalesque inversions of gender roles offer prominent examples of the typically double-edged potential of comedy, to both reinforce and undermine established norms. Characters such as those played by Bunny, Langdon and Laurel and Hardy are comic partly because of their inability to meet certain conventional gender expectations: put crudely, that (in a patriarchal society) a man should be master of his own house. To find their plight comic is implicitly to acknowledge the existence of the dominant expectation, to reinforce the stereotypical image of a more dominant and assertive masculinity (it might also entail an acknowledgment of the greater power of women within the confines of the domestic setting, but it is usually more excessive, and hence comic, than that alone would allow). Awareness of the departure from the norm – and hence awareness *of* the norm – is one of the key ingredients of the comic effect, here as elsewhere. This is one dynamic involved in the comedy of gender inversion: laughter at the breach is predicated on and can help to sustain the norm.

The same might be said of comedy produced by the presence of unusually assertive or supposedly 'masculinised' women. This includes minor and repressive characters, ranging from the domestic tyrants faced by Bunny and company to the bizarre maternal caricature produced in *Throw Momma From the Train* (1987), and those played by the relatively small number of more positively framed women comedy stars. Many women performers have failed to receive the same recognition as their male peers. Largely forgotten from the silent era are names such as Gale Henry, Alice Howell, Dorothy DeVore and Fay Tincher. The latter plays against conventional gender stereotypes in films such as *Rowdy Ann* (1919), in which her character is the tomboy daughter of a cattle rancher, riding astride her horse in cowboy attire and as handy with her rope, gun and fists as any male western hero. The film eventually offers some reconciliation of gender roles. Ann is sent east to college 'to larn [sic] to be a lady', eventually becoming 'tamed' sufficiently to wear dresses but not so much as to lose the ability to lasso and punch to the ground a con artist with designs on a rich heiress. The negotiation of gender roles found in comedies such as this can be related to an early twentieth-century social context in which efforts were made to maintain nineteenth-century ideals of domesticated womanhood in the face of disruptive social changes resulting from industrialisation (Jenkins 1991).

The disruptive and comically 'unruly' woman has a long history, in various specific historical contexts, appearing as a central figure in the repertoire of carnival in medieval and early modern Europe and in the burlesque and music-hall traditions on which early film comedy drew as one of its major sources.[1] A tradition of strongly assertive and disruptive female performers has continued in film, from Mae West to Whoopi Goldberg, although not in anything like the numbers of their male counterparts. Sustaining characters based on such performers has often proved difficult within the more general confines of patriarchal culture, as Kathleen Rowe suggests. Mae West is a dominating and gender-role-subverting presence in *She Done Him Wrong* (1933), treating men as interchangeable sex objects and sources of money. Her scope of activity is severely constrained, however, when compared with that of a male comedian comic such as Chaplin: 'West is limited to the single narrative of a woman's life: of her relation to men. West's persona bursts out of the narrative of the whore with a heart of gold, which is the only narrative that would make her acceptable to a mainstream audience. And yet, that narrative confines her to a single-note performance' (1995a: 124). Another notably disruptive performer from the early sound era in Hollywood is Charlotte Greenwood, the noisy and highly physical star of *So Long Letty* (1929), a figure whose unruly characteristics are also to some extent contained by the narrative frame (see Jenkins 1991).

Romantic comedy is one of the few arenas in which the unruly woman has been given rein with any regularity, perhaps because it is more likely than most comedy to be targeted at women, although the narrative conventions of the format tend towards the achievement of domesticated heterosexual containment. In Hollywood romantic comedies of the 1930s and 1940s such as *Bringing Up Baby, Ball of Fire* (1941) and *The Lady Eve* (1941), the unruly woman is portrayed as a positive influence, a source of zest that transforms dull and lifeless male characters. Rowe traces a shift away from this tendency in post-war America in the context of a range of social-cultural developments, including the immediate post-war effort to reconstruct myths of feminine domesticity and more openly combative struggles over gender and power from the 1960s; contexts in which the figure of the unruly and powerful woman 'became too threatening to stand as a comedic figure of mutual liberation and play' (1995a: 193). By the late 1980s and early 1990s, Rowe suggests, the 'woman on top' became a figure more likely to be portrayed as crazy, in the domains of the thriller and the horror film, than as a figure of liberating comic play. Any such change is not absolute, however. Vivian in *Pretty Woman* is a more recent example of a brash, willful woman whose example has a transformative effect on an all-work/no-play repressed male lead, even if she starts as the powerless figure in the equation. Her unruliness is contained, to some extent, through her induction into a more 'classy' and 'refined' lifestyle, but this process is only partial. Crucial to the dynamic of the film is the assumption that she maintains her original spirit. To the extent that she is 'tamed', the difference between this and the fate of some of the central figures of the films cited above is only relative.

The characters of unruly or 'masculinised' women, like those of the 'feminised' male, are comic partly by dint of their difference from – and implicit recognition of – the more 'passive' roles usually ascribed to women in patriarchal societies. Other possibilities also exist in these forms of comedy, however, including the potential for subversion of and liberation from restrictive binary gender categories. Comic pleasure might come from the reaffirmation of our conventionally assigned gender characteristics: we laugh at figures that do not conform, thus reinforcing the solidity of our own often precarious identities. But it might also offer a pleasurable form of release from such confines, a vicarious form of transgression into usually forbidden territories. If dominantly prescribed gender roles operate in only a narrow band of the spectrum of possible orientations, as is suggested from both social-cultural and psychoanalytical perspectives on gender-role formation, comedies of gender inversion or ambiguity can offer imaginary experiences of other dimensions. Conventional gender assumptions can be held up to ridicule, not just those who fail or refuse to meet their requirements. This may be one way of accounting for the relative absence of women associated with sustained comedian-comic personae in film. Male comics are allowed much scope for unruliness and disruption, whether the target is the 'feminine' realm of domestic responsibility or 'masculine' institutions such as the police or army. Women performers have not generally been permitted such licence. Where they have, their contributions have been more sporadic, forgotten or subject to disciplines such as the introduction of the Hollywood Production Code of 1934, the formalisation of which was partly promoted by, and put an end to, the more unruly dimensions of the screen persona of Mae West.

How many women comedian comics strongly associated with a particular unruly comic persona can be named in recent or contemporary Hollywood? Not many. Prominent exceptions to the rule include Whoopi Goldberg, a loud, garish and classically disruptive figure in films such as *Jumpin' Jack Flash* (1986) and *Sister Act* (1992), of which more below. Other examples have been found in British cinema, but often requiring qualification rather than clearly being disruptive or in the realm of comedian comedy. The free-wheeling, gag-centred format of the *Carry On* films provides some opportunities for disruptive performance on the part of the regular women performers Barbara Windsor,

Hattie Jacques and Joan Simms, Frances Gray suggests, cutting across the limited gender stereotypical roles within which they are situated by the narrative. The regular viewer would be aware of watching Barbara Windsor playing a 'Windsor part', including a dimension of assertive freedom, 'rather than a stereotype which happened to be played by Windsor' (1998: 102). Collective instances of unruly women are found in some cases, examples including pupils and teachers in *The Belles of St. Trinians* (1954) and its sequels, striking fear into the local community and representatives of authority. A consistent version of unruliness is found in many performances by Julie Walters, in films such as *Educating Rita* (1983), *Personal Services* (1987) and *Billy Elliot* (2000), although often mixed with grittier and bittersweet elements and coded as more 'serious' acting. One of the most striking European examples is the imposing German performer Marianne Sägebrecht in the offbeat films of Percy Adlon, especially *Rosalie Goes Shopping* (1989), in which her central character blithely disregards all usual social and legal restraints in regard to money; she forges and defrauds her way through the world of American consumerism, eventually neglecting some of her maternal duties in pursuit of computer-mediated control over the realm of business and finance.

An explanation for the striking absence of many more such performers might simply be that the question of women remaining 'in their place' is of greater sensitivity than that of men, with more at stake. The unruly comic male is less potentially subversive, exploiting just one of many available avenues of power and freedom. The unruly woman represents a more serious challenge to the gender hierarchies on which so many social relationships are based. The dominant norms of many cultures give women less licence than men to depart from prevailing inhibitions, especially in public forms such as performance (Apte 1985: 69–72). The disruptive figure cut by the mother, Ellen, when her body is occupied by the teenage daughter, Annabel, in *Freaky Friday* is liberating and comic but also potentially disturbing to patriarchal norms. She fails to achieve basic requirements of her allocated domestic role, which is portrayed as oppressive, and flirts playfully with the boy from across the street, even if all is resolved through the magic of comedy in the end. It is, perhaps, not surprising that such a figure, the film's principal source of comic and performative spectacle, has been less subject to reiteration than that of the regressive/disruptive male.

Comic subversion of gender codes can be achieved through a variety of approaches, including the inversion, deconstruction and exaggeration of dominant conventions. One way to explore this question in more detail is to examine some examples in which gender inversion is carried a step further, to the point of masquerade: the comedy of cross-dressing or of male/female impersonation. The comedy of cross-dressing is largely one of incongruity: the spectacle of a member of one gender group assuming the guise of another, with varying degrees of success. The initial comic *frisson* is based on the first sight of the character in drag, a moment that is sometimes delayed to increase its impact. In *Some Like It Hot* (1959) Joe/Josephine (Tony Curtis) and Gerry/Daphne (Jack Lemon) are first glimpsed from behind, at leg level, before the full-frontal revelation of the pair in drag, as they pose as members of an all-girl band in order to escape a gang of Chicago mobsters. In *Mrs Doubtfire*, the make-over that transforms Daniel Hillard into the eponymous cleaner, cook and child-minder (in an attempt to remain close to his children after divorce) is evoked in a series of close shots that deny the viewer the spectacle of the overall effect until the following scene. A similar delayed-revelation effect is offered in *Big Momma's House* (2000), in which detective Malcolm Turner (Martin Lawrence) impersonates the long-lost grandmother of a woman suspected to have knowledge about the location of the proceeds of a bank job. The quality of drag is relatively 'convincing' in these cases, creating quite plausible illusions of gender transformation. Once the cross-dressed version is established, however, and the initial novelty begins to fade, heightened moments of gender-related comedy tend to shift location, away from the spectacle of the finished article to moments of slippage between 'real' and 'fake' gender identities or in which both are on show at the same time.

Both *Some Like It Hot* and *Mrs Doubtfire* include madcap sequences in which the principals are required to make rapid-fire movements from one gendered identity to another in order to sustain their masquerades. Joe/Josephine is caught at one moment in the make-up (but not the wig) of Josephine while attired in the blazer and cravat of the millionaire figure 'Junior' he has adopted in an attempt to win the affections of Sugar Kane (Marilyn Monroe); the fact that he is also covered with suds after hiding the male attire of his body in the bath only adds to the incongruity of the spectacle. Daniel Hillard has two major sequences of rapid transformation (with foregrounded performance by Williams): trying to maintain both identities in the presence of a court liaison officer at his apartment and flitting between two dinner dates at an up-market restaurant. Incongruity is sometimes established between image and sound: Joe speaking on the phone in falsetto voice and made-up face but without the wig; Hillard mixing gender voices and appearances in various combinations while talking, from one room, to the liaison officer, in another; or in full middle-aged-woman drag while seeing off a mugger with a masculine-toned 'back off, asshole'. Similar moments of partial transformation are offered as comic spectacle on numerous occasions in *Big Momma's House*.

What happens in such comic moments of frantic gender reinvention or mixed signification? Are gender lines blurred or reinforced? Either possibility might be available, depending on both textual detail and how it is taken by the viewer. Historical context also shapes the extent to which any real questions of gender identity are likely to be raised. As Rebecca Bell-Metereau (1993) suggests, the silent and early sound eras in Hollywood saw a number of subtle and potentially subversive examples of cross-dressing comedy, including Chaplin's performance in *The Masquerader* (1914) and *A Woman* (1915). The 'moral' crackdown represented by the enforcement of the Production Code

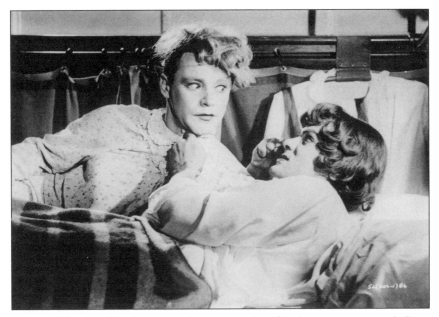

Figure 16 Slippage of identities: gender incongruity as Gerry/Daphne's wig goes astray in *Some Like it Hot* (1959)

from 1934 outlawed acts of gender impersonation that might be too convincing or risked any blurring of boundaries. Exaggerated and farcical treatments only were permitted, comedies such as the much re-made *Charley's Aunt* in which the masculine identity and heterosexual orientation of the cross-dressing male are clearly maintained throughout (Bell-Metereau 1993: 39). A greater range of possibilities was created in the social climate that led to the demise of the Code in the 1960s, including the appearance in popular films of previously taboo subjects such as homosexuality and transvestism.

In some cases, a slippage of gender boundaries is recuperated towards the norm. But the resonances often remain ambiguous. Take two similar but slightly different examples from *Mrs Doubtfire*. One occurs during Hillard's frantic restaurant performance, when he has to move between the role of Doubtfire out for dinner with Hillard's family and an important meeting with the owner of a television station, Jonathan Lundy (Robert Prosky). Hillard returns to Lundy's table from one speedy changeover with an excess of Doubtfire perfume and with lipstick still intact. He claims to have acquired both in a close encounter with a former girlfriend who works at the restaurant as a waitress. 'You dog!' enthuses Lundy, in a spirit of boisterous male-bonding-through-assumptions-of-potency. The signifiers of gender slippage (a man in lipstick and perfume) are reinterpreted, in other words, to support conventional attributes of the norm they might otherwise threaten to undermine (traces of lipstick and perfume as signifiers of 'proper' heterosexual contact with a woman).

Another example, with more complex resonances, comes when a bus driver flirts with Hillard-as-Doubtfire. As Hillard takes his seat his skirt is pulled up and his tights are askew, revealing a conventionally masculine-seeming hairy leg: comic as a fissure in the cross-dressing façade. The driver might be expected to be shocked or repelled by the revelation of so 'masculine' a signifier, a potential threat to his own male gender identity, perhaps (if he has fallen for a 'woman' who is really a man, a typical example of homophobic dread). This is not how it is played, however. The joke is the driver's comment that he likes 'that Mediterranean look' and, with an irony often found in comedies of cross-dressing, he adds that it is 'natural, just the way God made you'. The hairy leg is taken as a signifier not of dishonest masquerade but of more than usually honest and unvarnished femininity. Hillard's presence in the scene is not disruptive of gender identities within the world of the fiction, as it might have been; but a point is implied about the cosmetic interventions that help to construct or fabricate *conventional* female identity.

Both *Mrs Doubtfire* and *Some Like It Hot* provide other comic material that contributes potentially to a sense of the constructed nature of established gender identities, not just those adopted in the central masquerades. One source is the presence in 'straight' secondary roles of performers with pre-established reputations as the epitomes of their respective gender positions: Pierce Brosnan (as Stu Dunmier, Hillard's replacement in the affections of his ex-wife) and Marilyn Monroe as Sugar Kane. Brosnan's idealised masculinity (established primarily in his role as James Bond) is undermined by Hillard/Doubtfire's references to the liposuction and exercise regimes that create such bodies (and, when visiting Dunmier's exclusive club/pool, Hillard's comment: 'not a single body that exists in nature'). Attention is not drawn so explicitly to Monroe's incarnation of ideal femininity in *Some Like It Hot*, but it seems exaggerated close to the point of caricature.

Some Like It Hot is the more radical of these films in its treatment of gender, offering less stable anchorage for the identities of Joe and Gerry. The latter, especially, has to keep convincing himself of his position. 'I'm a girl, I'm a girl, I'm a girl,' he reminds himself, to keep his male ardour at bay when sharing a sleeping carriage with the female members of the band. Later, however, it is his 'real' gender identity that has to be reinforced in such a manner: 'I'm a boy, I'm a boy, I'm a boy', becomes the refrain towards the end of the film when he has successfully been romanced by the multiple-married millionaire Osgood Fielding (Joe E. Brown). Once the masquerade has begun, neither character is permitted much time entirely in the guise of his 'real' identity: Gerry remains Daphne, and seems increasingly comfortable in the role, beyond the initial stage of gaining a privileged position from which to ogle his female companions. Joe oscillates between alternative masquerades as Josephine and Junior, finding little space in between for his 'original' self. Gerry-as-Daphne eventually accepts Osgood's proposal of marriage. He plans to reveal the truth after the ceremony, to secure a profitable annulment, but this cynicism does not appear entirely to erase what seems like a genuine seduction (he has been shown, throughout the film, to be easily led by the schemes of others). The crowning moment of gender inversion in *Some Like It Hot* is Osgood's concluding comment when Gerry confesses to being a man: 'Well, nobody's perfect.' Biological gender fixture, it seems, is not of transcendent importance but just one factor among others: a potentially radical suggestion even when played for laughs that mark its departure from supposedly 'normal' behaviour.

Mrs Doubtfire is, generally, more restrictive in its strategies. Daniel Hillard's sexual orientations are never placed in doubt by his masquerade. Any sugges- tion that dressing up as a woman might offer sexual satisfaction in its own right is disavowed by the presence of Hillard's brother (Harvey Fierstein) and his brother's lover: a real – clichéd and theatrical – gay couple. Their existence marks out the difference between Hillard-in-drag-for-a-practical-purpose and any more substantial blurring of dominant gender identities, such as transves- tism. A similar device is found in *Billy Elliot*, the story of an 11-year-old boy from a mining community in the north-east of England who takes up ballet amid the macho-coded conflicts of the miner's strike of the mid-1980s. 'Just because I like ballet it doesn't mean I'm a poof,' he declares, aware of the gender-role complications caused by his activities; and to make clear this distinction, a real homosexual is inserted in the shape of his cross-dressing school-friend Michael (Stuart Wells). The dread of any real homosexual subtext in *Mrs Doubtfire* is reflected most strongly in the reaction to Hillard's masquerade by his adolescent son Chris (Matthew Lawrence), a key figure in this regard as a male child at a supposedly 'vulnerable' stage of development. Chris is keen to establish that his father does not 'actually like wearing that stuff' and is reluc- tant to join him in an embrace immediately after the moment of revelation.

A similar keenness to disavow any gay subtext is found in *Tootsie* (1982), in which the 'difficult' actor Michael Dorsey (Dustin Hoffman) becomes a hit after taking on a female identity as Dorothy Michaels in order to find work. Assorted comic complications and confusions ensure. His former girlfriend Sandy (Terri Garr) thinks he is gay; the women with whom he falls in love, Julie (Jessica Lange), thinks he/she is a lesbian; her father proposes marriage. The question of his sexual orientation is put directly by his male flat-mate Jeff (Bill Murray), but only in order to be dismissed, largely for our benefit, it seems, so that the spectacle of gender confusion can be enjoyed from a position of substantial stability. The grounding of our own knowledge of the 'real' underlying gender of the character is usually a major factor in our ability to find specifically *comic* the various errors and confusions that result from the masquerade. Cross-dressing that involves more radical uncertainty of underlying identity, or deliberate deception of the viewer, might be more likely to be found in more 'disturbing' formats such as the thriller or the horror film (Kuhn 1985: 62–3).

Dorsey is presented as learning important lessons from his experiences in drag. The film offers a critique of sexist male behaviour from various figures, including Dorsey himself. He complains about the way he is treated, as a woman, realising that this is precisely the way he treats Sandy. His experience as Dorothy is educative: 'I was a better man with you as a woman than I ever was with a woman as a man,' he tells Julie at the end; 'I've just got to learn to do it without the dress.' A brief period in drag is also part of the learning process that helps to loosen-up the excessively rigid David in *Bringing Up Baby*: he puts on a fluffy and frilly robe after being deprived of his clothes by Susan. The shedding of conventional gender signifiers offers both comic spectacle – David looks utterly ridiculous in the robe – and a stage en route towards other forms of transformation.

If gender-bending or cross-dressing comedy can be used to reinforce dominant stereotypes, it can also be a source of criticism. This can entail a degree of gender imperialism. In *Tootsie*, the man-as-woman is the only woman presented as capable of becoming an assertive heroic role-model for large numbers of women fans, a source of a good deal of criticism of the film from a feminist perspective.[2] If women are often positioned as characters who put pressure on regressive male comic figures to grow up, this process is achieved through an internalisation of female gender characteristics in films such as *Tootsie* and *Mrs Doubtfire*, a reconciliation of the opposition between the two that leaves little place for women themselves. The figure of the assertively unruly woman is taken over by male characters, a key ingredient of *Some Like It Hot*.

For Rowe, this is an indicator of a more general displacement of the unruly woman in the postwar decades. Other examples can be found that precede these specific developments in Hollywood. In British film comedy, for example, the cross-dressed figure of Old Mother Riley (Arthur Lucan) cut a disruptive swathe through a range of institutions in a series of films running from the late 1930s to the early 1950s; a classic instance of the loud, outspoken and unruly 'woman' from the lower classes who stands as an 'authentic' voice of the people and rises to unlikely heights, such as member of parliament and cabinet minister in *Old Mother Riley, MP* (1939). Arthur Lucan's man-as-Irish-washerwoman act is an inheritance from the world of comic gender-bending in music-hall and burlesque. Another, more extreme and further-reaching, example of male appropriation of the unruly woman is the deeply transgressive transsexual figure of Divine in the films of John Waters.

In the postwar Hollywood context, films such as *Tootsie* and *Mrs Doubtfire* might be understood alongside a number of comic and non-comic productions of the late 1970s and 1980s – from *Kramer vs. Kramer* (1979) to *Three Men and a Baby* (1987) – that have been seen as part of a backlash against second-wave feminism, presenting male characters successfully replacing women in conventionally 'female' domains such as the care of children.[3] One problem with such interpretations, however, is that they risk ignoring the specific and more ambivalent characteristics of cross-dressing, reducing them to issues of binary gender politics (Garber 1993: 7–8). The more sustained sense of binary gender deconstruction found in *Some Like It Hot* is related by Ed Sikov (1994) to the particular climate of suppressed sexual hysteria of the 1950s. The film, he suggests, is one of several comic manifestations of repressed desires that were to be given more overt expression in the 1960s and 1970s.

Some comedies go further in offering a deconstruction of dominant signifiers of masculinity, again through the introduction of gender shifts or instability. *La Cage aux Folles* (1978), its close Hollywood remake *The Birdcage* (1996) and *In and Out* (1997) offer variations on this theme. *La Cage aux Folles* and *The Birdcage* have an almost identical set-piece sequence in which a strongly 'effeminate' gay man is taught a lesson in more 'masculine' behaviour. What results is a caricature of macho posturing. How to butter a slice of toast like a man: 'hold it firmly and decisively' (*La Cage*); 'hold the knife boldly and with strength', don't 'dribble' mustard onto the toast but smear: 'men smear' (*The Birdcage*). Each includes attempts at an exaggeratedly masculine (but still decidedly camp) version of a John Wayne swagger. Crotch-adjustment, spitting and high-fives conclude the proceedings in *The Birdcage*, the kind of macho gestures that are also mocked in *In and Out*, in which English teacher Howard Brackett (Kevin Kline) seeks to reassert his heterosexuality after being wrongly identified as gay during one of the speeches at the Oscar awards ceremony. His efforts include a session with a book and cassette recording titled 'Explore Your Masculinity'. 'Stand straight and tall,' it commands; untuck your shirt, but just from one side. 'You want to be neat and tidy?' it queries, suspiciously. Men do not dance, under any circumstances, and must at all costs 'avoid rhythm, grace and pleasure'. Brackett cannot avoid the temptation when the tape plays dance music, his body rebelling against his will. 'I'm gay,' he subsequently announces during his marriage ceremony, the film offering an uneasy balancing act between criticising and playing on homophobic assumptions.

At least some of the comedy in these films is aimed critically at dominant masculine conventions. If Howard Brackett is a 'smart, clean, totally decent human being', then of course he must be gay, one character observes, implying that 'normal' heterosexual males are messy, dirty and something other than decent human beings. The extreme nature of the proposition still leaves plenty of room for recuperation, of course, as is so often the case in comedy. A more 'ordinary' or 'normal' masculinity might be implied as the norm against which such routines are based. But comedy can go some way towards revealing the status of certain aspects of the masculine 'norm' as themselves a masquerade, a matter of performance that requires on-going work and reinforcement, rather than as characteristics unproblematically rooted in nature. The enactment of all dominant gender roles entails a form of masquerade or imitation of constructed ideals.[4] Gender identities are seen here as fluid and subject to various forms of instability, which might be understood from psychoanalytical or social-cultural perspectives. The performance of identities that conform to dominant cultural expectations requires constant reinforcement, but this can easily shift over into an exaggerated deployment of conventional gender signifiers that offers further fruitful ground for comedy.

One source of this kind of exaggeration is the 'drag queen' comedy in films such as *The Adventures of Priscilla, Queen of the Desert* (1994) and *To Wong Foo, Thanks for Everything! Julie Newmar* (1995). The signifiers of femininity are exaggerated, sometimes to ludicrously performative extremes, and a number of different versions of cross-dressing are offered as comic spectacle: from 'men in women's clothing' at one end of the scale, as it is put in *To Wong Foo*, to transsexual reassignment of physiological gender identity. Numerous comic incongruities are found here, as in other comedies of cross-dressing. The fact that 'men' in women's bodies have unexpected strength and the ability to deal out appropriate treatment to bullies is a frequent and somewhat predictable source of humour. Binary gender divisions are complicated and played around with in both films. Unconventionally gendered characters from the 'sophisti-cated' metropolises of Sydney and New York land up in rural communities in the middle of nowhere and, in both cases, the latter prove less resistant to their gender-bending influence than might have been expected. The comedy lies as much in the openness of some backwoods characters to what is repre-sented by the drag queen as in the incongruity of the latter's appearance outside his/her 'natural' environment. The ultimate in gender reassignment is achieved in *Switch* (1991, a remake of *Goodbye Charlie* (1964)), in which divine intervention results in the reincarnation of a sexist male as a woman (Ellen Barkin) whose incongruously 'masculine' behaviour – slouching, thrusting hands into pockets, adopting a posture of casual dominance and handy with 'her' fists – creates a more complexly located spectacle of the unruly woman.

Exaggeration of gender signifiers is not only found in the person of charac-ters in drag. In *Some Like It Hot* the drag acts of Joe and Gerry are juxtaposed to Monroe's exaggerated figure of female sexuality, especially when she appears in a preposterously clinging and almost transparent flimsy-backed outfit for one of her songs and for a trip out to the millionaire's yacht. If they are the fake and she is the genuine, in terms of physiological gender orien-tation, it is Monroe's version of femininity that in some respects seems the more excessive and implausible. How this plays is potentially double-edged. Monroe has often been taken as a male fantasy-ideal figure of the woman; at the same time, the excessive nature of her version might also point to the fantastic nature of the supposedly ideal.[5] Monroe, like Mae West before her, might be described as a 'female female impersonator', presenting a version of the gendered self that appears to be a visual construct 'created through a performance of femininity that exaggerates its attributes and thus denatu-ralises it' (Rowe 1995a: 119). The crucial difference between the two is that the West character in a film such as *She Done Him Wrong* appears to be in control of the process of masquerade, shaping and performing her version of female spectacle for her own profitable ends (both within the fictional world and without, West having contributed to the creation of her own comic screen persona). Monroe, in contrast, is presented in *Some Like It Hot* as the 'dumb blonde' whose performance and its comic results are entirely unselfconscious.

Any disruption or unruliness offered by this figure is marked as the outcome of dimness rather than any more radical or liberating impulse.

If exaggerated figures of femininity can create a sense of the artificial and constructed nature of gender characteristics, the same can be said of comically excessive figures of the masculine. The macho action heroics of muscled performers such as Sylvester Stallone and Arnold Schwarzenegger verge close to parodies of idealised versions of masculinity, as many commentators have noted. A hyperbolic inflation of the masculine suggests its ultimate lack of any 'natural' grounding and its status as masquerade.[6] If some of the comedy in the 'straight' version of the action film is unintentional (along with the requisite dose of intended comic quips), the same performers have also ventured into deliberate self-parody. The basic concepts of the Schwarzenegger vehicles *Kindergarten Cop* and *Twins* (1988), for example, are rooted in jokes at the expense of the star's excessive physicality: incongruously located in an assignment in a nursery in the former and as unlikely twin brother of the diminutive Danny DeVito in the latter, although the oppositions are largely reconciled in both cases.

Cases of female-to-male drag appear less frequently in film comedy than male-to-female, for reasons that are not difficult to suggest. Males masquerading as female generally provide more fertile ground for comedy in patriarchal societies, in which the male is usually taken as the neutral unmarked norm. The female is the marked term, designated as more specific, more problematic and more visible, requiring a seemingly more active process of transformation: all those montage sequences in which make-up, wigs, foundation garments and other accessories are applied. For a man to dress as a woman, in this context, creates more scope for comic incongruity (unless, that is, a woman were to attempt an impersonation of the hyperbolic muscularity of a Stallone or a Schwarzenegger!). Female impersonation is an additive process, one of incongruous display. Male impersonation, in contrast, relies largely on concealment, of breasts, long hair and other physical characteristics, a potential but generally less immediate source of comedy.

Power and status differentials are also significant. For a woman to seek to 'pass' as a man might seem less comical, ridiculous or absurd, given the greater access to power and resources likely to result. For a man to dress as a woman is to trade downwards, in patriarchal terms, a seemingly less 'rational' and therefore potentially more comic manoeuvre. As one study of cross-dressing puts it: 'she cross-dresses because she wants to be taken seriously; he generally cross-dresses because he doesn't' (Kirk & Heath 1984: 9, quoted in Garber 1993: 215). Even in comedy, a clear narrative rationale of some kind is required for acts of cross-dressing that are not motivated by the presence of characters established as drag queens, homosexuals or transsexuals: access to children in *Mrs Doubtfire*; in pursuit of an acting job in *Tootsie*; as part of a criminal investigation in *Big Momma's House*; in order for a French officer to gain entry to the United States with his American army wife in *I Was a Male War*

Bride (1949). As Marjorie Garber suggests, a 'progress' narrative underlies the interpretation of many fictional versions of cross-dressing, the central figures of which are 'compelled' by social and economic forces to disguise themselves: 'Each, that is, is said to embrace transvestism unwillingly, as an instrumental strategy rather than as an erotic pleasure and play space' (1993: 70).

In *Know Thy Wife* (1918), Betty (Dorothy DeVore) assumes male appearance in suit, tie and a short-haired wig in order to pose as a male friend of her new husband on a visit to his family, who are expecting him to marry a rich heiress instead. The drag act is subdued and boyish, conventional formal male attire of the day leaving little room here, as in many other cases, for comically extravagant transformations. Comic incongruity comes in the form of how the couple's behaviour appears to others – the pair are caught kissing, a corset is found in their room – and in moments when Betty removes her wig, revealing long tresses while still wearing the man's suit. A more striking mix of gender signifiers is found in *Rowdy Ann*, when Ann is called for lessons in classical dance after being dispatched to college: the outfit in which she appears combines the requisite flimsy/flouncy white dress and tights with incongruous western hat, boots and gunbelt.

The usual complications and multiple ironies are found in more recent female-to-male cross-dressing features such as *Victor/Victoria* (1982) and *Yentl* (1983). In the former, Julie Andrews plays a singer posing as a female impersonator in 1930s Paris, immediately adding an additional layer to the gender confusions. In the latter, the title character (Barbra Streisand) poses as a young man in order to gain access to a male world of Jewish learning and ideas in early twentieth-century Eastern Europe. Both become drawn sexually and emotionally to figures of the same gender as that which they have falsely adopted, creating a range of comic tensions and gender ambiguities. Victoria falls for the Chicago gangster and club owner King Marchand (James Garner), who goes through a number of comic transformations of orientation towards her/him (initial attraction to the woman on stage; internal gender crisis when she is 'revealed' on stage to be a man; suspicion that 'he' is really a she; discovery of the truth; reluctant agreement to go along with a public façade in which both are assumed to be homosexual men; engagement in male-bonding rituals – provoking a fight in a workingmen's bar – to reassert his masculinity; and so on). Gender orientations are upset in some cases, most notably when Marchand's apparent homosexuality provides his tough bodyguard with the courage to confess his repressed homosexuality. Some gender fluidity is permitted in the margins, as is often the case in comedies of this variety, but the central romantic narrative, the relationship between Victoria and Marchand, is underpinned by, (a) his 'instinctive' recognition of her real gender status, and the fact that the viewer knows him to be right, and (b) the strong romantic-comedy-conventional expectation that their union will successfully be achieved. Yentl falls in love with her friend and 'study partner' Avigdor (Mandy Patinkin), after suffering typical comical cross-dressed dilemmas such as being forced to share a bed with him, but ends up 'marrying' the woman originally intended to be Avigdor's bride, Hadass (Amy Irving), and being put in a similarly awkward position. The denouement does not, in this case, unite the couple, Avigdor being unable to accept Yentl's demands to maintain her freedom; a narrative trajectory of feminist empowerment, and escape to the presumed freedoms of the United States, overrides the imperatives of romance.

Moments of gender-appearance transition do not play the same comic role in these films as in the examples of male-to-female impersonation considered above. Little of the process of transformation or of in-between incongruity is depicted. The first time Victoria dresses in a man's suit, she walks into frame already transformed, with only the hat missing to complete the effect (and the hat is already in place on her head the next time she appears). We see her gay friend Toddy (Robert Preston) cutting her hair, but only snipping off at the back, not effecting any visual transformation for the viewer. The first cut of hair is also seen in *Yentl*, a little more dramatically, but only before a swift move to a subsequent scene in which the Streisand character is already fully in her imposture as a boy, dressed in cap, glasses, jacket, trousers and scarf. A moment of transition is offered later, in which Yentl unbuttons her shirt to reveal, and unwind, the cloth used to bind her breasts (although no naked breast is revealed). The moment of disclosure to the male admirer is handled similarly in both films. Marchand obtains confirmation of Victoria's true gender status by spying on her as she strips in readiness for a bath; Yentl reveals herself deliberately to Avigdor. In each case, the physiological evidence is displayed to the character but not to the viewer, and in neither is the process of unveiling presented as in itself comically incongruous. Victoria is witnessed in a half-way state, dressed up for the 'drag' act but without wig or headdress, but, again, not offered as anything like the source of comic spectacle found in the male-to-female drag comedy.

Racial, ethnic and national dimensions[7]

If Whoopi Goldberg is one of relatively few women to have established a persona as a disruptive comedian-comic in Hollywood in recent decades – albeit somewhat sporadically – it is perhaps no accident that she should also be a black, African-American performer. To be a loud, crazy, unruly figure is to go against dominant stereotypes of 'acceptable' female behaviour and is something of a rarity in film, even in the realm of comedy. The same qualities might fit more easily into the parameters of long-standing racial stereotypes, however, most notably that of the 'coon': the racist version of the African-American as black buffoon and object of amusement.

Comedy is often used to ridicule and mock other groups in society, whether on gender, racial/ethnic or any other lines, a tendency that is widespread in human cultures (see Apte 1985). Comedy of this kind becomes pernicious where it is used to reinforce inequalities, which need not always be the case. Laughter at others is one way social groups define themselves, a process consisting to a large extent of distinctions between self and other. It is common for one culture to find the norms of another to be foolish or 'unclean' in one way or another, a potential source of comedy that helps to mark the bounds of the former. In considerations of racial or ethnic mockery in film, the point is sometimes made that racial and ethnic 'others' are not the only victims of comedy of this kind. A long tradition of racist representation exists in American film animation, for example. Without seeking to defend this, Terry Lindvall and Ben Fraser point out that African-Americans or other racially/ethnically defined 'others' are far from alone in being objects of distorted and exaggerated representation. Distortion and exaggeration are basic tools of the animated medium, they suggest, an argument that might apply to comedy more generally. The cartoon 'makes buffoons of everyone, regardless of ethnic or national identity' (1998: 123); 'To show consideration to whites, Indians, Japanese, German, or blacks would negate the very nature of a cartoon: lampoonery' (125). The stupid redneck Elmer Fudd, antagonist of Bugs Bunny, is just as much a stereotype as the dimwit black character who also features in some of the same cartoons. The difference, however, is one of context, specifically in relation to broader structural inequalities in society. White and black characters might be equally subject to mockery but the implications are different. Where relationships of inequality exist between one group and another, comedy of this kind can contribute to the legitimation of the dominance of those in power. The other is seen as laughably foolish or incompetent, and so not capable of taking on greater power or responsibility. This is more likely to play its part (among very many other factors) in shoring up discursive and other structures of inequality, I would argue, than any mockery of those in power is likely to reduce the basis of their dominance. Lampoonery is qualitatively different, in its implications, according to the nature of its target.

Women are sometimes represented in this way in patriarchal culture. They are often reduced to objects of comedy or ridicule, and not just in films defined primarily as comedies: the comic spectacle of the stereotypically 'flustered' and incompetent woman who cannot cope with adversity or extremity in the action-adventure film, for example, such as Willie Scott (Kate Capshaw) in *Indiana Jones and the Temple of Doom* (1984). The effect is to reinforce, through opposition, the construction of the assured and competent male hero. Dynamics such as this can work both ways, however, sometimes moving closer to a realisation of the disruptive potential of the figure of the unruly woman. Comedy represented by the antics of the incompetent can open up the possibility of criticism of the norms from which such characters depart, as we have seen. An example of such potential in comedy at the expense of a woman can be found in the characterisation of the eponymous figure played by Goldie Hawn in *Private Benjamin*. Hawn's incarnation of Judy Benjamin owes much to the stereotype of the comic dizzy blonde. Her induction into the army begins with a catalogue of jokes at the expense of her incompetence or the inappropriateness of her 'feminine' characteristics in this context (she complains at the absence of curtains on the barrack-room windows, for example). She is a figure of fun. But she is also disruptive of the institution, making it appear foolish; and, eventually, she prevails, in a combination of its and her own terms, in classic comedian-comedy style. Something of the same double-edged potential can be found in comedy that emerges from representations of racial or ethnic groups.

There can be little doubt that comic representation of African-Americans has been used as a way to aid the legitimation of racial inequalities. Early American film inherited a set of racist caricatures from forms such as vaudeville, the minstrel show and the dominant culture at large, including that of the 'coon' (Leab 1975). Early 'coon' comedies, often featuring white performers in blackface, include titles such as *The Wooing and Wedding of a Coon* (1907), *The Pickaninnies* (1908) and *Rastus in Zululand* (1910) (Waller 1992: 3). Racist stereotypes such as that of the 'coon' have proved hard to shake throughout the subsequent history of American cinema, despite decades of protest from black organisations and the relative breakthroughs in the representation of black Americans achieved since the civil rights protests of the 1950s and 1960s.

Whoopi Goldberg is one of a number of African-American comedy performers to have gained substantial box-office success since the early 1980s. Others include Richard Pryor, considered highly bankable from the start of the decade, and Eddie Murphy, rated as the biggest star in Hollywood, with the possible exception of Sylvester Stallone, by 1987 (Bogle 1989: 280, 286). Success has also come for a more recent generation of comic black performers such as Martin Lawrence, Chris Tucker and Chris Rock. To what extent might the success of these performers, in the format of comedian comedy, be explained by the degree to which their antics conform to racist stereotypes such as that of the 'coon'? If the comedian comic in general is frequently portrayed as crazy, irrational, childlike and disruptive, the difficulty here is the closeness of fit between these characteristics, when manifested by African-American performers, and elements of racist ideologies that have functioned for many decades to legitimate racial discrimination. Is the comic spectacle offered by performers such as Goldberg, Pryor, Murphy, Lawrence and Tucker implicitly racist? The answer, as usual in the case of comedy, is not so clear cut.

Goldberg's character in *Sister Act* is the epitome of the disruptive comedian presence. Dolores Van Cartier, a brash lounge singer, is sent to a convent for safety while waiting to appear as the key witness at the trial of her former lover, the mobster Vince (Harvey Keitel). 'I will not tolerate any disruption whatsoever,' decrees the frosty Reverend Mother (Maggie Smith), reluctantly agreeing to the arrangement. The convent is a classic example of the kind of repressed institution into which the comedian comic intrudes. Dolores is obliged to swap big frizzy hair, gold coat and jewelry for plain nun's habit; her attitude, however, is less easy to keep under wraps. Before long she has taken over the inept choir and transformed it into a rousing and jazzy pop ensemble that appalls the Reverend Mother but revives the status of the failing church. The whole institution learns to unwind, including eventually the Reverend Mother herself, and to open itself up to the rough neighbourhood from which it had previous hidden in fear. Dolores herself is also changed by the experience. If not entirely tamed, she gains a calmer and more relaxed demeanor that appears to save her life: the hit-men dispatched by Vince cannot bring themselves to finish the job because, it seems, her new-found aura convinces them that she is a real nun.

All very much the familiar stuff of comedian comedy. The gender issue is avoided in most of *Sister Act* by the choice of a largely all-women setting. Dolores is not set in initial opposition to a repressive male figure in the convent but to a woman authority figure, the Reverend Mother. It is notable that male authorities in the church approve of the non-traditional antics of the choir; both the priest and, to add extra comic implausibility, the Pope, who requests a special performance. The difference represented by Dolores in the convent is not figured in terms of gender but of race. Hers is the only black face in sight. The intended opposition is between the worldliness of funky street-level culture and the cloistered repression of the convent. In effect, however, it is posed in terms that translate into a familiar racist dynamic, in this case put in more positive terms: the figure of the African-American as a source of renewal of a desiccated white culture. White America has often adopted elements of black culture as supposed sources of more 'natural' and 'authentic' qualities that can cut through the effects of deadening institutionalisation, whether the funky choir music of *Sister Act* or rap-as-source-of-insight in *Bulworth* (a tendency that can be traced more generally, in literary and cultural circles, to the 'Harlem Renaissance' of the 1920s).

This kind of dynamic is also present in *Jumpin' Jack Flash* (1986), in which Goldberg plays Terri Doolittle, a brash, outspoken and disruptive character who rubs up against authority in various forms, including her employer, the police and British consular officials with whom she becomes involved during a spy-caper narrative. Repressive authority is male and almost exclusively white, giving Terri's acts of rebellion a potentially double-coded quality. Her appearance and actions are often clown-like, especially during a series of scenes in which she is dressed in baggy trousers, braces, a broad checked shirt and white bow-tie while engaged in an assortment of slapstick escapades. Several factors distinguish this figure from the stereotype of the 'coon', however, the purpose of which, along with other stereotypes, was 'to entertain by stressing Negro inferiority' (Bogle 1989: 4). Terri may be loud and unconventional, but she is no hapless buffoon. Instead, she is shown to be highly proficient at her job, computer-based, in the foreign exchange trading room of a New York bank. She also proves resourceful, even if in the unconventional manner typical of the comedian comic, when dragged into the world of a Cold War conspiracy thriller, as does Dolores Van Cartier in *Sister Act*. Both are presented as strong and appealing zany characters. Certain qualities that carry associations of the 'coon' – plenty of screaming and shouting combined with eye-popping looks in moments of extremity – are mixed with more positive and assertive dimensions.

The same can be said of the roles played by other recent or contemporary African-American comedian comic stars in Hollywood. The most sustained comic superstar career has been that of Eddie Murphy, whose screen persona is based to a large extent on a supply of loud, demonstrative and highly performative comic 'turns', elements of which are sometimes uncomfortably close to 'coon' style. From *48Hrs* (1982) to *Nutty Professor 2: The Klumps* (2000), Murphy's routines are marked by a tendency towards mock-outraged high-pitched voices, popping eyes and other excesses of diction and gesture. Similar qualities are often found in the performances of Richard Pryor, Martin Lawrence and Chris Tucker. To condemn this as *simply* a reenactment of old racist stereotypes is to miss a number of different possible dimensions of such performances, however, some of which can be identified in *The Nutty Professor*.

The narrative dimension of *The Nutty Professor* is itself critical of the loud, excessive and motor-mouthed aspects of Murphy's performance. As did Jerry Lewis in the original, Murphy plays two central roles: Dr Sherman Klump, an obese genetic scientist, and Buddy Love, the egotistical alter ego released through the application of a formula that restructures Klump's DNA to reduce his weight. Klump is a calm and resigned figure. Love is pushy, sassy, sexy and attractive to women but unbearably arrogant. The moral weight of the narrative structure is behind Klump, who eventually beats Love in a battle for control of his soul. One of the major attractions of the film, however, along with the special effects that create and morphologically transform the enormous bulk of Klump, is the spectacle of Murphy as Buddy Love. Or, really, Buddy Love as Murphy: what the transformation of Klump brings out is the dominant Murphy persona, in outrageously performative overdrive. The narrative theme is not without significance, even if its moral about exterior appearance being less important than internal qualities is somewhat glib and ironic in the context of the kinds of body images favoured by Hollywood. But the performative dimension is the major source of pleasure promised by the film, with Murphy playing not just Klump and Love but also transformed into another five outlandish members of the Klump household.

The viewer is also invited to experience Murphy's act *as* one of performative skill. In *The Nutty Professor* and *Nutty Professor 2: The Klumps*, Murphy plays a range of different characters. A number of performative turns are also provided in many of the films in which he plays only one character, as a result of their tendency to adopt multiple guises. In *Beverly Hills Cop* (1984), for example, Axel Foley (Murphy) poses variously as an undercover cop, a writer for *Rolling Stone*, a customs inspector, a 'dumb nigger' and a homosexual: acts that foreground his performative skills. It is in these kinds of personae that the 'crazy coon' aspects of Murphy's act are more likely to come to the fore, although it should be stressed that they are far from the only elements at work: the performance, like that of Goldberg, is also in many cases more assertive and successful in gaining its desired ends than anything associated with the traditional figure of the 'coon'. Where this is the case, and the performance is coded explicitly as a show, joke or comic routine, a degree of distance might be created between the style and any potentially racist overtones.[8]

A similar effect is created by the performance of Martin Lawrence in *Blue Streak* (1999), a film that functions almost as a remake of *Beverly Hills Cop*. Lawrence, another comedian comic figure with a background in television, is Miles Logan, a member of a criminal gang who poses as a detective in an attempt to recover a jewel hidden on a building site that turned into a police station while was in jail. Like Axel Foley, Logan is a clownish and disruptive presence within the LAPD, but also extremely effective in the role, if not always by intention. As an ex-con, he knows how the criminal world operates, his insider knowledge leading him eventually to prevail against a drugs-and-antiques smuggling plot, very similar to that of the Murphy vehicle, and to recover his jewel. Logan is partnered, in typical fashion, with a rookie detective who is a stickler for rules and procedure, highlighting the unconventional activities of the star. Lawrence does the usual range of performative turns, peppered with 'coonish' outbursts and excesses of behaviour.

The performative nature of a number of black *and* white roles is emphasised in *True Identity* (1991), a showcase in which the character played by the British comedian Lenny Henry undergoes a series of transformations that include 'whiting-up', a transformation used as disguise to avoid the unhealthy attentions of a Mafia hit-man. From the start, before the narrative-proper is underway, the fact that racial characterisation is performed, according to dominant stereotype, is suggested in a sequence in which the actor Miles (Henry) is encouraged by a theatre director to do an exaggerated impression of clichéd, funky 'black' behaviour. The handling of sequences in which Miles appears in whiteface owes much to the style found in the gender cross-dressing comedies considered above. The transformation effect itself is highly effective, producing initially a *frisson* of the uncanny: the figure of Miles posing as white yuppie or as Italian-American hood is only barely recognisable as either Miles or Henry. Much of the comedy that follows is based on the exposure (or threat of exposure) of the character in various states of transition or with non-whitened parts of the body on display. That Miles is an actor motivates his performative skills, in black and white roles, perhaps reducing the potential of the film to undermine their status as anything other than series of cultural constructs.

Comically foregrounding the performative nature of ethnic roles could be a source of pleasure in its own right in the early decades of the twentieth century, a period in which large numbers of recent arrivals to the United States were attempting to cope with the pressures of life in a new country. Role-playing was a central dimension of the immigrant experience, Charles Musser (1991) suggests, as many new arrivals were obliged to conceal aspects of their identity in order to gain success beyond the confines of the immediate ethnic neighbourhood. Comic treatments of this process offered a form of psychic release for those involved, an important segment of the urban film-going public: 'Ethnicity is shown to be a constraint – and a construction – from which characters and audiences can be at least temporarily liberated. Role-playing, which was necessary and typically alienating, could become pleasurable, subversive, and affirming of self' (1991: 43). In *Animal Crackers* (1930), one of the principal examples used by Musser, the Marx Brothers are presented as 'Jewish hustlers insinuating themselves into WASP high society ... an aggressive assault on the exclusionary policies being applied to Jews by WASP-dominated universities, country clubs, and other public and private institutions' (63).

How the performances of more recent African-American comedian stars are likely to be taken remains subject to audience interpretations that are likely to vary on a number of scores, including race itself. Potentially racist elements in the mix might make performative comedian acts more acceptable to white audiences and might have contributed to the scale of success enjoyed by these performers in territories such as the United States and Britain, in which racism remains deeply rooted (the deliberate use of racist stereotypes in this way, to gain commercial success, is satirized in Spike Lee's *Bamboozled* (2001)). The high-pitched demonstrative and often childish tone in which the disruptive performance often occurs seems largely unthreatening to the racial status quo. This seems to be the case even in an example such as the central performative scene of *48Hrs* in which Eddie Murphy's character Reggie Hammond rousts a redneck bar (in parody of, or homage to, a scene in *The French Connection* (1971)), proclaiming to one occupant: 'I'm your worst nightmare, man. I'm a nigger with a badge. That means I got permission to kick your backwoods ass whenever I feel like it.' The principal source of comedy is the reversal of the norm (the oppression meted out by racist white policing). The fact that this scene is coded as comedy – and that it is a masquerade anyway, within the narrative frame – is likely to reduce any threat created by the spectacle of a seemingly dominating black character.

Race is another arena in which comedy can function as a safety net, permitting the use of material that might otherwise be controversial or impossible to include in mainstream film. In *48Hrs*, for example, Reggie and the white cop Jack Cates (Nick Nolte), with whom he shares an initially hostile 'buddy movie' relationship, fight and trade insults including numerous racist epithets on the part of Cates ('watermelon', 'spear-chucker', 'overdressed charcoal loser') that would be far more controversial in a non-comic treatment. Comedy licenses the usage without entirely removing the racist edge. We are expected to laugh at Cates or to anticipate an improvement in the relationship, according to the lightweight buddy formula; or simply to treat the entire relationship unseriously. Such a reaction is far from guaranteed, however.

The historical context of these films is an important factor in their adoption of comic strategies to handle race-related material. The rise to superstar prominence of Murphy, Pryor and Goldberg can be understood in the context of the earlier 'blaxploitation' era in Hollywood in the early 1970s, a period in which a number of unusually assertive (violent and sexually active) roles were given to black performers, male and female, in films ranging from *Sweet Sweetback's Baadasssss Song* (1971) and *Shaft* (1971) to *Coffy* (1973) and *Foxy Brown* (1974). Hollywood courted an urban black audience in this period as part of its efforts to escape from economic difficulties. When stability returned to the studios in the later part of the decade they sought to keep this audience without alienating white viewers. The result was a series of black/white buddy partnerships including comedies such as *Stir Crazy* (1980) and *Trading Places* (1983) and comedy-thriller blends such as *48Hrs* and the enormously successful *Lethal Weapon* series (1987, 1989, 1992, 1998), along with the black comedian comic vehicles discussed above.

Black star performers were either kept in 'protective custody', as Ed Guerrero terms it, by being paired with white co-stars, or removed from any on-screen presence within a broader black community (1993: 128). It is in this guise, as comic sidekick (Pryor in *Silver Streak* (1976) and *Stir Crazy*) or transplanted into an all-white milieu (Murphy in *Trading Places* and the *Beverly Hills Cop* films) that they have enjoyed their greatest box-office success. Black performers had been confined primarily to comic roles for decades preceding the blaxploitation era, Donald Bogle suggests, following the controversy ignited by the presence of a threatening black male villain in *The Birth of a Nation* (1915), a position to which they returned to some extent from the 1980s. The very fact that comedy – coded as ultimately unthreatening, unserious – has been the primary realm in which black performers have consistently achieved superstar status in film speaks volumes about the racial politics of American society. Comedy offers, in heightened form, the possibility of fantastic resolution, containment or evasion of contentious social issues such as race and racism.

The mobilisation of elements of apparently racist stereotypes in the acts of African-American comic performers has been a subject of criticism among members of black communities, for the same reason that it might appeal to a white racist tendency. It can also be read more positively in some cases, however, and might be able to appeal to a black audience (or to anti-racist white viewers) as a transcendence or parody of the stereotype. This, for Bogle, is one way black performers in Hollywood have historically been able to go beyond the confines of the stereotypical roles to which they have been limited. The 1930s, for example, was the 'Age of the Negro Servant', in which the antics of a number of black performers were offered as sources of comic absurdity and relief from the realities of the Depression. What was involved was an

Figure 17   Protective custody: Eddie Murphy paired with co-star Nick Nolte in *48Hrs* (1982)

enactment of racist stereotypes, including the 'coon' and the 'mammy'. In the hands of some performers, however, notably Stepin Fetchit (Lincoln Perry) as the 'coon' and Hattie McDaniel as the 'mammy', these figures were taken to extremes that transcended the limitations of the stereotype, Bogle suggests.

Fetchit presented an image of the 'arch-coon', an extravagant and stylised character detached from the fictional world in which he was situated (as in *Judge Priest* (1934), for example, in which it seems hard to take the extreme lassitude of his servant character as anything other than self-parody), while McDaniel developed the cantankerous qualities of the 'mammy' to an assertive point at which she appeared the equal of her white 'superiors'.[9]

It is possible to read some of the comic antics of Goldberg, Pryor, Murphy, Lawrence, Tucker or other performers in a similar manner, as excessive and stylised caricatures of racial stereotype. In some instances, the process is explicitly marked as parodic. In *Stir Crazy* (1980), for example, Harry (Pryor) puts on a show, affecting an absurdly exaggerated jivey swagger from the shoulders and hip to play the part of the 'baad' black man – and to encourage his partner Skip (Gene Wilder) to do the same – in an attempt to act tough and avoid any unsavoury attentions in jail. A similar routine involving the same performers is enacted in *Silver Streak*. The various personae used by Axel Foley in *Beverly Hills Cop* include self-consciously 'black' turns such as an 'outraged-at-apparent-racism' outburst, when he is told that no room is available at a luxury hotel, and the adoption of a clumsy 'dumb black' manner to approach and eventually disarm a gunman in a bar. The black sheriff, Bart, in *Blazing Saddles*, which was co-written by Pryor, also does a 'coon' turn – whining 'oh, lordy, lordy' – when he pretends to take himself at gunpoint to escape from an angry crowd after arriving in town; thus proving himself far more clever than the ignorantly racist white townspeople, the principal targets of comedy in the film. Much of the performance of Lawrence in *Big Momma's House* can be read as parody of the 'mammy' stereotype, although the stereotype is also enacted, still, in its cross-dressed incarnation, with Malcom-as-Momma offering 'real' maternal advice. The line between exaggeration, parody and simple re-enactment of stereotypes is often hard to draw, however: another factor that is likely to depend to a large extent on the way the material is read by particular viewers.

Adopting and occupying existing stereotypes is a strategy that has been used elsewhere in comedy of a distinctive racial or ethnic slant. It is a characteristic associated particularly with Jewish humour, found in the films of Woody Allen and Mel Brooks among others. The exaggeration to the point of absurdity of negative stereotypes has also been identified, as a strategy of subversion, in the performances of Richard 'Cheech' Marin in the highly successful Cheech and Chong comedies. The cartoon-like style of films such as *Up in Smoke* (1978) and *Cheech and Chong's Next Movie* (1980) undermines any suggestion that the Mexican-American stereotype to which Cheech often conforms is to be taken realistically, at face value, suggests Christine List: 'With the underlying self-consciousness of the trickster, Cheech's character conveys the image of the Chicano as someone who knows he is stereotyped and always tries to resist by showing he is aware of the typing' (1994: 378). In *Up in Smoke* (1978), 'Cheech resorts to stereotype in order to evade the narcotics detective when both end up in the men's room. Cheech plays the Mexican buffoon, making silly references to his own penis. When he leaves we find out that he was actually urinating on the detective's leg. We are gratified at this clever mode of simultaneous masquerade and revenge' (377).

Jewish humour is often characterised as self-deprecating, a form of self-defence that involves the internalisation of negative stereotypes: 'An "I'll-Say-It-About-Myself-Before-You-Say-It-About-Me" attitude represents a defensive strategy strengthened by centuries of persecution, powerlessness, and paranoia' (Desser & Friedman 1993: 15). The films of Woody Allen are filled with images of self-doubt and parodies of Jewish fears of persecution, such as the paranoia of Alvy Singer (Allen) in *Annie Hall* (1977), who insists on hearing the phrase 'do you eat' as the slur 'Jew eat'). The issue of assimilation of the Jew into other cultures is another subject of comic treatment, in the work of both Allen and Brooks, reaching its absurd heights in *Zelig* (1983), in which Allen plays a 'human chameleon' figure so keen to fit in that he metamorphoses to blend in with any social group, from black or Chinese to the ultimate hate figure of the Nazi.

Caricature Jewish figures regularly turn up in unlikely places in the work of Mel Books, a manifestation perhaps of an American-Jewish sense of always being out of place: a Jewish-Indian chief in *Blazing Saddles*, for example, and a rabbi with a wagon-load of sacramental wine in the Sherwood Forest of *Robin Hood: Men in Tights* (1993). The penchant of Brooks for parody might also be explained by his identity as a cultural outsider. The love-hate relationship between parody and its object provides the ideal setting for a combination of criticism of mainstream American mythology and yearning to take part in its traditions, a combination often taken to be typical of the American-Jewish identity (Desser & Friedman 1993: 112). Obscure in-jokes and references also populate the films of Allen and Brooks, many of them rooted in Jewish culture or the use of Yiddish. The comedy is often one of incongruity. The simple fact of an Indian chief uttering Yiddish phrases is comic in itself. To gain the full effect of this kind of comedy requires a knowledge of the language, however, which highlights another dimension of comedy based on ethnic, national or other social categories: the issue of the translatability of particular comic forms.

Comedy, as we have seen, is often founded on prior knowledge of one kind or another, such as familiarity with the norms from which it departs. Mass-market comedy, such as that produced in Hollywood, generally casts its net fairly wide, rather than depending on too narrow a constituency with sufficient familiarity with its comic points of reference. In some cases, comedy is designed carefully to offer different points of access to different members of the audience, examples including films targeted primarily at children that include jokes likely only to be picked up by adults, a source of pleasure planted to maintain the interest of those accompanying young viewers. The DreamWorks animated feature *Shrek* (2001), for example, uses a number of comic devices to distance itself (if only relatively) from the more sugary-sentimental Disney style. One sequence, in which a princess sings sweetly in ever-higher notes to the accompaniment of a bluebird, reaches a climactic pitch at which the latter explodes, just off-screen. Gestures such as this are designed to position the film as appealing to an audience of older, more cynical or knowing children, and adults, as well as to younger generations. More exclusively adult or older adolescent oriented gags include the phallic implications of Shrek's comment on first sight of the enormous castle of the diminutive villainous prince ('Do you think he's compensating for something?'), his donkey-companion's urging later, in reference to the princess, to 'wake up and smell the pheromones', and an intertextual visual gag in which the princess performs a freeze-frame mid-air kung fu kicking routine from *The Matrix* (1999).

Comedy of a particular ethnic, national or other in-group slant might be more restrictive, appealing or offering an extra dimension to those with special competence to pick up nuances inaccessible to a wider audience. The Yiddish-speaking Indian in *Blazing Saddles*, for example, wears a headband bearing Hebrew characters saying 'Kosher for Passover' (Erens 1984: 328). Some of the non-ethnic comic points of reference in Woody Allen films are likely to remain obscure to any other than a particular (metropolitan, 'intellectual') audience. In addition to numerous bites of obscure philosophy-speak in the dialogue between Boris (Allen) and Sonja (Diane Keaton), *Love and Death* (1975), for example, makes puns out of references to Russian literature and art cinema, the source of which is likely to be obscure to the non-cognoscenti. In one case, a night of passion between Boris and Sonja is followed by three shots of a statue of a lion: lying down, standing and then sprawled with its tongue hanging out in an attitude of exhaustion. The full experience of the gag is unavailable to anyone unfamiliar with the sequence it spoofs – three shots of lion statues linked by montage to suggest the rousing of revolutionary forces – in Sergei Eisenstein's *Battleship Potemkin* (1925). The issue of the accessibility of such jokes is acknowledged in *Annie Hall* when, following one of Alvy's standup routines, Diane Keaton's title character comments: 'I think that I'm starting to get more of the references.' The specific resonances of comic sequences can vary considerably from one type of viewer to another, a factor that can allow comedy of a ethnically-coded variety to appeal to wider audiences. This might be the case in *Animal Crackers* (1930), as Charles Musser suggests. What he reads as an angry attack on anti-Semitism could also be taken simply as zany, anarchistic comedy, the specifically Jewish edge remaining invisible to a more general audience. Different interpretations might be made of individual gags. When Groucho's character, Captain Spaulding, is hailed as an 'explorer', he mishears the term as *schnorrer* (a beggar or leech, exactly what he is). The viewer unfamiliar with the Yiddish might hear it as 'snorer', Musser suggests, 'an association that makes perfect sense because he is carried in on a sedan' (1991: 70).

The comedy of *Animal Crackers* is launched not just from a Jewish but also from an urban, metropolitan perspective – like that of Woody Allen – another requirement for an appreciation of the specific qualities of some of the gag routines. The difference in how these might be taken is put well by Musser, in reference to a parody by Groucho of Eugene O'Neill's play *Strange Interlude*: 'If the spectator is in the know, the spoof is outrageously delightful; if the spectator is not, it is delightfully nonsensical' (70). In some cases, the comedy could work both ways, for either audience, but economic pressures grew during the 1930s for a reduction of urban-specific elements, including jokes, in order to make films more suitable for a broader, national audience. Jewish points of reference were largely eliminated from the films of Eddie Cantor after *Whoopee* (1930), the other main example of pleasurable ethnic role-playing interaction discussed by Musser.[10] A similar process occurred with the Marx Brothers, although to a more gradual and lesser extent, Musser suggests, the ethnic images of Groucho and Chico being so central to their comic personae and their films less expensive than those of Cantor, and hence under less commercial pressure.

Comedy is one of the forms through which membership of a particular group identity can be reinforced: the fact that one 'gets' exclusive jokes is a signifier of group belonging and distinction from those to whom the comedy is inaccessible. As Henri Bergson puts it: 'However spontaneous it seems, laughter always implies a kind of secret freemasonry, or even complicity, with other laughers, real or imaginary' (1956: 64). Another notable example is found in a brand of comedy produced in Hong Kong in the early 1990s known as 'nonsense comedy', a form that makes intensive use of Cantonese slang. These films celebrate and construct a distinct Hong Kong identity 'by addressing the Cantonese-speaking Hong Kong insider as a privileged viewer who alone can understand the puns, jokes, and generic allusions of the films' (Chiu-han Lai 1997: 95). One of the gags in *Dai fu zhi jia* ('It's a Wonderful Life', 1994), for example, comes from a play on language in which, in Cantonese slang, pronunciation of the English word 'sexy' means 'eat shit' (Stokes and Hoover 1997: 207). Films featuring Stephen Chiau are particularly noted for the 'nonsense' variety of Hong Kong comedy (Teo 1997: 246–7). The form is not unique to Hong Kong, as we saw in Chapter One, in the case of the Mexican comedian Cantinflas, but it takes on particular resonances in a particular national context.

The significance of this particular usage can be seen in the context of efforts to maintain or construct aspects of Hong Kong identity in the years preceding the takeover by China in 1997, the linguistic distinction being made from both English colonial and Mandarin Chinese languages. Comedy was the principal vehicle through which the Cantonese-language film industry made a recovery from the mid-1970s after its demise in the face of competition from more extravagant and Hollywood-style Mandarin films (Lau 1998: 24–5). Comedy has since become the most popular form of cinema in Hong Kong, accounting for nine of the top ten best-sellers in the 1980s and 1990s. The importance of comedy to Hong Kong cinema has generally been ignored in the

West, Jenny Lau suggests, in favour of the dominant association of Hong Kong with the martial arts tradition. The reasons for this are not hard to understand: a combination of the general lack of serious attention often paid to comedy and the specific difficulties raised by comedy produced in social contexts distant from that of the potential Western viewer. The latter is a problem both for the general viewer, and thus for the overseas market of the films, and for academic analysis. As Lau puts it: 'the analysis of comedy is an exceptionally difficult task because the recognition of humor depends heavily upon the understanding of the complex dynamics involved in the interaction of the symbolics, such as gestures, icons, linguistics, and so on, which are defined by their own social and cultural traditions' (24).

The importance of Cantonese dialogue gags to Hong Kong comedy makes it a particularly difficult (but by no means unique) case for study, or enjoyment in all of its dimensions, by the outside observer. Plenty of slapstick and comic action is offered by Hong Kong comedies such those starring, and often written and/or directed by, Michael Hui, which played a key role in the recovery of the 1970s, or those featuring Stephen Chiau in the 1990s. Much of this is easily available to overseas audiences. But many of the dialogue jokes, and other resonances, including some of the more pointed dimensions of broad comedies such as those of Hui, are likely to remain invisible to viewers lacking the necessary cultural capital. The madcap comic routines of Hui's *Modern Bo Biu* ('Modern Security Guards' aka 'Security Unlimited', 1981), for example, contain a number of dimensions that depend on local knowledge for their full effect. In one sequence Chow (Michael Hui), an arrogant officer in a private security firm, demonstrates an alarm system activated when an intruder steps onto a doormat. Before he has connected the wires, one of his underlings arrives late, steps on the mat and subjects Chow to a series of electric shocks. The broad and generally accessible slapstick of this routine, Lau suggests, plays into more specific thematic issues around which the film is structured, principally the relationship between the 'old' and 'traditional' (of which problems of punctuality would be a 'Chinese' example, familiar to the local viewer) and the 'modern' and technological, for which Hong Kong is taken to stand.

Another example cited by Lau is a ludicrous method of teaching driving skills to security guard recruits, who spend most of their lessons in a classroom learning mechanistically by rote (a practice shown to be highly ineffective). This is a parody, Lau suggests of 'a learning experience common among Hui's audience, namely, that of forced memorization and coerced acceptance of outdated teaching' (1998: 28). *Modern Bo Biu* also includes a sub-plot involving two crooks who seek to make a corrupt killing on the racetrack, a series of routines likely to appear to be arbitrary distractions from the narrative to the viewer unaware of the strong local association between horse-racing and key aspects of the distinct nature of Hong Kong society, and thus of the place of these scenes in the broader fabric of the film.[11]

Comedy is often used in the representation of other nations, their peoples and customs. Comic stereotypes abound, in film as elsewhere. The gangsters who seek to rob an exhibition in *Modern Bo Biu* are presented in a manner associated in Hong Kong with the Chinese mainland, Lau suggests: crude, ignorant and backward, characteristics typical of those often attributed to others. From its earliest years, American film comedy has been filled with stereotypes grounded in reductive notions of national character, both external and in the internal form of the 'hyphenated' American immigrant (Irish-American, Italian-American, and so on). The Irish are stereotypically associated with comic drunkenness and fisticuffs, for example, in cases ranging from *Irish Ways of Discussing Politics* (1896), set in a bar-room, to John Wayne's sidekick Sgt Quincannon (Victor McLaglen) in the John Ford western *She Wore a Yellow Ribbon* (1949); or with stupidity, as in *The Finish of Bridget McKeen* (1901), in which a caricatured Irish maid (played by a man in drag) is blown up after using kerosene to light a stove (Musser 1991: 45).

American stereotypes of Canadians – as excessively clean, prissy and polite – are mobilised as a source of humour in *Canadian Bacon* (1995), although with an extra edge in some instances. Detainees in a prison cell include a man held for putting regular gasoline in an unleaded tank, another 'for being in too many bad moods' and a third – treated most negatively, and a joke that operates on a different level given the socialist politics of the director, Michael Moore – for raiding a company, merging it with his own conglomerate and then firing all the employees. A stereotypical version of 'Englishness' – in terms including hopeless 'niceness' and a 'silly accent' – is a major source of the comedy of *Mickey Blue Eyes* (1999), in which the quintessential contemporary embodiment of 'posh, effeminate' Englishness, Hugh Grant, plays Michael Felgate, an English auctioneer entangled with a New York Mafia family. Here, as in some other examples, the comedy can cut both ways: Felgate's hilariously inadequate effort to mimic a Mafiosi accent is a joke at the expense of both imitator and imitated. The attribution of particular qualities to others is, in general, likely to say as much about the producers of the comedy as the ostensible target. Traits towards which groups have negative attitudes are often projected onto others. By finding them comic in others, a group implicitly defines itself as free of such traits.

'British' comedy and beyond

To what extent do individual nations or regions have their own distinct brands of comedy? If what we laugh at is one way of defining us, through reference to in-group or external characteristics, can we identify comic traits particular to one nation or another? Is there such a thing, for example, as a specifically British style of film comedy? The short answer is almost certainly: no, in any unqualified manner. Any attempt to define a distinctively 'British' form of comedy runs into a host of difficulties – as does any attempt to mark out a singularly distinctly British cinema more generally or, indeed, to define 'British' itself. Nations are complex constructs, existing in the realms of myth and fiction as much as in reality.[12] They are marked by divisions that put into question any notion of singular national identity. Any construction of 'Britain' or the 'British' is subject to challenge at the level of constituent parts ranging from the national (England, Wales, Scotland, Northern Ireland) and the regional to those of class, gender and ethnicity; none of which are likely to be simple, single or coherent entities in themselves, let alone when combined along multiple and overlapping dimensions.

Particular *versions* of 'Britishness', or of 'British comedy', have historically been favoured in particular circumstances, however, for reasons that are worth exploration. The idea of a distinctively British type of comedy has existed, as a form of discourse, even if its claims are subject to qualification on various levels. Take the comedy produced at Ealing Studios from 1949, for example, particularly the celebrated group of films constituted primarily by *Passport to Pimlico* (1949), *Kind Hearts and Coronets* (1949), *Whisky Galore* (1949), *The Lavender Hill Mob* (1951), *The Man in the White Suit* (1953), *The Titfield Thunderbolt* (1953) and *The Ladykillers* (1955). Ealing comedy has probably been described more often than any other as typically or 'essentially' British/English (again, that uncertainty of terminology/location that immediately complicates the picture). A particular view of the world is usually associated with Ealing comedy. As Jeffrey Richards puts it:

> It is a world that is essentially quaint, cosy, whimsical and backward-looking ... It is a world that enshrines what are seen as quintessentially English qualities: a stubborn individuality that is heroic to the point of eccentricity ('It's because we're English that we are sticking to our right to be Burgundians,' says a character in *Passport to Pimlico*); a hatred of authoritarianism and bureaucracy coupled with a belief in tolerance and consensus; a philosophy that can be summed up by the slogan 'Small is beautiful; old is good'. (1997: 134)

Is this a distinctively British/English perspective, yielding a distinctive brand of comedy? It appears to have been *designed* with this in mind, to some extent at least. A conscious effort was made by Michael Balcon, head of the studio, to project a picture of Britain and the 'British character'. This can be understood, as Charles Barr suggests, in the context of a wartime period in which 'an authentic national cinema was being called for – in order to encourage and interpret to itself Britain at war' (1993: 81). The style of film-making embodied in the Ealing comedies is a product of the time and the national context, blending elements of comic fantasy and documentary-style naturalism to explore difficult postwar issues, such as the merits of rationing versus those

Figure 18 Postwar spirit: relieving the besieged after the local declaration of independence in *Passport to Pimlico* (1949)

of an unfettered market, for example, in *Passport to Pimlico*. What resulted was a very particular projection, however: one version of what it was to be British in the late 1940s or 1950s. It is very much a middle-class perspective – if also a liberal one, as Barr suggests – in terms of both content and style of comedy.

If Ealing comedy has often been celebrated for its subtle, eccentric and restrained style, this is in opposition, implicitly at least, to cruder, more vulgar or slapstick varieties of comedy, such as those derived from the music-hall tradition. British comedy has not been short on the latter, including some of its most popular and, by other accounts, most indigenous forms. To construct the Ealing variety as the quintessentially British/English is to use the concept of nation and national style as cover for what is really a distinction on the lines of class-taste formations. 'Nation' is invoked here, as often elsewhere, as a way of making hegemonic claims for the preferences of particular interest groups, very often those of the middle or upper-middle classes. A particular view of the world, and a particular style of comedy, is elevated to some more generally representative status, largely as a result of the control certain social groups have over the media in which such matters are debated. One aspect of this debate in the 1950s was an attempt by certain self-appointed 'guardians' of culture to celebrate aspects of indigenous culture that might serve as a bulwark against a perceived threat of being 'swamped' by 'lower' forms of culture imported from the United States.

Processes such as this are probably inevitable in any attempt to single out an individually 'national' form or style of comedy. Much gets left out of the picture (including, as Barr suggests, the fact that 'Ealing comedy' was not a single phenomenon, but included different strains, a distinction being made between the mainstream Ealing world of the 'nice, wholesome and harmless' and the return of some of what is repressed in these films – principally, class divisions and sex – in more prickly examples such as *Kind Hearts and Coronets* and *Whisky Galore*) (Barr 1993: 110–11). If Ealing eccentricity is the 'quintessential' British/English comedy, where does that leave the very many other varieties of British film comedy? They might, in some accounts, be relegated to a secondary status. The extremely popular 1930s films of Gracie Fields and George Formby, for example, are often seen as part of a distinctively 'northern' regional comic tradition, complete with Lancashire settings and strong accents that might seem to deny them a more 'nationally' representative status. Are these films any less 'British' than those associated with the Ealing comedy tradition (leaving aside the fact that many Fields and Formby films were made at Ealing, under the earlier regime of Basil Dean)? Not at all. Fields and Formby gained the status of national as well as regional figures, without sacrificing their distinctive regional personality traits; they were, respectively, the biggest female and male stars in Britain in the late 1930s (Richards 1997: 258). In the case of Formby, Jeffrey Richards suggests, a move was made to nationalise his appeal, transplanting him into the south in many of his films, into the suburbs or the countryside. While specifically northern in some respects, his screen persona offered the wider comedian-comic appeal of the hapless 'little man' who wins through against the odds (261).

Can any distinctly 'British' elements be found in common, across such different types and sources of comedy? The formal characteristics of the best-known 'Ealing comedies' are generally rather different from those of the films of Fields and Formby. The former are narrative-led while the latter are highly performative, designed to create opportunities to showcase the musical comedy talents of star performers doing turns familiar from the world of the music hall. It is in this formal dimension, to a large extent, that their different social-class basis lies, along lines similar to those explored earlier in this book. Some similarities might be identified at the thematic level, however. The world of Balcon's Ealing and that of George Formby comedies such as *No Limit* (1935) and *Keep Your Seats Please* (1936) share an appeal to the values of both eccentric individuality and the kind of small-scale community into which such eccentricity might be fitted. These are values that might, in some formulations, be seen as typically 'British', even if only as the preferred view of some sectors of society. Even at this heavily qualified level, it is hard to make a case for any of this being the basis of a distinctively British approach, to comedy or more generally, because such values are hardly unique to Britain or to British comedy. Eccentric individuality, and a way of integrating this into established institutions, is an important dimension of a great deal of the comedy explored already in parts of this book, particularly in the comedian comedy tradition that has proved so popular in many different national contexts.

The problem of seeking to isolate distinctive 'national' comic traits is complicated from two directions: from both inside and outside the particular national context involved. To demonstrate that particular aspects of the comedy produced in one nation are uniquely characteristic of that country is extremely difficult, given the number of potential counter-examples that would have to be taken into account. It is possible to frame this issue into more manageable proportions, however. We can move away from broad claims about the nationally-representative-or-otherwise qualities of particular forms of comedy, to consider the question at the level of industrial strategies of audience-targeting. Some British comedies are *aimed* primarily at a domestic audience, while others are intended to reach a wider international audience, especially in the United States. The kinds of comic strategies employed might be determined to a significant extent by the choice of industrial/marketing approach, a factor related to considerations of the degree of national specificity of the comedy even if this does not constitute evidence of broader national representativeness or otherwise. Some forms of comedy are thought to travel easily overseas; others might be deemed comprehensible only to the domestic audience.

Both the Ealing comedies and the earlier films of Fields and Formby were produced primarily for the domestic market, one of two basic strategies open to British film-making since the achievement of global domination of film markets by the United States in the late 1910s and early 1920s. Films made on reasonably modest budgets have a realistic expectation of earning back their costs in the relatively small home market, plus maybe that of 'Empire', colonial or post-colonial territories overseas. The generally inexpensive nature of comedy is one of its attractions for many national cinemas, for this reason, which, in turn, permits the use of more locally-specific comic material. The other option, which has often been a temptation to British film-makers, is to attempt to break into an American market that is large and potentially profitable, but tightly controlled by the major US distribution companies. To do this a different approach has often been used: higher spending, to compete with the 'production values' of Hollywood, plus the construction of products designed to appeal more widely than just to the British or colonial/post-colonial audience. In the realm of comedy, this requires the use of forms assumed to translate with little difficulty for the American viewer.

In the 1930s, Andrew Higson suggests, citing trade press comment from the time, British comedy was seen as one of the most nationally specific genres in production, 'the only British genre that did consistently well at the box office' (1995: 110). Comedy, including the works of Fields and Formby, was one format in which British films could more than hold their own against Hollywood competition in the domestic market. The impression was mutual, according to a number of sources cited by Higson: 'wise-cracking' American comedy did not go down well in most British cinemas, while British comedy was considered 'pretty deadly' and unappealing in the American market. A Gracie Fields vehicle such as *Sing as We Go* (1934) would be considered 'virtually inexportable' on both sides of the Atlantic (111–12). Its appeal was located in the performative context from which Fields emerged, including strong regional accent and cultural reference points that might not be expected to travel well overseas, even if the film resonated at the broader national level at home. Industrially, the film was a product of Associated Talking Pictures, a sizeable independent production company that aimed its product at the domestic and Empire markets. Higson contrasts the strategy used in *Sing as We Go* with that of the contemporaneous *Evergreen* (1934), another musical-comedy star vehicle, featuring Jessie Matthews, a performer who, unlike Fields, achieved some degree of stardom in the US as well as at home. *Evergreen* was a product of the larger Gaumont-British studio and was structured differently, with a classically-integrated narrative structure and a more 'cosmopolitan' London setting, in keeping with the aim of the studio to break into the American market.

An examination of industrial strategies such as these is one way of making more concrete sense of which kinds of film comedy are considered to be more or less nationally specific in particular circumstances and, therefore, potentially suited to one marketplace or another. Definitions of the 'national' often prove to be relative rather than absolute: a 'British' style is likely to be defined to a large extent in terms of its difference from the high production-value gloss of the dominant Hollywood style. The reality remains complex, however. Ealing comedy was generally successful in America, as it turned out, although it was not designed with that as a priority. It is not the case that British comedies that have succeeded in America have always been the most similar to the traditions of classical Hollywood comedy; quite the contrary, in many cases. Quirky, offbeat and eccentric comedies of various kinds have broken into the US market, if often relegated to niche-sector 'art-house' releases, by trading precisely on theirs status as something distinct from the Hollywood mainstream. Examples include Ealing comedies, the films of Monty Python and more recent productions such as the serio-tragi-comic *Trainspotting* (1996) and *The Full Monty*.

Trainspotting and *The Full Monty* were made for a modest $3.5 million apiece, budgets that could be recouped at home. The former grossed $16.5 million in the US and $12.3 million in the UK. The latter crossed successfully into a larger mainstream market both at home and abroad, taking $45.8 million in the US, $51.9 million in the UK and a total of some $243 million worldwide.[13] Other varieties of British comedy have been designed more consciously for their potential in the American market, sometimes employing larger budgets. Recent examples of this tendency include the romantic comedies *Four*

Weddings and a Funeral, which trades on glossy images of British upper-class life similar to those offered by the 'heritage' film or the literary adaptation, and *Notting Hill*, with its emblematic relationship between the very 'English' bookseller Will Thacker (Hugh Grant) and the Hollywood-star-character-played-by-actual-Hollywood-star, Anna Scott (Julia Roberts). *Four Weddings* (still quite modestly budgeted, at about $7.5 million) took $52.7 million in the US and a worldwide total of $191.4 million; *Notting Hill* (on a much more Hollywood-proportioned budget of $42 million) earned $116 million in the US market and a blockbuster-worthy total of $300 million globally. Lower budgets and less dependence on the American market generally allows for the production of grittier, quirkier or potentially more troublesome varieties of comedy, or blends of comedy and more serious material such as those found in both *Trainspotting* and *The Fully Monty*.

Particular varieties of British comedy might be rooted to a substantial extent in particular British situations, defined in terms of social, historical, industrial or other contexts, but these are themselves variable. Examples (and there are also many others) include the musical comedies of Fields and Formby, offering a particular form of optimistic cheer during the depression of the 1930s; the Ealing blend of 'realism' and fantasy in the context of postwar adjustment; the *Carry On* and *Confessions* series, comically negotiating issues of class and gender relationships, among others, from the 1950s to the late 1970s (see Hunt 1998); the subcultural or intercultural dynamics explored in British-Asian centred films such as *Bhaji on the Beach* (1993) and *East in East* (1999). Some continuities can be traced across different examples. Something of the Ealing inheritance might be felt, for example, in the quirky Scottish comedies of writer-director Bill Forsyth, films such as *That Sinking Feeling* (1979), *Gregory's Girl* (1981), *Local Hero* (1983) and *Comfort and Joy* (1984), partly in their reliance on off-beat 'literary' qualities, centred on script more than performative turns.[14] Whether this is a matter of influence, given the canonical place of Ealing in recent British comedy tradition, or of tapping into some more amorphously 'British' qualities, preferences or ideologies is hard to say; the burden of proof has to fall on anyone arguing for the latter (as we have seen, the 'literary' tradition is far from the only important strain in British comedy, and any consideration of Forsyth in national terms would also have to take account of any potentially distinctive Scottish dimension). There may be some broad tendencies, rooted to some extent in certain aspects of the mixture of cultures found in Britain in any one place or time. The difficulty comes when an attempt is made to reduce a wide range of comedy to any particular 'national' essence, a process that almost inevitably results in acts of internal cultural imperialism of one kind or another.

The difficulty of isolating distinct national tendencies in comedy results to a significant extent from the similar histories of film comedy, along with film more generally, in the main producing countries. Similar modes of comedy were shaped in the early years in America, Britain and France, each of which witnessed a comparable split and negotiations between narrative-led-situational and more performative or slapstick traditions. Similar backgrounds, in forms such as vaudeville, music hall, variety and, later, radio, television and standup, have shaped the styles of many performers, while the relative fluidity of the film business in the early decades led to an exchange of forms between the comedy of one nation and another. It is easy to forget, for example, that France was generally considered to be the leader in film comedy in the period up to the start of the First World War. American comedy drew heavily on the early French tradition, from Chaplin's debt to Max Linder to the influence of Jean Durand's troupe Les Pouics on the Keystone Kops. Comedy was 'the most specifically French genre' in the pre-war period, Susan Hayward suggests, and has continued to enjoy the most sustained success of all forms of popular cinema in France ever since (1993: 90). The international dominance of Hollywood comedy since the First World War created a situation in which it is not always easy to separate out distinctly national dimensions, so strongly has the Hollywood version become associated with the fundamentals of the form.

What results is often a mixture of Hollywood or more general, international characteristics – the two overlapping considerably, partly as a result of Hollywood's global hegemony – and some more specifically national features. The comic persona represented by Paul Hogan in *Crocodile Dundee*, for example, exhibits characteristics specific to the Australian post-colonial context, sharing with other Australian comic performers such as Barry Humphries (as Edna Everage) and Norman Gunston a 'combination of colonial naivety and ironic rebellion' (McCallum 1998: 210). In his confrontation with urban New York society, however, Mick Dundee embodies the features of both an Australian national mythic character – 'the tough, laconic outback hero', specific to a particular cultural context – and a provincial or frontier figure that resonates more widely and in the particular American context important to the success of the film (213). Some of the comic numbers in the German film *Hallo Caesar!* (1927) are direct borrowings from the Hollywood slapstick tradition that was highly popular in Germany in the 1920s, Thomas Elsaesser suggests; at the same time, however, characters and situations were tailored to 'recognisable German issues and conditions' (1992: 79). The style of comic performance offered by the star and director Reinhold Schünzel raises the general question of performativity versus narrative integration, but in this dimension, too, Elsaesser suggests, the non-narrative form with which the film engages has a specifically German dimension, in the shape of the operetta tradition.

A distinctive blend of *commedia all'italiana* has been identified in Italian cinema in the 1950s and 1960s, the product, again, of a particular twist being given to more widely used comic forms. *Commedia all'italiana* is a dark, often cynical brand of comedy, rooted in a society undergoing rapid change and plagued by corruption, bribery and fraud. Comedies of the period play to some extent on the earlier Italian neorealist tradition. *I soliti ignoti* ('Big Deal

Figure 19   Webbed-feet whimsy: Ealing inheritance in *Local Hero* (1983)

on Madonna Street', 1958), for example, has a texture of bleak background locations that gives a distinctive neorealist impression to a robbery-caper comedy. The mood of such films is very different from that of their neorealist equivalents, however, darker and more ironic than 'the sometimes facile and optimistic humanitarianism typical of neorealist comedy' (Bondanella 1983: 145). Other examples, such as *Divorzio all'italiana* ('Divorce, Italian Style', 1961), are rooted in geographically-specific social customs, in this case Sicilian codes of behaviour that give the selfish nobleman Ferdinando Cefalu (Marcello Mastroianni) the opportunity to murder his wife in order to pursue a younger woman if he can devise a scenario that enables him to frame it as an act of 'honour', and thus guarantee a light prison sentence. The typical character-type portrayed in this kind of *commedia all'italiana*, Peter Bondanella suggests, 'is an inept, self-centred, shallow, yet lovable individual, the eternal adolescent whose lack of self-awareness sometimes borders on the grotesque' (145). A variation, that is, of the type of regressive comic character examined in Chapter Two, but a particular embodiment that is the product of a particular national-historical context.

The popular Finnish comic figure Uuno Turhapuro (Vesa-Matti Loiri) can be read, similarly, as an embodiment of both general and specific factors. Uuno appears to be a classic instance of the Bakhtinian grotesque or trickster figure: lazy, overeating, boasting, physically disheveled and disruptive of various institutions in a series of low-budget films launched with *Uuno Turhapuro* (1973). Fully to understand the appeal or meaning of this figure, however, it is necessary to look at some of the specifics of the dominant projections of Finnish culture to which its is largely opposed, including the construction of white, middle-aged masculinity in terms such as 'endurance, obstinacy, shyness, inability to show emotions, repressed aggressivity, speechlessness and excessive drinking (which, in the Uuno films, is metaphorised in the mode of excessive eating)' (Hietala *et al.* 1992: 139). Some of these characteristics are similar to those found in other national cultures, and to which other grotesquely comic figures are opposed. Uuno is far from a unique figure. On the one hand, he participates in a broader tradition of grotesquely disruptive figures, in terms of both wider cultural processes and comic performers in film; on the other, he offers a version some of the resonances of which are more specific to the particular national context.

Quite how the balance between such elements works out varies from one national-historical context to another, and among particular brands of comedy within any individual context. Comedian comedy appears to offer similar elements of appeal in many different national and historical contexts, as was suggested in Chapter One. The similarities are sometimes striking, but specific resonances are still likely to be found in particular examples, the more closely they are examined, as in the case of Uuno Turhapuro or comedians from very different regions, such as Adel Imam in Egypt or Jagua in Nigeria. Some national or geopolitical-historical contexts create particular problems for the production of comedy. Highly politicised contexts raise a number of difficult issues, on the part of either film-makers or institutional authorities. Indigenous film production in Africa, for example, usually with limited resources, has sometimes leaned towards politically didactic forms, seeking to express a voice distinct from that of Hollywood or former European colonial powers. This has led some to complain about a neglect of more popular forms such as comedy.[15] A strategy adopted by some film-makers in the late 1980s led to a greater use of such forms in 'social realist' productions that reached a wider audiences than other varieties of politically-engaged African cinema. For Manthia Diawara, films such as *La vie est belle* ('Life is Sweet', 1986) 'broke the intellectualist tradition of African cinema and adopted populist themes that are dear to the working class and the unemployed. The aim of the film-makers was to transform the polemics against the elite into jokes made at the expense of the elite and to make films that appeal to the African masses because they can identify with the characters in them' (Diawara 1992: 142). *La vie est belle*, a Zaire/Belgium co-production set in Kinshasa, features a lowly 'everyman' type figure, Kouru, played by the popular Zairean musician Papa Wemba. Much of the comedy, which is subtle and understated, is aimed at the rich businessman Nvouandou (Kanku Kasongo) into whose orbit Kouru falls, especially the former's efforts to produce an heir through taking a younger second wife. *Bal poussière* ('Dancing in the Dust', 1988) and *Finzan* ('A Dance Sung in a Hero's Honour', 1989), Diawara suggests, also use comedy to address issues of modernisation and women's liberation, making central male characters into comic figures for their insistence on holding on to traditional patriarchal practices such as polygamy (144–5). *Finzan*, from Mali, is a strongly-felt polemic against the exploitation of African women, in which a dramatic and political modality outweighs the comic touches, however. Its mockery of the defence by men of their traditional powers and privileges is angry and heartfelt, and laughter at a male character who regularly drinks and acts the fool (and who is fed a powerful laxative to induce a gross-out-worthy spasm of farting and subsequent diarrhoea) becomes uncomfortable once it is established that the character suffers from mental incapacity.

Comedy represented a substantial problem to authorities in the Soviet Union of the 1920s. An effort was made to 'Sovietize' existing film formats, especially 'bourgeois' genres such as melodrama, adventure and comedy that remained the most popular with the mass audience (Youngblood 1993: 37). Comedy provided particularly difficult territory for this process, Denise Youngblood suggests, a format about which more was written at the time than any other. Part of the problem was finding subjects that could safely be the target of comedy. Religion, foreigners and other anti-revolutionary forces were considered the best bets. But even here, the potentially double-edged quality of comedy made this a risky business, as was suggested in some of the satirical examples discussed in the previous chapter. The relative freedoms of the early-to-mid-1920s were withdrawn as comedy became increasingly subordinated to political ends. Decrees were issued by the state stipulating the types of comedy that should or should not be pursued: 'Comedy should not, for example, feature an "idiot" hero like American comedies, nor should it be "physical". Rather, it needed to be infused with "ideology" and "social significance" (though no one speculated how this could be achieved without robbing comedy of its humor)' (Youngblood 1993: 41).

An edict of 1935 by Boris Shumiatsky, head of Soviet cinema at the time, ordered film-makers to combine ideology with mass entertainment, emphasising the importance of forms such as drama, comedy and the fairytale as sources of 'joyful Soviet laughter' under the rule of Stalin. Two musical comedies directed by Grigory Alexandrov are used by Moira Ratchford to underline the shift in policy that this represented. In *Veselye rebyata* ('Happy Guys', 1934), 'Alexandrov strove to "de-ideologize" the script, defending the importance of laughter for its own sake and producing 'an eccentric, slapstick jazz review with only a hint of ideology compared to his subsequent productions ... [The stars] basically sang, danced, romanced, and just goofed around' (1993: 84). *Tsirk* ('Circus', 1936) reflected the very different context created by Shumiatsky's prescription and the centralisation of film production into the hands of a single state agency. A strong dose of ideology is injected into a musical comedy plot revolving around the move to the Soviet Union of a circus performer, Marion Dixon (Lyubov Orlova), who is hounded by a lynch mob in the United States because she has a young child of mixed race. Elements of knockabout comedy, musical numbers, circus-act performances and melodrama are overlaid with an ideological fabric designed to assert the superior and harmonious nature of Soviet society.

One distinction between officially sanctioned Soviet comedies and many of the examples discussed in this book is their treatment of the relationship between the individual and society. The former People's Commissar for Enlightenment, Anatoly Lunacharsky, writing in 1931, argued that the collective should be the standard of value: those who were out of touch with the needs of society should be the targets of comedy (P. Christensen 1993: 49). Pressure should be put on the individual to conform; in other words, the opposite of the emphasis often found in forms such as comedian comedy, in which individuals may become reconciled to social institutions but usually on their own terms and in a manner in which individual eccentricity is celebrated as a source of both entertainment and renewal. The counter example of Soviet comedy offers a useful reminder of the specific social, cultural or political grounds on which all forms of comedy ultimately lie. The wide spread of formats such as comedian comedy, in their dominant incarnations, can lead to an essentialisation of forms that risks ignoring their more specific roots and implications in particular contexts. Film comics such as Chaplin and Keaton are commonly referred to as 'universal' in their appeal, on the strength of the popularity they have demonstrated in many parts of the world. Many important issues may be elided by such formulations.

Some forms of comedy might translate particularly effectively across cultural and geographical boundaries, and they might be all the more likely to be favoured by commercial film-makers on that basis. Physical slapstick, for example, is freed from dependence on local or specific meanings rooted in language. Like sequences of 'action', spectacle and special effects, it has the potential to sell disproportionately well in the international market that has always been a crucial source of revenue for Hollywood and some other national cinemas. To sell abroad is not the same as being rooted in some single, universal source of appeal, however. Attempts to identify such sources are found in many general theories of comedy. At best, accounts based on the identification of supposedly 'universal' comic mechanisms are incomplete, leaving out specific meanings and effects that might attach even to the most apparently 'basic' physical comedy in one social context or another, including some of those explored in this chapter. The most simple pratfall has potentially different implications in our culture, for example, depending on contextual detail, if performed by figures of different gender or racial/ethnic backgrounds. Many of the central dynamics of the classical American silent slapstick tradition are explained by Mark Winokur (1991), for example, in terms specific to the experiences of mass immigration in the early years of the twentieth century, a plausible argument given the importance of members of the recent immigrant and 'ethnic' community in both the Hollywood hierarchy (including most of the studio heads) and the mass audience.

The comedy of Chaplin, the figure most often cited as an example of 'universal appeal', is read by Winokur as a dramatisation of the immigrant experience of acclimatisation to an alien and hostile environment. American comedy relied heavily on slapstick at a time when it was becoming less central to the development of comedy in Europe, Winokur suggests, because slapstick was appropriate 'to a culture whose most important encounters were with physical danger because such comedy was *about* physical danger – from either the city or the country – and about fantasy methods for avoiding that danger' (1991: 47). Explicitly ethnic representation was repressed, as part of a drive for 'respectable' assimilation on the part of studio heads, emerging instead in the form of a comic eccentricity battling with the world of contemporary America; especially, Winokur argues, that of the machine age, many of the more recent waves of immigration having come from poor and less urbanised parts of southern and eastern Europe. Chaplin's comedy is characterised as 'transformational' in nature, 'an immigrant phenomenon derived from the need for transforming both the old and new cultures to which one belongs' (75). Pleasure is provided by transformations enacted on otherwise oppressive institutions. The assembly line of *Modern Times* (1936), classically, becomes a playground: 'American comedy thus began by reading the activities forced onto its audience as instinctual activities ambiguously accessible to all, turning a technological, economic, or social exigency (the fact that many recent arrivals might find themselves chained to the production line or its equivalents) into a volitional virtue' (48).[16]

The virtue of Winokur's argument – whether or not its every detail is accepted – is to suggest nationally and historically specific explanations for the production and mass consumption of particular comic forms in a particular time and place; explanations that open up specific and detailed questions rather than closing them down, which tends to be the effect of theories based on notions of 'universal' appeal. The basis of Chaplin's comedy suggested by Winokur might also help to explain its popularity in other times and places but, again, in specific rather than universal terms. The confrontation between misfit individual and oppressive machine has potential resonance in other cultural contexts within the world of industrialised/industrialising capitalism, or elsewhere. The global dominance of particular economic-social structures, particularly the ideology of 'individualism' that underpins so much Western comedy, has become such that it is easy to mistake the particular for the universal.

five

comedy beyond comedy

A police officer, beaten and bloodied, taped to a chair. A member of a robbery gang, more than a little unhinged, with torture on his mind. Generally, a rather violent, threatening and unpleasant situation. The two are left together, the former at the mercy of the latter, Vick Vega, aka Mr Blonde (Michael Madsen), and we can expect the worst. Vega calmly informs the officer he is going to torture him, regardless of whether he has any information about who betrayed the gang and led to their jewelry heist going wrong. His reason: 'It's amusing to me to torture a cop.' He takes out a gun and points it at the head of his victim. He laughs at the officer's writhing response and produces a knife from his boot, asking, a little incongruously, 'You ever listen to K Billy's Super Sounds of the Seventies?' (a nostalgia radio station to which previous reference has been made in the film). He switches on a radio and tunes in as the monotonously-toned DJ introduces 'Stuck in the Middle with You' by Steeler's Wheel. The music starts, quietly, over a shot of Vega half kneeling to inspect the unconscious and bleeding figure of another member of the gang, Mr Orange (Tim Roth), unaware of his status as an undercover detective. Cut to a close shot of the cop's face as the volume of the music increases. Cut back to Vega, who stands and begins a shuffling kind of dance step as he sings along to the music, knife poised readily in hand...

It is very hard not to be amused at this moment in *Reservoir Dogs* (1992). There is something clearly incongruous in the figure of Vega dancing with the knife, partly in the combination of his menacing bulk and lightness of the step, while the title and some lyrics of the song seem excessively appropriate to the scene; too much so, perhaps, for us to remain entirely caught up in the action. Vega shuffles over to the cop and slashes him across the face, before moving in to perform the act for which the film gained much of its notoriety; he severs the officer's ear, an event that occurs off-screen after the camera tilts up and away to focus on an empty corner of the warehouse in which the action unfolds. 'Was that as good for you as it was to me?' quips Vega, his voice breaking into a laugh. 'Hey, what's going on?' he says, holding the detached ear up to his mouth; 'You hear that?' he adds, chuckling.

What are we to make of the comic dimension in a sequence such as this? It invites us to laugh, on one level at least, rather than merely presenting a 'straight' and chilling or horrific depiction of the actions of a character already established as given to violent instability. As such, it might be rather discomforting. The structuring and tone of the sequence invites the viewer both to remain detached and to share, to some extent, the amusement experienced by Vega.

The deployment of the song is a major factor in creating these effects. In its first moments, the music is quiet and stays in the background. It remains within the diegetic sphere, generated plausibly from a source within the fictional space of the film. On the close-up of the cop, however, and especially in the cut back to Vega and the start of his dance, the volume increases. This might be motivated diegetically, the radio broadcast building from a quieter beginning as the number gets into its stride. But the effect is stronger than that would suggest; the music is of greater volume and richer tone than is likely to have been produced by the diegetic source. The music is taken up, at this point, at a non-diegetic level, sound added from the outside, as part of an imposed soundtrack. This kind of sound transition, from diegetic to non-diegetic, is used quite commonly in Hollywood films as a way of smoothing over distinctions between different levels of fictional construction. External musical impositions, used to establish tone and mood, are given a degree of plausible motivation within the 'reality' of the on-screen events. The effect in this sequence is to relocate the amusing dimension – the incongruity and incongruously-appropriate lyrics – from the specific perspective of the crazed Vick Vega, and his antics, to a position closer to that presented by the film itself and, by implication, a position offered to the viewer.

Distinctions or confusions between levels of engagement such as these can be one source of the controversy associated with films such as *Reservoir Dogs* that offer a mixture of comic and darker or more violent tones. The main question to be explored in this chapter is the function, or effect, of the presence of comedy in contexts that are not usually considered to be primarily those of 'comedy' in its more substantial or clear-cut forms, whether these are put in adjectival or noun-based terms. In some cases the mixture or merging of comedy with other dimensions can be complex, challenging and unsettling. Elsewhere it seems to have the opposite effect, reducing the potential for the production of any disturbing qualities, a factor that helps to explain its appeal in many products aimed at a mass audience.

Comic relief

Comedy beyond the realm of films designated principally as comedies is often used as a source of relief from the otherwise more serious implications of the material presented. Comedy in general tends to offer a safety net, as suggested in the Introduction, a guarantee that events are not to be taken too seriously and so should not have too much potential to disturb; that they remain firmly rooted in the domain of 'harmless entertainment', even when they contain more dramatically-engaging dimensions. Comedy scenes are often included strategically in otherwise primarily non-comedy films, to moderate the overall effect, reducing the weight of seriousness in some cases or offering moments of relief from tension or excitement. As such, comedy is a valuable commodity for mainstream commercial film-makers, a leavening ingredient that can help to make some forms more palatable to wider audiences than might otherwise be the case. Many films add some measure of comedy to their mix of non-comic ingredients, a tendency that can be so far-reaching – as in much of recent and contemporary Hollywood – that to contain a degree of comedy often appears to be the norm rather than the exception. In such circumstances, films that entirely avoid comedy, in the pursuit of greater dramatic seriousness or tragedy, might become the more specific and marked cases; the absence of comedy can be as particular and significant as its presence.

Overt moments of comedy relief can have varying degrees of impact and effect, depending on the context in which they appear. At one extreme, they might serve further to underline the avowedly non-serious, 'just entertainment' and pleasure-offering status of films that are already clearly operating in such a mode on other levels. Elsewhere they can offer stronger contrast to more 'serious' and substantial modality. The first category includes the widespread use of comic quips in Hollywood formats such as the action film of recent decades, or the action-science fiction hybrid, a form that sometimes merges more substantially into the comedy arena. A familiar feature of the contemporary Hollywood action film is the use of comic one-liners, often at the climax of a major action set-piece. A lengthy chase sequence in *The Rock* (1996), for example, ends with the destruction of a sports car from which the central character Stanley Goodspeed (Nicolas Cage) effects a last-second escape. 'Hey man, you just fucked up your Ferrari,' observes a passing motorcyclist. 'It's not mine,' Goodspeed growls; 'Neither's this,' he adds, shoving the owner from his mount and using it to continue the pursuit.

The effect is to offer a moment of comedy (two quips, in this case, one building on the other) that releases some of the tension built up in the extended chase sequence. The chase itself could hardly be described as terribly serious, however, in this as in many other examples of recent Hollywood action cinema. The chase is to a large extent in the domain of comic exaggeration, complete with some one-liners worked into the sequence itself. Part of the pleasure it offers is a self-conscious awareness of its own excessiveness. The chase has a structure not unlike that of many gag sequences: an escalating series of unlikely stunts ordered largely on the principle of one move 'topping' the effect of another and concluding with an effort to 'top the topper', to out-do a previous high point attraction that might have been expected to be the climax.

A series of obstacles and hazards are presented, in more or less ascending order, to complicate what begins as a standard high-speed pursuit through the streets of San Francisco. First there are roadworks to avoid by crashing through a line of parked vehicles. Then there is a truck loaded with water cooler bottles blocking an intersection, through which escaped convict John Mason (Sean Connery) blasts in a stolen vehicle. He hits more vehicles, bringing down a telegraph pole, an obstacle that sends one police car flying into the air. 'I hope you're insured,' quips Mason, a comment inserted between two shots of the car in the air; thus, it seems, undercutting any likelihood of real concern about the consequences for its occupants. Goodspeed avoids the blockage by driving into a garage and ('Oh well, why not') accelerating out through its window to resume the chase. A series of shots of ultra-fast driving is followed by the sound of a phone ringing in the stolen vehicle, an expensive military-style 'Humvee' (High Mobility Multiperson Wheeled Vehicle); the German-speaking owner is on the line and to his complaints Mason replies: 'I'm only *borrowing* your Humvee,' as he crashes it through a pile of refuse. Shortly after this we cut away to a cable car, a shot (like that of the truck, earlier) that serves the same function as the preparatory stage of a gag, setting up the expectation that it will soon be brought into the mayhem. The sequence is concluded with the final topper, an even more extravagant display of destruction in which Mason swerves to avoid an elderly lady, hitting the cable car and sending it out of control; the cable car explodes into the air and slides downhill towards Goodspeed's Ferrari.

The chase is not to be taken entirely seriously, but it is not wholly in the realm of comedy either. What is offered is a balance between real action-excitement and comic relief. Moments of real tension are offered – will one vehicle or another hit this pedestrian, that group of wheelchairs, and so on, the viewer often being taken very close to the action through the use of unsteady, quasi-subjective camerawork – but they are lightened by the expectation that no serious damage will really be done. Such an expectation is the outcome of a number of factors. These include the generally familiar conventions of this kind of 'excessive' action film, a format that became known in the 1990s as a speciality of the producers Don Simpson and Jerry Bruckheimer, and the specific use in this recipe of elements of comedy such as exaggeration and the insertion of comic quips. Exaggeration serves to establish a level of implausibility that removes the events from the world of harsher dramatic realism, where the consequences of the destruction unleashed might be felt more painfully. Examples of the latter are the edgy, quip-free car chases of the mercenary-gang espionage-thriller *Ronin* (1998): equally fictional and conventional but operating in a modality in which comedy is largely absent and collateral damage appears to have more consequences for those involved. In the big-budget action film, the use of exaggeration and the comic quip is a strategy drawn from the highly successful James Bond franchise, in which the witticism preceding or following the dispatch of an enemy – 'beg your pardon, forgot to knock,' as Bond (Pierce Brosnan), dangling upside-down above a toilet cubicle, comments to a Russian officer before knocking him cold in the pre-credit sequence of *GoldenEye* (1995) – lessens its violent impact and marks the ability of the title character to rise above the level of such behaviour.

The balance between action-excitement and comedy is variable in films such as *The Rock* (1996), some sliding more to one end of the scale than the other. No entirely objective measure is available to locate the position of individual examples, the identification of particular traits as comic being so dependent on potentially variable individual and group perspectives. *The Rock*, however, appears to be *structured* with the intention that the dimension of comedy should not go too far towards undermining the dynamics of action-excitement-thrills. The same goes for *Con Air* (1997), another product from the same stable (producer Jerry Bruckheimer and star Nicolas Cage) that balances comedy and more 'straight' material. Comedy is, again, introduced into the mix to underline and ensure the modality of the film as ultimately unserious, without going so far as to undercut the dimensions of action-excitement and action-thriller-suspense. Similar strategies are employed. The film centres around a hijacked plane-load of ultra-nasty convicts, using devices such as exaggeration and the deployment of comic one-liners to establish their *ultimately* comic-book rather than disturbing nature, even if real nastiness and threat is also manifested sufficiently to provide the *frissons* appropriate to a thriller that retains some degree of edge. The group includes a multiple rapist who menaces a female prison guard on more than one occasion who is not taken as a subject for comedy, for example. There is also the mass-killer Garland Greene (Steve Buscemi) whose crimes, we are told, make 'the Manson Family look like the Partridge Family' (serious crimes, then, even if leavened by the quip). Greene's unsavoury nature appears to be realised, or on the verge of realisation, in a sequence towards the end of the film in which he 'befriends' a little girl in a disused swimming pool and is subsequently seen walking from the scene, ominously, carrying her doll.

Such characters are not all handled in the same manner. The rapist is not granted much in the way of comic relief or qualification of character; he remains solely in the realm of implacable threat. Others are lightened, through their access to the realm of the comic quip, offered as a source of pleasure to the viewer, even while ostensibly confirming their unhinged status. Asked at one point if he has lost his mind, the ringleader Cyrus 'The Virus' Grissom (John Malkovich) replies, flatly: 'According to my last psyche evaluation … yes.' As an aside to Greene, later, he observes: 'Love your work.' The latter has his own comic or partially comic lines; recalling the mass murder for which he gained notoriety he says: 'One girl; I drove through three states wearing her head as a hat.' In another context this, and the sequence in which he befriends the young girl, might have far more disturbing connotations. Here, however, these are assuaged. In this context, a film filled with comic quips, the comment about wearing the girl's head as a hat is designed to be taken in the same spirit; the viewer can also be reasonably safe in the expectation that the incident in the swimming pool will prove to have ended without the atrocity that is implied on one level, as proves to be the case.

The comic quip is used in classic contemporary Hollywood action-movie style when Cyrus kills Francisco Cindino (Jesse Borrego), a convict with South American drug connections that have paid for the escape attempt. Cindino betrays the others, attempting to abandon them and escape in an executive jet, which is then impeded and crashes on the runway. Cindino climbs out of the gasoline-leaking wreckage and appeals to Cyrus for mercy. Cyrus takes a lighted cigarette and completes Cindino's imploring 'Cy…' with '…anora' (= sayanora) before torching him: horrific death in flames leavened by the throw-away style of the witticism. Quips such as these offer pleasure in their own right – in this case, and others, through a comic play with language – while also implying a level of detachment from the otherwise unpleasant nature of the material into which they are inserted. The presence of the quip, aimed primarily at the viewer – if also used often to establish the cool and controlled persona of the character – is a reminder of the nature of the product as a fictional construct that should not be taken too seriously.

Comic interludes, in which the focus moves briefly away from the main action, are also used as relief from the tension of the action-thriller dimension in *Con Air* (1997). One revolves around the removal of the location-tracing transponder from the hijacked plane. It is placed in a light aircraft, belonging to Uncle Bob's Scenic Tours and about to take passengers on a pleasure flight over the Grand Canyon, to lead the pursuing authorities astray. The unwitting accuracy of the guide's comment to his passengers ('This is gonna be a day you'll never forget') is ensured, as we are led to expect, when the plane is eventually confronted by a flight of heavily armed attack helicopters on the trail of the convicts. Another comic cutaway scene features a middle-aged couple in their car, accompanied by light music from their radio that clearly establishes a comic modality. The man complains when a bird defecates on his windscreen. The viewer is conditioned to expect what is to follow, in comic anticipation, having witnessed a preceding scene in which a body is dropped from the hijacked plane: a pair of comically coded overhead shots show the body plummeting towards the car before it lands on the bonnet and sets off a multi-vehicle collision over which the light and airy music continues to play.

Comedy plays an important part in the overall mix offered by *Con Air*, but it does not dominate the film. The film presents itself as an over-the-top action-thriller *with* comedy, rather than a comedy-action-thriller. It is not the kind of film that is generally noted for its subtlety, given its tendency towards lurid characterisation and excessive scenes of action and destruction, but the balance between comedy and non-comedy elements appears to have been carefully established through a series of checks and balances between one dimension and another. The notoriously nasty convicts on the plane are exaggerations, on the whole, especially in combination, but they are not as crudely drawn or grotesque as would have been possible. Some of the performances are restrained rather than of the scenery-chewing variety that might be expected, and is often found in portrayals of Hollywood villains, especially those of Malkovich and Buscemi. Drooling and scowling is generally kept to a minimum, given the subject matter. The film moves from elements of knockabout relationships and banter between characters into clashes and reconciliations that are coded as more serious or sincere. This is true of the convicts and of the assorted representatives of law-enforcement agencies. Tensions between the bookish federal agent Vince Larkin (John Cusack) and the blunt Drug Enforcement Agency officer Duncan Malloy (Colm Meaney) are played for laughs at some times, more seriously at others. In the former dimension, for example, Malloy's prized sports car is borrowed by Vince and eventually wrecked and dropped at its owners feet after it gets pulled into air behind the plane as it makes a final escape from a remote airfield; in the latter, Vince has to make an impassioned last-minute intervention to prevent the gung-ho Malloy leading a missile attack that would destroy the aircraft and everyone on board.

Comic devices used in the film are generally handled lightly rather than being milked or over-played, as might be the case if the film was located more clearly as a *comedy* thriller, in which the comedy was allowed to dominate the overall tone. Expectation of the comic confrontation with the scenic tours plane, for example, is established a considerable time before it comes to fruition. In the meantime, its comic dimension recedes largely into the background. When the attack helicopters are dispatched on the aircraft's trail, mistakenly, with Malloy on board, the plot device is taken seriously within the narrative, especially in terms of the objections of Vince, a character with whose position viewers are encouraged to sympathise (if only because the destruction of the convict jet intended by Malloy is structurally impossible at this point because it would kill the hero and bring the film to an premature end). The joke remains in play, at some level, but it is not the main operative mode of the film at this moment. And when it does come to fruition, the moment is passed over rather rapidly and lightly – the startled reaction of the pilot, a brief bemused wave from an elderly woman passenger, the anger of Malloy – without the scenes of tourist-panic-in-the-plane that might have been expected. The wider framing device of the film (Cage's character, unfairly convicted parolee Cameron Poe, becoming caught up in the hijack while on his way home for reunion with his wife and a first meeting with his eight-year-old daughter on her birthday) might be somewhat implausible, but it is played straight in its own melodramatic terms, as is Poe's on-board reluctance to abandon either a close friend inmate (in urgent need of an insulin injection) or the rape-threatened female guard.

Con Air remains, for all its relatively straight dimensions – as established within the terms of its genre confines – a slice of hokum with little pretension to any real seriousness. Comic relief can also be used in films of darker shading or that explore more substantial issues. A striking example is offered by *The Searchers* (1956), as mentioned in the Introduction. At the heart of *The Searchers* is an exploration of the dark side of the American frontier hero, as manifested by the figure of Ethan Edwards (John Wayne). Ethan is presented, in key respects, as the classically heroic man of the frontier; a towering and implacable figure, skilled in the ways of the West, in tune with his environment, fluent in the reading of its signs and meanings and ambiguously located on the edges of, rather than fully inside, the developing society of the West. At the same time, however, Ethan is an obsessive racist, to the extent that his intention throughout the film appears to be to kill his niece, should he find her alive, years after she is kidnapped by a Comanche chief; so badly, in his view, would she have been tainted by the experience. Ethan is a central, heroic figure, then, but one who is deeply disturbing in what he represents. It may be for this reason that the film includes a number of forms of comic relief, sometimes given a clear-cut space of their own, sometimes used in closer relationship to darker moments in the narrative trajectory.

One source of relief is provided by foolish clown-like characters, a prominent example in *The Searchers* being the figure of old Mose Harper (Hank Worden). Mose is used as a source of relief at one key point in the development of the initial narrative situation that drives the remainder of the film. A group of characters, including Ethan and Mose, ride out from their settlements to investigate a series of incidents that might signify hostility from the Comanche. They realise that they have been tricked, the men deliberately lured away from their homes, leaving them vulnerable to attack. It is a moment of helpless desperation for the characters, most of whom rush off in vain attempt to protect their families. Ethan and Mose remain, their horses needing rest, and at this point Mose does a foolish little Indian-style dance; in response, Ethan kicks him, slapstick style, in the rear. This is just a brief interlude of comedy, followed by a worried look on the part of Ethan, seriously-toned music on the soundtrack and a cut to the tense scene at the home of Ethan's brother's family that culminates in the attack (not depicted) and the looming of a Comanche shadow over Ethan's other young niece, Lucy. The moment of comedy is carefully positioned in between two highly charged and serious narrative moments. Later, while preparing for a charge by a Comanche posse, Mose provides something closer to the action-movie comic quip. The enemy will be 'right in your lap in a minute', Ethan informs another member of his group, as they dig in on the bank of a river: 'That we are about to receive, we thank thee, oh Lord,' offers Mose.

A series of comic routines in *The Searchers* revolves around a group of secondary characters including Martin 'Marty' Pawley (Jeffrey Hunter), who accompanies Ethan on his years-long search, his would-be fiancée Laurie Jorgensen (Vera Miles) and her oafish suitor Charlie (Ken Curtis). These, again, are used to offer relief from the darker moments of the film. Ethan and Marty turn back at one point, although planning to resume their quest, after Lucy is found dead (and, it is implied, raped) and her fiancé dies after riding madly into the Indian camp. A light-hearted sequence follows, in which Laurie teases Marty after interrupting him while he is taking a bath. This creates a marked break from the sombre mood that is reestablished when Marty tells Laurie of his fears about what will happen if Ethan finds Debbie alive, the first clear intimation of the dark twist the film is to offer on the familiar American format of the rescue-from-Indian-captivity narrative. More serio-comic banter occurs between Marty and Laurie before the former sets off in pursuit of Ethan.

Another shift into the register of broad comedy occurs during a sequence in which Marty and Ethan leave an Indian trading post, the former discovering that he has unwittingly bought a Native American bride, a subject of much laughter and teasing on the part of the latter. The comedy of this sequence is increased through its placement within the frame of a letter from Marty to Laurie, which she reads in increasing (and, to the viewer, comic) infuriation in the company of Charlie, the possessor of a ludicrous southern accent. When Marty's new bride, Look (Beulah Archuletta), lies down beside him, he gets up and kicks her down a slope, to which Ethan responds with a loud laugh and the quip: 'That's grounds for divorce in Texas.' Marty replies that he does not think it is funny. 'If you really want to do some good,' he suggests, 'why don't you ask her where to find Scar?' – the Comanche suspected of having taken Debbie. At this point the mood shifts abruptly: dark, lowering strings on the soundtrack and Ethan getting up, now very serious, to interrogate Look (whose existence primarily as a comic device is shifted in a later scene in which her body is found as one of many victims of a cavalry attack on a Comanche village).

A further sequence of knockabout comedy occurs later in the film, in which Marty and Ethan return to the Jorgensen household just as Laurie is about to marry Charlie ('I'll thunk yew to unhiyund my fiyancey'), a situation that leads to a comic brawl between the two suitors. The comic interlude is, again, located between dramatically highly-charged sequences: first, a series of scenes including a confrontation with Debbie, who says she does not want to return home, and Ethan appearing to be thwarted in an attempt to shoot her only by the intervention of an Indian attack; second, the climactic scenes, an attack on Scar's village, in which Ethan starts out still wanting Debbie's death but ends up somehow reconciled and takes her home to the Jorgensens. The fate of Debbie, and the resolution of the narrative, hang in the balance during the comic interlude, the end of which is signaled by a conversation in which even Laurie – the good-hearted school teacher, a classic 'civilising' influence in the pantheon of characters familiar to the western – demonstrates agreement with the stance of Ethan ('fetch *what* home?' she asks, in relation to Debbie), suggesting that even the girl's mother would want him to put a bullet in her brain.

That *The Searchers* should have recourse to moments of comic relief is hardly surprising, given the dark and brooding take on the frontier hero that it offers. A questioning of aspects of frontier mythology was not entirely alien to the time in which the film was made, the 1950s, or before, even if wholesale deconstruction of the genre had to wait another decade or so, in films such as *Little Big Man* (1970). *The Searchers* is an example of the more adult-focused western, whether understood in terms of the evolving work of the director John Ford or more general tendencies in post-war Hollywood, in which the industry sought to respond to a loss of much of the audience on which it had previously relied. It remains a western, however, a format still associated to a large extent with less complicated or challenging forms of entertainment, which might explain the perceived need to leaven the darker material with regular doses of comedy. Plenty of avowedly 'serious' or 'adult' films of 1950s Hollywood did not feel such a need, examples including the family melodramas of the period or 'social conscience' films dealing with issues such as racial or ethnic discrimination. A variety of factors are likely to influence the extent to which particular types of film might or might not add elements of comedy to the mix. For film-makers wishing to assert 'serious' credentials, comedy might be something carefully to be avoided rather than deployed. But elements of humour are found very widely, even in seemingly unlikely contexts such as Steven Spielberg's heart-on-sleeve and super-avowedly-serious Holocaust drama, *Schindler's List* (1993).

Humour is an important ingredient in the modulations of tone found in *Schindler's List*, especially in the first hour, before the onset of the worst Nazi labour-camp atrocities (Thomas 2000: 42–56). A vein of wry, deadpan comedy runs through the establishment of the character of Oskar Schindler (Liam Neeson): his suavity, the smoothness with which he bribes and flatters Nazi officialdom, the unspoken attachment that develops in his relationship with the reluctant accountant Itzhak Stern (Ben Kingsley), his womanising. The latter is established through classic, if understated, comic editing techniques: a jump-cut sequence in which he tries out a procession of secretaries, his degree of interest determined by physical appearance rather than typing skills; a comic-ellipsis-cut in which his wife's offer to stay with him if he remains faithful ('Promise me, Oskar: no doorman or *maître d'* will ever presume I'm anyone other than Mrs Schindler') is followed by a shot of her departing by train. The effect of the humour is to lighten an otherwise oppressive mood on occasion, although subtly, without disrupting the serious modality established from the start and in advance publicity surrounding the film. Much of the humour is mordant, pointing with painful irony towards what is to follow. Subdued *pre*-Holocaust jokes of the 'it cannot get worse than this' variety form part of the narrative fabric. Based on assumptions of audience foreknowledge – a superior position to that of the characters, in the hierarchy of knowledge – they establish a protective degree of ironic distance for the viewer (Thomas 2000).

Exactly how comedy works in association with darker or more serious dimensions is not always easy to determine, however, as we have seen elsewhere, particularly in the context of political satire. Do the comic interludes in *The Searchers* undercut, or leaven, the disturbing material? Or do they reinforce its impact, through the point of contrast, the light and shade, they offer? They are certainly much broader and represent a greater break from serious modality than the more subtly integrated elements of humour in *Schindler's List*. Changes of tone can themselves be disturbing, more so, in some cases, than clear-cut or unrelenting 'seriousness'. Comedy can be offered as a dimension that merges or intermingles with other modes of address, as in the example from *Reservoir Dogs* cited at the start of this chapter, a process that can create complex, ambiguous and potentially disturbing effects.

Mixing tones

An important distinction between the use of comedy in *The Searchers* and the 'Stuck in the Middle with You' sequence in *Reservoir Dogs* is that the former does not at any point render comic any of the disturbing material *itself* with which the film engages. Comic relief might sometimes heighten the shift into darker dimensions, and the comedy associated with or at the expense of a number of minor characters plays a part in establishing the edifice that is Ethan Edwards (*never* himself rendered comical); but the two are essentially kept separate. Action films such as *The Rock* and *Con Air* apply comedy to some potentially disturbing material, particularly violent death, which might be a source of criticism from some observers, but the overall generic context and modality limits the extent to which any of this is meant to be taken very seriously. Some films go a great deal further, merging comedy with extremes of dark and disturbing behaviour – and in a more subversive manner than the subtle and contained modulations of *Schindler's List* – as will be seen later in this chapter. First, though, it is worth looking at some more examples of the effects that can result from a shifting of tone between comedy and more serious modes of presentation. A landmark film in Hollywood, in this respect, is *Bonnie and Clyde* (1967). Much of the critical furore that surrounded the film on release revolved around its use of comedy in conjunction with other qualities, especially the graphic portrayal of violence.

Bonnie and Clyde is characterised throughout by abrupt and unsettling shifts of tone in which comedy plays an important part. One of the sequences most often cited in this regard is the first bank robbery staged after the recruitment of C. W. Moss (Michael J. Pollard) as Bonnie and Clyde's getaway driver. Farcical comedy ensues when C. W. backs the car into a parking space during the robbery, rather than waiting on the street outside; the getaway is delayed as he tries hurriedly to manoeuvre out of the space, bashing into the vehicles on either side. The car is eventually freed but, as the trio make their escape, a bank official jumps onto the running board and is shot in the face by Clyde Barrow (Warren Beatty), a moment of sudden and graphic violence that alters the mood entirely. A jaunty banjo theme accompanies many of the gang's getaways and sequences in which they are chased by the police, giving them a flavour of Keystone Kops slapstick, but it is markedly absent in this case, as later in the film when members of the gang end up bleeding and screaming in pain in the back of the car. The mixture of violence and comedy offered by the film offended the sensibilities of some critics, mostly notoriously Bosley Crowther in *The New York Times*. Despite his other reservations, he suggests, 'the film might be passed off as a candidly commercial movie comedy, nothing more, if the film weren't reddened with blotches of violence of the most grisly sort'. The 'blending of farce with brutal killings,' Crowther declared, 'is as pointless as it is lacking in taste' (in Friedman 2000: 178). But the power of the film lies precisely in these shifting tones, as Pauline Kael of *The New Yorker* suggested in her lengthy riposte to hostile critics such as Crowther. The joke is partly on the audience, Kael suggests: 'Instead of the movie spoof, which tells the audience that it doesn't need to feel or care, that it's all just in fun, that "we were only kidding", *Bonnie and Clyde* disrupts us with "And you thought we were only kidding"' (in Friedman 2000: 181). The effect is to keep the viewer off guard, 'in a kind of eager, nervous imbalance,' rather than in any secure mode of relation to the events on screen.

A similar effect is created in *Three Kings*, set in Iraq in the immediate aftermath of the Gulf War. *Three Kings* shifts tone with an abruptness very much like that of *Bonnie and Clyde*, moving speedily from elements of comedy to action-adventure (a plot to 'liberate' a fortune in stolen Kuwaiti gold bullion), tragedy and melodrama (the shooting of a mother in front of her young child; the plight of refugees seeking to escape across the border into Iran) and political comment (an explicit indictment of the Bush administration for encouraging Iraqi dissidents to rise against Saddam Hussein without providing the support they are led to expect). The inclusion of a dimension of comedy is likely to have been seen as important in commercial terms, leavening the seriousness of the overall impression, given the potentially controversial nature of some of the issues raised. Its effect, however, is to create exactly the kind of imbalance identified by Kael in *Bonnie and Clyde*, potentially wrong-footing the audience through sudden shifts of tone, a strategy that is risky from an industrial point of view as it can upset audience expectations, a quality that is not usually a good source of the positive 'word of mouth' recommendation on which success in the cinema often depends (the cinema screening I attended included several moments in which laughs were heard from some viewers at deadly serious moments when this did not appear to be the intention of the film-makers).

If the bounds of what is deemed to be comedy, or acceptably presented in a comic mode, are defined to a large extent by matters of social context, they can also be policed by institutional factors more specific to a medium such as film. The Production Code in Hollywood, for example, enforced from the 1930s until it began to break down during the 1950s and especially in the later 1960s, ruled out the explicit degree of tonal shift found in a film such as *Bonnie and Clyde* on numerous grounds (including the possibility of showing sympathy for criminals or depicting such graphic violence). *Bonnie and Clyde* was one of a series of films in the 1950s and 1960s that challenged and led to the eventual dismantling of the Code, a development that, among other things, permitted the use of comedy in contexts where it would not previously have been allowed in Hollywood, including some of the darker satirical works considered in Chapter Three.

The relationship between the Production Code and the creation of comedy could be an ambiguous one, however. In numerous cases, the presence of comedy was itself much of the problem for the administrators of the Code, making light of matters it decreed should only be treated with due seriousness and careful apportionment of 'moral' values and punishment for those who transgress. Objection was made to the script for *Red-Headed Woman* (1932), for example, featuring the successful rise of a character played by Jean Harlow through a series of affairs, because it 'made comedy out of what had previously been the material for melodrama' (Maltby 1993: 53). This was an issue in many films of the first half of the 1930s, the period in which the operation of the Code took its final form with the creation of the Production Code Administration (PCA) in 1934. The films of Mae West came in for constant attention, both during the scripting process and in the interventions of state censorship boards. Comic punch-lines and other double entendres referring to the West character's active sexual desire outside marriage were removed from *Goin' to Town* (1935), for example. In one exchange, asked if she consented to marry another character, Cleo Borden (West) replies: 'I certainly did – twice.' The word 'twice' was removed by the Ohio censorship board, and thus the entire point of the joke, to eliminate the implication of pre-marital sex (Curry 1995: 225). Comedy continued to be a source of difficulties into the 1950s, challenges to the Code including *The Moon is Blue* (1953), which violated restrictions on the use of seduction or suggestions of illicit sex as a source of comedy (F. Miller 1994: 161). The film was eventually released amid much controversy without the Seal of Approval from the Motion Picture Association of America that was usually required to gain distribution in the United States.

Comedy could also be used to serve the requirements of the Code, however, reducing the edge of materials that might otherwise be deemed beyond the bounds of the permissible. This was the attitude taken in some cases with the work of Mae West. Presented with the script for an adaptation of her play *Diamond Lil* in 1932 (which subsequently became the film *She Done Him Wrong*), James Wingate, director of the Studio Relations Committee, the forerunner of the PCA, advised the studio to 'develop the comedy elements, so that the treatment will invest the picture with such exaggerated qualities as automatically to take care of possible offensiveness' (quoted in Maltby 1993: 55). Taken sufficiently far, into the realms of farce, comedy could offer protection rather than a source of difficulty, although this did not always work sufficiently to prevent official intervention in the case of West, as suggested above.[1] In some cases, a strong dose of madcap comedy enabled films of the Production Code era to get away with material that seems wildly transgressive of its norms, as in *The Miracle of Morgan's Creek* (1944), directed by Preston Sturges. Trudy (Betty Hutton) becomes pregnant after, apparently, marrying a serviceman on his last night before going off to war. Having drunk too much and danced with many different men, she cannot remember exactly what happened or the name of her new husband. Various complications and confusions ensue, involving her innocent admirer-since-childhood, Norval (Eddie Bracken), who is prepared to marry her, bigamously, in order to recover the situation. Trudy conceives in wedlock, it seems – of crucial importance to the Code – but in a manner, and resulting in a trail of chaotic events and attempted deceptions, that offends strongly against its usual spirit; not least in scenes towards the end of the film when, Trudy having become world famous after giving birth to sextuplets, the state governor colludes, for the sake of the local image, in the confection of a series of farcical retrospective adjustments of reality designed to repair assorted fissures in the moral fabric of the case. The judge who performed the initial marriage is to be 'annulled', for example, although it is far from clear that anyone will be able to determine his identity.

The Code could be a source of comic creativity in its own right, for screenwriters obliged to seek ways to evade its restrictions, which might be the case with manic inventiveness of *The Miracle of Morgan's Creek*. More obviously, evasion of the Code led to the reinforcement of the tradition of comic *double entendre*, suggestive lines of dialogue that could be defended, literally, as within the confines of the Code, while their connotations suggested otherwise. In one example, from the ultra-fast-talking newspaper comedy *His Girl Friday* (1940), reference is made to a character being shot 'right in the classified ads' (cited by Maltby 1993: 40). The pilot Sobinski (Robert Stack) in *To Be or Not to Be* (1942) refers, in all innocence, to the capabilities of his 'bomber'; 'I can drop three tons of dynamite in two minutes,' he says, earnestly. Sexual innuendo is supplied through the tone and gleaming-eyed gaze accompanying the – in itself harmless – 'Really?' with which Maria (Carole Lombard) responds. 'Does that interest you?' he asks: 'Certainly does,' she replies, heavy with sexual undercurrents. This is a particularly good example of the 'deniability' of innuendo, the effect lying in an overall impression that cannot be pinned onto any of the individual utterances taken alone. Phallic connotations are also irresistible in the repeated references to David Huxley's missing 'bone' in *Bringing Up Baby* (1938). Non-verbal comic devices could also be used to suggest actions that could not be depicted directly on screen, as in the final image of *The Awful Truth* (1925; 1937): consummation of the restored relationship between the romantic principles is implied through a shot of two figurines on a clock, both retiring into the same compartment (Neale & Krutnik 1990: 162).

Comic and darker tones were sometimes mixed, to potentially disturbing effect, in the era of the Production Code, although the more violent ingredients had to be represented indirectly. The films of Alfred Hitchcock offer many examples. Humour is often used in conjunction with the creation of suspense in Hitchcock's films, as Susan Smith suggests, but its location is liable to shift, with potentially unsettling effect: 'humour often appears to offer some form of relief from the darker aspects of the narrative worlds only to become implicated, retrospectively, within it' (2000: 12–13). In *Shadow of a Doubt* (1943) comic relief is offered by two characters, Herb (Hume Cronyn) and Joe (Henry Travers), a pair of harmless-seeming crime-fiction enthusiasts whose hobby is to speculate on committing the 'perfect' murder. Three of their discussions are presented in the film. The first two are placed before the viewer has been made aware of the film's 'real' murder plot; dark intimations have been provided but nothing specific. A sense is given, Smith suggests, 'of the film constructing an initially self-contained comic space where such murder fantasies can safely be indulged and observed' (50). A third comic interchange between Herb and Joe comes after the narrative enigma has been revealed: the fact that the central character, Charles (Joseph Cotton), is the so-called 'Merry Widow Killer'. The timing of this encounter, for Smith, coming immediately after a disturbing diatribe by Charles against widows, 'problematises the humour and our relationship to it considerably by now making us unavoidably aware of how these two comic characters are linked, via their shared concerns with murder, to a male character whose psychopathology has just been revealed to us in such uncompromising terms' (52). The film sets out to snare the viewer, we might say, offering the pleasure of light relief that returns with more bite.

Moments of comedy in Hitchcock films contribute to the construction of suspense, the quality for which the director is best known. In a famous sequence in *Sabotage* (1936), for example, a young boy is sent on an errand. The audience is aware that he has been made to carry a bomb, due to explode at a pre-set time, and needs to arrive at his destination before it goes off: a classic suspense scenario. He is delayed on the way, adding to the suspense but also offering a comic interlude, in which his teeth are brushed and his hair is greased by a street peddler who tells the boy afterwards that he is 'groomed for stardom'. A complex blend of tones is in operation in this sequence, as Smith suggests. On the one hand, the delay, and the change of tone, adds to our anxiety about the boy's fate; on the other, the peddler's comment has an ironic, playful and distancing effect typical of much of Hitchcock's work. Disturbing shifts of tone also surround the climax of the sequence, in which the boy is eventually killed by the bomb. From the explosion itself, we cut immediately to two characters laughing; this is followed by a sequence in which the boy's adult sister, in a state of distress after being told the news, joins in with the laughter of an audience of children watching a Disney cartoon. The effect, as Smith suggests, is to heighten and complicate the disturbing impact of the act of violence.

The first two discussions by Herb and Joe also serve a suspense-related function in *Shadow of a Doubt* (1943), 'through Hitchcock's strategy of cutting straight from their discussions to an important point in the thriller plot' (Smith 2000: 51). We might question, as a result, the extent to which these constitute quite so self-contained a comic space as suggested by Smith. What is found generally in this and many other Hitchcock films is a subtle and nuanced blend of comic and non-comic tones that, like the other examples considered in this section, adds up to something more than the sum of the parts. The implication of the viewer suggested, relatively mildly, in *Shadow of a Doubt*, is extended in *Rope* (1948), in which we are to some extent invited to laugh along *with* the witty and urbane (if arrogant and manipulative) central character, Brandon (John Dall), in full knowledge from the start that he is guilty of murder. *Rope* also follows and goes further than *Shadow of a Doubt* in including its own critique of the humorous dimension. The third exchange between Herb and Joe provokes an outraged outburst by Charlie (Teresa Wright), the principle source of audience sympathy in *Shadow of a Doubt*, while more than one character in *Rope* complains to Brandon about the warped and morbid nature of his sense of humour. In the first case, as Smith suggests, the outburst seems to mark a watershed in the film: a point from which contrasts rather than parallels are emphasised between the comic duo and Charles, reducing any sense of parallel between their playful discussions of murder and the real thing, and from which the element of comedy subsides. In the latter, space seems to be opened up for a position more distanced from that of Brandon, from the comic strategies employed by the film and, by extension, from the director himself, given his penchant for the morbid style of humour practiced by Brandon: 'Rather than simply defining *Rope* as a black comedy, then, it might be more accurate to describe it as a film centrally *about* the nature and role of humour within a Hitchcock film' (59).

Painting it black

The combination of comedy and dark, often violent material has become relatively commonplace in contemporary Hollywood, although still often a source of media and sometimes political controversy. If *Reservoir Dogs* is one prominent example, others have also been associated with the work of its director, Quentin Tarantino, including *Pulp Fiction* (1994) and *Natural Born Killers* (1994), for which he supplied the initial story. A strong vein of comedy runs through both films, often merged closely with outbreaks of violence. *Pulp Fiction* owes much of its reputation to the comically quirky relationship established between the two hit-men Vincent (John Travolta) and Jules (Samuel L. Jackson). The comedy arises largely from incongruity, from mismatches between the level of investment displayed in different elements within the situation on screen; especially between the unredeemably violent and the trivial or off-hand. Thus, the much-celebrated banter between Vincent and Jules in advance of their arrival at an apartment where they are to perform a series of killings. The pair engage, avidly, in a discussion of subjects such as the French name for a particular kind of burger or the merits of foot-massage, mixed up with reference to one apparently brutal killing by their employer Marsellus (Ving Rhames). Some of this material is continued, especially on the subject of fast-food, once they are inside the apartment, occupied by a group of younger men who are about to pay with their lives for what appears to have been an attempt to double-cross Marcellus. Jules, particularly, is voluble and excessively articulate on the subject. When he shoots dead one of the young men, however, he does so in manner that is so casual and off-hand – he barely glances in his victim's direction – as to be shocking, on one level, but also comic. The effect, both comic and shocking, is created by the sudden drop from a level of lively engagement, in something trivial, to a level of engagement that hardly registers, on a matter of life and death.[2]

A similar sense of mismatch, with blackly comic effect, continues to run through the sequence as Jules interrogates another of the men, Brett (Frank Whaley), in the stunned aftermath of the shooting. Brett is rendered capable of little answer beyond a stammered and repeated 'what?'; Jules threatens to shoot him if he says 'what' one more time. Brett manages to articulate a proper answer to only one question before reverting to 'what' and receiving a bullet in the leg for his trouble. He gets shot, in other words, a serious outcome that might be expected in the broader narrative context, but the reason for the shooting itself, at this point, is entirely trivial. There is a gap, as before, in what might be termed the 'syntax' of the chain of events, the logic through which one event follows another seems to be astray; a feature common to the world of comedy although, as here, capable of having more than *just* comic effect. A further disjuncture follows, between behaviour appropriate to a man of god and hit-man, when Jules goes on to quote his favourite passage from the Bible before delivering the *coup de grace*.

Editing is used to highlight this kind of darkly comic disjunction later in the film, when the multi-stranded narrative returns to the scene in the apartment, initially from the perspective of another member of the group hiding in the toilet. He bursts out shouting 'die, you motherfuckers', emptying his gun in the direction of the two hit-men. Cut to Vincent and Jules. They stand, bemused, clearly not having been hit. Each looks down, to one side, back down to the other side and up at their adversary, before filling him with lead. The comic dimension seems to lie in the contrast, underpinned by its expression through a cut, between the manner and competence of the two parties (quiet, cool and self-possessed hit-men; noisy, excitable, seemingly incompetent adversary) and in the denial of what otherwise might be expected (hails of gunfire, in non-comic contexts, not usually being followed by expressions of calm bemusement).

Perhaps the most comically-black moment of disjunction in *Pulp Fiction* comes in the following scene, in which Vincent and Jules debate whether or not their survival was a miracle, as the latter insists, while driving away with the surviving member of the group, Marvin (Phil LaMarr) in the back seat of their car. Vincent turns around, gun in hand, to ask Marvin's opinion, and accidentally blows off his head. His response is a deadpan: 'Oh, man, I shot Marvin in the face.' The mismatch this time is more extreme, an extension almost to the point of parody of the effect created in the sequences described above. The level of engagement in the shooting is reduced to nil. It is entirely an accident this time, but the violence is more explicit, the interior of the car being splattered with blood and gore. The stretching of disjunction between the two may be the source of the less ambiguously comic tone of this incident. The shooting sets in train a series of events revolving around the effort to get the car safely cleaned up before it is spotted by the police, with incongruity again a major source of the comedy that ensues. Vincent, Jules, Marcellus and the fixer 'Mr Wolf' (Harvey Keitel), who comes to their aid, are all hardened mobsters. In this case, however, the threat that they take most seriously is the reaction of the wife of the man in whose home the clean-up operation occurs, should she come home from work before they have finished. An incongruous-seeming emphasis is put on social niceties, given the casual horror of Marvin's fate, including Vincent's insistence that he be asked politely, rather than being bluntly ordered, to perform his share of the task. The resonance of these strands of *Pulp Fiction*, including but also extending beyond the comic dimension, lies to a large extent in the maintenance of relatively 'normal' interpersonal dynamics such as these – including the earlier banter between Vincent and Jules – within the more highly charged and generically-coded world of the gangland/hit-man thriller.

Violence in film comedy is nothing new, of course. It was a major source of laughs in the era of silent slapstick and has remained so ever since. Violent slapstick has always been a cause for concern for some viewers, critics and would-be guardians of public morality. In earlier incarnations, however, especially those governed by the Hollywood Production Code and its forerunners, the comedy of violence was usually clearly established as part of a world apart, free from the consequences of real violence. When performers such as Laurel and Hardy poke one another firmly in they eye, for example, or the seats of their pants are set on fire, there is no suggestion that they really suffer any infirmity, even within the fictional space on screen. The violence is clearly coded as exaggerated, cartoon-like and not to be taken seriously. What makes films such as *Bonnie and Clyde*, *Reservoir Dogs* and *Pulp Fiction* more controversial, in general, is the way they mix elements of comedy with representations of violence that are more graphic and explicit, that have real and painful consequences in their own contexts and are not likely to be experienced as entirely comic by most viewers either. Characters who are shot at close range in *Pulp Fiction* do not bounce back unharmed in the next scene (a partial exception to this rule is the death of Vincent, who appears alive in a later sequence as a result of the non-linear narrative structure of the film; further departures occur in the Tarantino-scripted *From Dusk till Dawn* (1996), but only once it has shifted generic gear into the mode of over-the-top, and hence largely parodic, vampire-horror).

Questions of moral propriety are often raised, particularly in non-specialist media coverage, in connection with films that offer the representation of torture or killing as a source of comedy, which is hardly surprising. Torture and death are not meant to be 'funny', according to our dominant cultural norms. To make them so on the screen, for many cultural critics, is either a symptom of the decline of moral norms, a contribution to such decline or a combination of the two: judgements that beg a number of rather more complex questions than can be considered here about the nature of the relationship between films and the societies in which they are produced and consumed. Clear-cut comedy-with-violence, unmixed with other dimensions, is less likely to be seen as a problem; like it or not, it is generally seen as being confined to its own separate realm. The difficulty comes when comedy is blended with, or into, more 'serious' or ambiguous treatments of dark subject matter. It can be accused of undermining the seriousness with which serious issues should be handled, of creating a 'dangerous' ambiguity of approach to material on which no such ambiguity should be encouraged. Alternatively, dark forms of comedy can create unsettling effects that might be all the more effective in handling material of a disturbing nature.

Different kinds of rationales are available for the use of comedy in these areas. Satire is one source of potential 'justification'. Comedy of a very dark nature might seem to be more justified if it is being put to more 'serious' critical-satirical ends that seems to be the case, for example, in *Pulp Fiction*. Distinctions such as these are not always easy to maintain, however. *Natural Born Killers* makes claims to the status of satire, particularly of the media, as discussed in Chapter Three, but some of the darkly comic features of the film have little to do with the more clearly satirical dimensions. The opening scene, in which the mass killers Mickey (Woody Harrelson) and Mallory (Juliette Lewis) wipe out the occupants of a redneck south-western state's restaurant, combines murder with a number of stylised and comic flourishes. When Mickey shoots at a large woman armed with a cleaver, we are given something close to a bullet's point-of-view shot in slow motion (in fact, just behind the object), the bullet halting in front of the woman's nose to the cartoonishly incongruous sound of brakes squealing and an operatic high-note, among other elements on the soundtrack, before we cut to the resulting splatt of blood on a nearby wall. In similar style, the camera follows the perspective of a knife thrown at one victim through a window; sound is reduced to the slowed-down *thwomp* of the knife, moving end-over-end, and a repetition of the aria used in the previous example. We are invited to enjoy the comedy-through-stylistic-excess of these moments, along with much other material that is excessive, in terms of the usual bounds of Hollywood style, in *Natural Born Killers*. The effect, as in other examples considered in this chapter, is to create a measure of detachment from the violent events themselves, so explicitly is attention drawn to the process of cinematic construction, but without reducing all emotional investment in the depiction of a series of killings that retain the potential to shock and disturb.

The viewer can also be implicated through such strategies, however, as part of the broader society that the film assaults. Taken in its entirety, the restaurant sequence in *Natural Born Killers* is, for those who enjoy such things, an exciting, thrilling and immensely stylish, if rather garish, use of the medium. The figures of Mickey and Mallory are very much to the fore in the creation of this effect, which might easily translate into something close to a celebration of *their* style and potency: the kinds of characteristics for which they are taken as folk heroes by members of the public interviewed in a television show made by another character in the film. Our enjoyment of the stylistic and comic flourishes of the film, therefore, might implicate us in the world on which it sets its satirical sights. This is one respect in which comedy can be particularly effective, because of the patterns of implicit allegiance that it usually involves: to share the joke entails at least some degree of shared perspective – if combined with a more detached awareness of its status as joke-construction – however uncomfortable that might feel. The fact that such allegiance is offered might help to explain the particularly virulent negative response of some critics, a response that might be interpreted as an effort to demonstrate (or to will) their distance from any such implication. A similar effect is created in *American Psycho*, another dark satirical comedy that does not entirely keep its distance from its target, the urbanely crazed serial killer Patrick Bateman (Christian Bale), in the midst of some of his appalling activities.

In one such sequence, Bateman kills a Wall Street rival, Paul Allen (Jared Leto). Allen has offended in two respects: he has produced a business card even more subtly and tastefully impressive that Bateman's own new design and he claims to have obtained a reservation at an exclusive restaurant to which Bateman has been denied access; both important currencies in the obsessively status-symbol-conscious subculture depicted by the film. The prospect of the murder is at least partially comic from the start, because of the absurdly petty grounds on which it is based. The staging of the deed greatly increases its blackly comic qualities, however, as in the case of many of the killings in *Pulp Fiction* and *Natural Born Killers*. Like Jules in *Pulp Fiction*, Bateman has a habit of mixing his violent deeds with incongruous and earnest closely-argued discussion of aspects of popular culture. With Allen back at his apartment (and newspaper in readiness on the floor: the style section, naturally), Bateman launches into an excursus on the qualities of the band Huey Lewis and the News as he puts on a plastic mac to protect his clothes, sashays around the floor (shades of Vince Vega) and eventually launches into Allen in a frenzied attack with an axe. Once again, if style is part of the subject of the film, the film's own stylistic flourishes, and the pleasure they offer to the viewer, create a potentially ambiguous relationship between protagonist, viewer and the text itself.

How far can the integration of elements of comedy with disturbing material be taken? The outer limits of the darkest comedy become particularly difficult to chart with any certainty because of the problem of varying subjective or group response. The more disturbing the disturbing element, it might be suggested, and the darker and more subdued the humour, the more variable and hard to predict the response might become. In some cases the comic and the disturbing might be kept relatively separate, even in profoundly disturbing contexts. In *La Vita è Bella* ('Life is Beautiful', 1997) a dimension of knockabout comedy and comedian performance is imported into the grim setting of a Nazi concentration camp, a source of much controversy at the time of the film's release. The mix is very different from that found in *Schindler's List* (1993) which did not provoke any such reaction. The humour of the latter is always wry, understated and subordinated to the demands of serious (melo)drama; that of the former is more farcical, opening up a larger and potentially uncomfortable gap between comedy and serious/important context. Roberto Benigni plays a variation on his familiar comic persona as Guido, an endearing, apparently-bumbling-but-in-fact-quick-witted-and-sharp-eyed waiter in Mussolini's Italy. The first half of the film mixes slapstick humour and Benigni's performative turns with mild satirical assault on stuffy fascist bureaucracy as Guido's seemingly magical ability to manipulate his environment secures his union with the woman of his desires. In the second half, however, Guido and his young son Giosuè, are hauled away to the death camp, an event the former translates to the latter as part of an elaborate game the fictional existence of which he works frantically to maintain during their period of internment, an effort in which he succeeds through the deployment of the imaginative skills and fast-thinking demonstrated in the preceding action.

La Vita è Bella does not set out to make the concentration camp experience itself a subject for comedy; its horrors are suggested, although the principal focus is on the fabrication Guido creates for Giosuè, a process that results in the creation of comedy seemingly out of keeping with – but also perhaps high-lighting the menacing undertones of – the situation. In one sequence shortly after their arrival at the camp, for example, Guido volunteers to translate a guard's instructions to the non-German-speaking occupants of the bunkhouse in which they are to be interned. Not a speaker of the language himself, Guido 'translates' into the terms of the game he has invented for his son (on his own role, the guard's words become: 'We play the part of the real mean guys

Figure 20 Inapt glee: Guido keeping up a comic front for his son on entry to their 'accommodation' at the concentration camp in *La Vita è Bella* (1997)

who yell'). Elements of broad comedy are not always restricted to the world as presented to Giosuè, however, a fact that complicates the modality of the film. Towards the end, when control in the camp is beginning to break down with the imminent end of the war, Guido makes an attempt to recover his wife Dora (Nicoletta Brasci) from the separate woman's section, dressing himself in farcical drag comprised of rolling up his trouser legs, donning a blanket as a skirt and using Giosuè's pullover as a scarf. His frantic efforts to find Dora are played straight and 'moving', on one level, but he looks comically absurd, like something out of Old Mother Riley. Eventually he is caught (very much serious; he is to be shot dead, abruptly and off-screen shortly afterwards, while his wife and son survive) but in a farcical position, picked out by a searchlight while hanging up a wall on a drainpipe, legs lifted to avoid being spotted but his 'skirts' dangling into the path of the beam. The mixture irritated and offended some commentators, unsurprisingly, the Holocaust being an event of such awfulness and sensitivity that its representation is subject to stringent policing. It is easy to argue that the presence of the comic dimension risks trivi-alising or misrepresenting the realities of the concentration camp experience, so much is it foregrounded in the film; at the same time, however, it could be said that the mixture of tones has the potential to offer a complex emotional experience that is less easy to resolve that the more obvious recourse to bleak and serious 'realism'.

Something close to a limit case in the merger of comic and very dark tones is offered by *C' Est Arrivé Près de Chez Vous* (translated, not literally, as 'Man Bites Dog' (1992)), an exceedingly dark spoof-documentary made by three Belgian film students who also play the lead roles. The subject is the life of a serial killer, although the style of the film is very different from that of the lurid *Natural Born Killers* or *American Psycho*. Hand-held black-and-white footage is used to create a stripped down cinéma-vérité documentary impression as we view what is, ostensibly, the film shot by a low-budget crew following the activities of Benoît (Benoît Poelvoorde), an amiable workaday mass killer in whose crimes the crew become increasingly implicated. The vérité approach used here is just as much a construct as the heavily stylised sound and visuals in the Hollywood examples considered above, but the effect is to a large extent responsible for the more disturbing quality of the film. Its outbursts of violence are coded as extremely raw and 'realistic', according to the conventional associations of the form, conventions that are rooted in the exigencies of real documentary production. The film also offers shifts of tone more violent and disturbing than anything seen so far in this chapter, cutting with startling abruptness from quieter and deadpan humorous scenes to moments of horribly 'realistic' brutality. The source of much of the comedy offered by the film is quite similar to that found in the likes of *Pulp Fiction* and *American Psycho*, however, even if it pushes the bounds a stage further.

In one sequence Benoît bursts into a house and dispatches a couple bare-handed with a force presented in a raw state that is extremely painful, the vérité impression making it almost unbearably harsh and immediate. A young boy walks in on the scene and is chased out into the garden by Benoît, with some help from the film crew, before escaping but eventually being captured and restrained. The reporter, Rémy (Rémy Belvaux), helps Benoît to hold down the child while he works to smother him with a pillow. Throughout this scene, Benoît and Rémy engage in a conversation typical of the exchanges that recur throughout the film, in stark and incongruous contrast to the awful subjects around which they often revolve. Earlier, for example, Benoît offers droll observations such as 'I usually start the month with a postman,' after killing one of the latter, particular favourites among his victims, and 'I like to try out new work methods,' after killing an old lady with a heart condition by shouting, suddenly, in her direction. On the occasion of the murder of the child, Rémy asks Benoît if he kills many children. No, the latter replies, 'I don't really have the knack in this department.' This is only his third or fourth in five years. 'Kids aren't good business,' they are not 'bankable', he offers in explanation, his usual strategy being to see his killings as a source of income through robbery of the victims. What about kidnapping, asks his interlocutor. Benoît: 'I think it's more of a nuisance than anything else. Especially when the media gets involved.'

This is an appalling scene, its effect created through the combination of form and content, far more so than anything in the other films examined above. But it utilises a similar strategy of disjuncture between the actions being performed and the kind of discourse with which they are surrounded. Phrases like 'I don't really have the knack in this department' and 'more of a nuisance than anything else' are simply not commensurate with the subject of child murder or kidnapping. They are too casual, too offhand, to be appropriate terms in which to discuss such activities. The main point of the film, and its principal source of comic incongruity, is the presentation of extreme behaviour enacted as if it were just another 'ordinary' routine, an extension of the approach used in *Pulp Fiction*. The presence of Benoît's comments invites us to find some degree of comedy in this sequence, although there is no guarantee that this will result. Horror might be just as likely a reaction (at the risk of oversimplification, it might be suggested that the cultural construction of gender in our society is such that women viewers might be more likely to respond in this manner than men). A number of factors intervene between text and individual viewer, ranging from broad socially-defined categories such as age-group and gender to more film-specific influences, such as the manner in which a film such as this is sold or covered by reviewers. The Tartan DVD cover, for example, emphasises (darkly) comic qualities, highlighting quotations from reviewers such as 'Very, very funny, very sharp', 'Deliciously Depraved' and 'Appallingly Funny'. Framings such as these do not by themselves determine the way texts are interpreted, but they form part of the general context in which acts of consumption and interpretation are performed, and are likely to increase the extent to which the viewer comes to the text at least *prepared* to laugh in some places.[3]

What happens if we *do* take this material as at least partially comic? It is unlikely, in a case such as this, I would suggest, that the disturbing quality of the film will be undermined by the admission of the comic dimension. More likely is that the effect of disturbance will be increased, for some of the reasons discussed in the case of tone-shifting or blending films such as *Bonnie and Clyde*, *Three Kings* (1999) and *Sabotage* (1936). To find a sequence such as the child murder in *C' Est Arrivé Près de Chez Vous* simultaneously disturbing and, to a degree, comic, might have a net effect of greater disturbance on the part of the viewer, because of the irresolvable nature of the relationship between the two. The film is genuinely shocking, horrific and *also* comic, in some cases at the same moment; a combination that is hard to synthesise into any neat and disposable formula, and thus possess potentially more lingering disturbing impact. The element of comedy has the ambiguous, double-edged quality we have seen in other examples, potentially both implicating and distancing the viewer from some degree of complicity in the action. Any tendency towards implication is heightened in this case by the role taken by the film crew in Benoît's violence. They become strongly implicated, assisting Benoît in some of his killings, in the disposal of the remains and joining him in

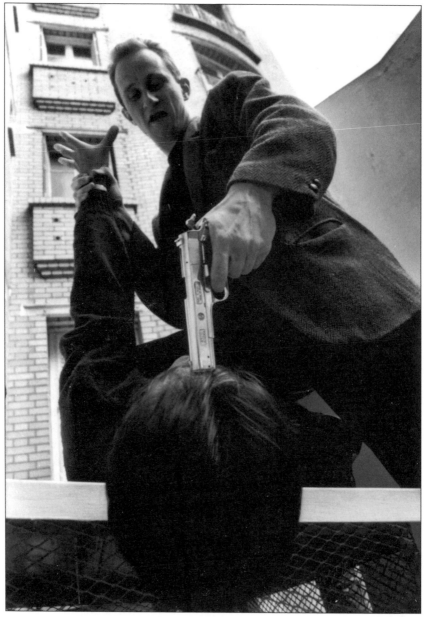

Figure 21 Is this meant to be funny? Benoît going about his daily routine in *C' Est Arrivé Près de Chez Vous* (1982)

the rape (followed by murder) of one victim. Their presence appears to be an encouragement to Benoît, implicating us, as viewers of the film, especially if we derive pleasure from the experience.

194

Viewer implication in dark, murderous comedy is also achieved, through formal means borrowed from other formats, in *Series 7: The Contenders* (2001), a satire or parody (depending on exactly how it is taken) of the broadcast 'reality TV'/game-show hybrid. Incongruity is created through the use of familiar television conventions – access to the sometimes banal, sometimes screamingly melodramatic world of 'ordinary' people – in an exaggerated context in which the winner is the contestant who succeeds in killing all the others. The texture is very much that of the real thing: hand-held 'actuality' camerawork, edited recapitulations of key moments, flash-forward mini-trailers of upcoming events, the seductive tones of the off-screen presenter. Within this context, the violent nature of the events is disjunctive: both comic and potentially disturbing, especially given that the defending champion is eight months pregnant (an incongruous and taboo-breaching mix of bringing new life and death) and has to seek the help of one of the rivals she was about to kill (a nurse) when, as we have been encouraged to expect, she goes into early labour at an inopportune moment.

Mixture of the comic and the serious, tragic or simply the desperate is also found in more quotidian territory in films such as *Happiness* (1998), written and directed by Todd Solondz, and the work of Mike Leigh. *Happiness* and Mike Leigh films such as *Life is Sweet* (1991) and *Secrets and Lies* (1996) tread an almost unbearable, exquisitely painful line between tragedy, banal awfulness and comedy, at times blending moods in a manner that is uncomfortably awkward and challenging to the viewer. *Happiness*, a portrait of a group of characters revolving around three sisters and their about-to-separate parents, offers moments of pointed comedy, blended with an unflinching treatment of issues such as isolation, obsession and sexual abuse. 'She's not like me, you know, she doesn't have it all,' opines the blindly but also comically self-satisfied Trish (Cynthia Stevenson) to her husband Bill (Dylan Baker) of her sister Joy (Jane Adams). Trish does, indeed, appear to possess the material accoutrements of well-heeled middle-class suburbia, unlike the inaptly named Joy. Her words, already smug and treated satirically, gain deeply ironic and painful resonance, however, the preceding scene having depicted Bill (who turns out to be a child sex abuser) masturbating in his car with the aid of a children's magazine. A scene in which Bill confesses, in some detail, to his son Billy (Rufus Read) is extraordinarily powerful, direct and unmelodramatic, yet followed by a 'six months later' sequence, at the end of the film, that climaxes (literally) with Billy's first achievement of ejaculation, a moment rendered into the form of gross-out comedy as the pet dog laps up his spilt semen and bounds off to lick the boy's mother in the face.

Happiness is a strong example of the potent effect that can be created by the irresolvable blending of comic and serious tones. 'You gotta laugh, ain't'ya, sweetheart. Else you'd cry,' says Cynthia (Brenda Blethyn) in *Secrets and Lies*. Taken this way, humour is a defence mechanism, as in Freud's account: 'The ego refuses to be distressed by the provocations of reality, to let itself be compelled to suffer. It insists that it cannot be affected by the traumas of the external world; it shows, in fact, that such traumas are no more than occasions for it to gain pleasure' (1990: 429). Films such as these do not use comedy in so purely ameliorative a manner however: they encourage us to laugh *and* cry. Lives of quiet, but occasionally hysterical – sometimes hysterically comic – desperation are depicted. Comedy is, partly, a coping strategy, as Cynthia suggests, a way of deflecting some of the emotion that might otherwise become overwhelmingly depressive. But, for the film-maker, it is also a way of heightening the overall emotional impact. Laughter is generated at the expense of some of the characters in these films, especially through elements of caricature of suburban/bourgeois aspiration, in figures such as Trish in *Happiness* and the house-proud Monica (Phillis Logan) in *Secrets and Lies*, who might seem rather easy targets. The space comedy permits for the viewer to become distanced or superior is restricted, however, by the painfully human contexts into which such figures are inserted.

Comedy plus seriousness results in something more than a simple sum of the parts in cases such as these. It generates, potentially, a state of unstable and contradictory emotional response, a quality that can be both disturbing and exhilarating in its refusal of the reconciliatory dynamics typical of mainstream film comedy. This is something found primarily in the commercial margins, its uncertain modality and the resulting tendency to create moments of discomfort not being seen as the best way to attract large audiences. Many examples, including the work of Solondz, are found in the lower-budget American independent sector, where comedy is often deadpan (the films of Jim Jarmusch, for example), low-key or mixed with painful and relatively unmelodramatic tales of dysfunctional relationships (films such as *Trust*, which works moments of absurd comedy into a generally bleak milieu of oppressive family life).

A perfect illustration of the merging of tones is found in the darkly comic 'Yosser's Story' episode of the BBC television series *Boys from the Blackstuff*, scripted by Alan Bleasdale (technically outside the brief of this book, although, unlike the rest of the series, this episode ran to feature length and was shot on film). Yosser Hughes (Bernard Hill), a stark and iconic representative of the high unemployment of early 1980s British society, is in a state of emotional breakdown, close to the end of his tether. 'I'm desperate, father,' he tells his priest in the confessional. 'Call me Dan, *Dan*,' urges the priest, seeking to establish more personal, human contact. 'I'm desperate, Dan,' says Yosser, before looking upwards and banging his head on the wall, an 'unintended' joke (Desperate Dan being a well-known British comic-book figure) that leaves the viewer, unaided, to decide what to do, emotionally, with an acute mixture of tragic and comic resonances, neither of which cancels out the other. As J. L. Styan puts it, in a different context: 'The detachment of comedy is not allowed us nor the sympathy of tragedy' (1962: 246). The inclusion of the comic element is the destabilising ingredient, as in some blends of horror and violence with comedy, increasing rather than diminishing the seriously affective charge.

Unintentional comedy

Intended comedy can be a fragile quality, easily subject to misapprehension, especially in particularly sensitive areas such as some of those considered in the previous section. The failure of comedy to be recognised as such might be a question of weakness of conception or of execution at the level of the film text. But it can also result from problems at the level of reception. Particular audience groups, or a wider and more general audience, might lack necessary cultural reference points, whether in-group, intertextual or of some other variety. Material that is comic to some is liable to be offensive to others, sometimes designedly so, as we saw in Chapter Two. A deliberate effort might be made *not* to find some forms comic, even if this is achieved largely through avoidance of exposure, as part of a process through which individuals or groups seek to distinguish themselves from others. To establish oneself as intellectually 'superior' might require the suppression of any tendency to laugh at incidents such as farting, shitting or other manifestations of the bodily grotesque, for example, unless they are given some 'higher' cultural resonances (or can be made 'legitimate' through academic study in a book such as this). Likewise, the avowed anti-racist or anti-sexist might be obliged to stifle any reaction to comedy based on appeals to racial or gender stereotypes that might otherwise manage to bypass their defences. Our responses to comedy can be a good test of the range of cultural assumptions we have internalised, to a large extent involuntarily and perhaps against our better judgements, and that we do or do not wish to make manifest. We might also *try* positively to find comedy in some material, as a way of demonstrating our belonging to other social categories (those sufficiently 'sophisticated' to pick up the references or to adopt a particular attitude; to be 'cool' enough, for example, to laugh at, rather than be appalled by, a film such as *C' Est Arrivé Près de Chez Vous*).

If comedy that *is* intended by its creators does not always make the transition to its viewers intact, for various reasons, comedy can also be found where it is *not* intended. The reason, again, can have much to do with the match between particular audiences and viewing contexts. The question of target audiences is an important one for the whole question of the success, failure or unintended emergence of comedy. A film such as *C' Est Arrivé Près de Chez Vous* is clearly designed to appeal to particular niche audiences considered likely to appreciate its darkly comic dimensions, however such audiences might be defined, rather than to a wider 'general' audience, or some more specific audiences, that might be expected to reject the possibility of finding comedy in such material. Gaps between target and actual audiences can account for a range of different reactions to the same textual material. Some viewers of *C' Est Arrivé Près de Chez Vous* (myself included) might take more offense at the ideological undertones of much of the avowedly 'sweet' and 'innocent' comedy found, for example, in the typical animated Disney feature. We all have our own multiple-determined cultural investments in the enjoyment, or otherwise, of one format or another. Differences of orientation occur between one set of subcultures and another.

Historical gaps provide some of the most obvious sources of unintentional comedy. The conventions on which comedy is based can lose their resonance with historical changes of context. What was once considered to be comedy, or comedy with a particular edge, does not always remain so for later generations. Viewed today, for example, the networks of innocence and seduction in *The Moon is Blue* hardly seem the risqué or controversial subject for comedy they were considered to be in the 1950s. Classical silent and early sound era film comedy retains its comic effects for many viewers, but leaves some cold, partly, it seems, as a result of the gap between the conventions of one era and those of another, despite some of the continuities traced elsewhere in this book.[4] *Non*-comic conventions are also subject to historical change that can be a source of unintentional comedy for audiences removed from the original viewing context. Silent melodrama is one of the most obvious cases. Taken out of context, some of the conventions of the form – especially the histrionic style of 'excessive' gesturing used to indicate emotional states – can easily appear exaggerated and absurd.[5] They are more than usually visible *as* conventions, and as conventions that have lost their original rationale, and so are vulnerable to appearing ludicrous. Comedy may fill the gap created, here and elsewhere, by the fact that a film is 'built around a greater intensity of dramatic tension than it makes an audience feel' (Durgnat 1969: 51).

The conventions of silent melodrama might have been parodied at the time, as we saw in Chapter Three, and may not always have been taken entirely straight in their original form. A test of the change that results from greater historical distance, however, might be that their use today could not be envisaged in any form *other than* as intentional comedy. Even without excessively heightened melodramatic gesturing, comedy can result from the experience, out of context, of so basic a silent-era convention as the use of intertitles to provide dialogue. In *The Son of the Sheik* (1926), for example, it may be hard for the historically-distanced viewer to keep a straight face during earnest declarations of love between the principals, Rudolph Valentino and Vilma Banky. This is less because they appear overplayed than the result of the – to the modern audience incongruous – gap that opens up between the mouthing of lines and their rendition in the form of titles. The comic potential of this fissure is exploited in the Mel Brooks spoof *Silent Movie* (1976), in which words of what appear to be snarling abuse by one character to another come up in the titles in the clearly mis-translated 'You're a bad boy!' Taken other than comically, the conventions of the classical Hollywood-style musical, even in its own fantasy terms, are another source of difficulty for many viewers of more recent decades. Many such films combined music with comedy but the comedy did not usually emerge from the basic conventions of the musical itself – such as the very act of characters bursting unannounced into song at regular intervals without the 'realistic' motivation provided by the backstage variety – as might seem to be the case from a more distant historical perspective.

The representation of wider social or cultural conventions from the past offers further potential for the production of comedy not intended by its makers. 'Outmoded' social attitudes or behaviour are often likely to be experienced as comic, largely as a result of incongruity from the perspective of the historically-distanced viewer. This might be another area in which the experience of comedy can to some extent be willed on the part of the viewer, as a deliberate rejection, for example, of what appear to be less enlightened representations of gender, racial or ethnic characteristics. Distance from the original point of production and consumption creates the possibility of a range of different kinds of reception. Is it possible, for example, for the viewer in later decades to enjoy the rather blatantly sexist and racist comedy of British 'low' cultural formats such as the *Carry On* films, or spin-offs from television series such as *On the Buses*, without substantially being implicated in their ideological dynamics? Distance might permit an 'ironic' positioning of the viewer, enjoying such forms of comedy *as* absurd examples of sexism or racism, from a perspective that rejects such representations; laughing *at* rather than laughing *with*, although there may be a good deal of slippage between the two. The claim to a position of ironic distance might, effectively, become cover for pleasure of a more unreconstructed variety.

Unintentional comedy can also be produced through changes in audience expectations at the level of the 'quality' of work achieved in particular areas. Special effects is one of the departments most likely to be cited in this regard. One of the principal aims for creators of high profile effects in recent Hollywood science fiction, for example, has been precisely to avoid any danger of the unintentional creation of comedy, something that has not always been achieved in the past, especially when the genre was usually allocated lower budgets. The aliens, flying saucers and rayguns of many 1950s science fiction films have become the stuff of comic cliché, as is the ardent and sincere attitude of many of their central characters. The low-budget 'special effects' monsters of earlier ages are liable to become ludicrous rather than frightening or impressive spectacles, from the 'intellectual carrot' of *The Thing from Another World* (1951) to the giant bunnies of *Night of the Lepus* (1972). Sheer incompetence of execution is another major source of unintentional comedy, whether on low budget or higher, the most celebrated ultra-cheap case being Ed Wood's *Plan 9 From Outer Space* (1959), a cult classic of the 'so awful its funny' variety (boasting, among other attractions, the line: 'One thing's sure. Inspector Clay is dead – murdered – and *somebody's responsible*,' and a sequence in which a bereaved man walks out of frame to the sound of squealing brakes and his supposed death under a car – although his shadow, still standing, remains clearly visible on the screen!).

Figure 22 You have to laugh... Christopher Reeve, struggling, in *The Bostonians* (1984)

In less extreme and exotic territory, any number of films, screenplays or performances might be received with laughter that was not intended by those involved, and not always as a result of historical or other contextual distance. The business of being taken as seriously as film-makers or performers intend can be a precarious one. Try, for example, Christopher Reeve's attempt at the accent and mannerisms of a 'gentleman' Southern lawyer in *The Bostonians* (1984). Literary adaptations such as this can be fruitful sources of unintentional comedy that lies in the gap between the qualities of the original and the aspirations of a particular offshoot. Another strong contender is *The Scarlet Letter* (1995), described with understatement in the opening titles as 'freely adapted from the novel by Nathaniel Hawthorne': a version that dips close to unintentional self-parody on numerous occasions, not the least being its soft-focus, almost soft-porn style of lush sexual encounters and overblown attempts to create a dramatic/emotional impact that is not likely to make the journey intact to anything like all viewers.

Material not intended to be in the realm of comedy can also be re-deployed to comic or partially comic effect by other film-makers. In *What's Up Tiger Lily?* (1966) Woody Allen turned a Japanese imitation of a James Bond film (*Kagi no Kag* ('Key of Keys', 1964) into comedy by redubbing it with comic dialogue: principal characters become Terri Yaki and Suki Yaki in a plot revolving around a stolen recipe for egg salad (perhaps not so much more absurd than that of the original). *The Atomic Café* (1982) re-presents a range of Cold War American anti-communist and pro-nuclear propaganda in a manner that renders it into an absurd although sometimes chilling form of comedy. Highlights include 'Bert' the turtle's 'duck and cover' drill, according to which schoolchildren were supposed to survive nuclear attack by covering their heads and faces, and a television presenter who breaks off from moralising about the alleged threat of communist takeover from within to give a lengthy plug for two local shopping centres. *Reefer Madness* (1936) is another favourite example of 'serious' warning turned by historical distance into ludicrous comedy, although in this case no outside intervention or re-focusing was required beyond the programming of the film – a stilted, comically inept and over-the-top 'exposure' of the dangers of marijuana use – as a late-night cult classic. Nothing, ultimately, is safe from becoming comic at some future date or from some unanticipated audience perspective. If film comedy has been around since the birth of the cinema, we can be sure it will be with us – intentional or otherwise – as long as the medium continues to exist.

notes

Introduction

1   Cited in Kramer 1999: 94; a survey of the viewing habits of 1,000 Americans.
2   *Screen Digest*, 12 December 1999: 334.
3   See J. King 2000.
4   Genres are also subject to a constant process of construction, change, redefinition and redeployment, as suggested by Rick Altman, 1999.
5   See Fowler 1982 and, especially, Altman 1999.
6   Collections which offers samples from a wide range of theorists include D. Palmer 1994 and Corrigan 1965.
7   For a sociologically-inclined account based on the principal of incongruity see M. Davis 1993: 11–13. Incongruity theory has also featured in many psychological accounts of comedy, humour or laughter, especially from a cognitive perspective. See, for example, various contributions to Goldstein & McGhee 1972 and Chapman & Foot 1977. The roots of incongruity approaches to comedy are usually traced back to a brief definition given by Immanuel Kant in his *Critique of Judgement* and later elaborations by commentators including Herbert Spencer, Arthur Schopenhauer and William Hazlitt.
8   For more general accounts of comedy in these terms, see D. Palmer 1984: 9; Nelson 1990: 2; Charney 1978: 88.
9   See, for example, Shaviro 1993.
10   In the terms of cognitive psychology, drawing on the work of Piaget, this is a question of whether the stimulus received by the viewer is subject to 'reality assimilation' or 'fantasy assimiliation'; that is to say, whether a stimulus discrepant with an established framework of meaning is to modify that framework, because it is taken as real, or can be accepted at another 'fantasy' level that leaves the framework intact. See McGhee 1972.
11   Superiority theories are usually traced back to the philosophical writings of Aristotle and Hobbes, the latter being most widely quoted for his notion of laughter as the passion 'caused either by some sudden act of their own, that pleaseth them; or by the apprehension of some deformed thing in another, by comparison whereof they suddenly applaud themselves' (1651/1909, Part 1, Chapter 6: 45). See Keith-Spiegel 1972 for an outline of this and other early theories of humour.
12   The terms are used here in the sense elaborated by Murray Smith (1995) to explore more generally the relationship between film character and viewer.

13 On this and much of the following detail, I am indebted to Dave Bessell for interpretation and translation of the relevant aspects of musical structure.

14 For more examples from Tati, see Mast 1979: 296.

15 An equivalent argument in psychological theories of humour is offered by Jerry Suls, who suggests that the perceiver must pass through two stages to find a joke funny: 'humor derives from experiencing a sudden incongruity which is then made congruous' (1972: 82). The punch-line of a joke may rely on incongruity, according to normal logic, but another cognitive rule is found according to which logic can be twisted to make it follow from the initial premise in some way.

16 There are similarities between Koestler's account and that of Schopenhauer, for whom comic incongruity results from a mismatch between abstract rational knowledge and knowledge resulting from sensory perception: 'The cause of laughter in every case is simply the sudden perception of the incongruity between a concept and the real objects which have been thought through with it in some relation ... It often occurs in this way: two or more real objects are thought through *one* concept, and the identity of the concept is transferred to the objects; it then becomes strikingly apparent from the entire difference of the objects in other respects, that the concept was only applicable to them from a one-sided point of view' (1818/1964, Vol. I, section 54: 76).

17 For psychological studies of the impact of the disposition of comedy viewers, in terms of factors affecting mood, see Zillmann & Bryant 1991.

18 'Release' theories, like those based on incongruity and superiority, are found quite widely in the general literature on humour, laughter and comedy. Examples in the realm of the psychological can be traced back to Kant and range from the well-known psychoanalytical writings of Freud to more recent empirical work on the role of entertainment choices in mood management; see Zillman & Bryant 1991.

19 Including Neale & Krutnik 1990 and Karnick & Jenkins' invaluable collection, *Classical Hollywood Comedy* (1995).

Chapter One

1 This is not always the case, especially in formats such as horror or science fiction, in which characters might comment on the extraordinary or unbelievable nature of events, according to normal logic; such events are usually explained, however, within the terms of the mode or genre involved.

2 The above examples are taken from Seidman 1979: 25–6.

3 For more background, see Gomery & Allen 1985.

4 See Neale & Krutnik 1990: 110; Karnick & Jenkins 1995: 65.

5 For a number of different takes on this issue see contributions to Karnick & Jenkins 1995 from Krutnik, Crafton and Gunning.

6 For more on this see Neale & Krutnik 1990: 52–3.

7 See Kramer 1988: 101; Gehring 1997: 33.

8 See Teo 1997: 246.

9 See Stokes & Hoover 1999: 202.

10 These examples are from a brief but useful survey; Dobson 1994.

11 For an analysis of the different kinds of relations often found between stars and their audiences, in a different context, see Stacey 1994.

12 See Kuleshov 1974; Bazin 1967.

13 For an account of this process in general, see Neale & Krutnik 1990: 33–5.

14 In this manipulation of narrative sequence, and other stylised comic effects, the film owes much to the innovations used in *Pulp Fiction* (1994), via the director's previous feature, *Lock, Stock and Two Smoking Barrels* (1998).

15 See Wells 1998: 151–2.

16 For more on the relationship between romantic comedy and melodrama see Neale & Krutnik 1990: 132–48 and Rowe 1995.

Chapter Two

1 *Rabelais and His World*, written in Russia in the 1930s but not published until 1965.

2 See, for example, Eco 1984.

3 This is a major theme of Henri Bergson's 1990 essay, 'Laughter'.

4 In Kristeva's (1982) version, this would be an acting out of the abject in an arena where it can be confronted, and its threat reduced; a process necessary to her account of subject formation. For an elaboration of this reading more generally, see Gross 1990. In Kristeva's own account, the works of writers such as Celine, Dostoyevksy, Lautréamont, Proust, Artaud and Kafka are viewed as substitutes for the role previously played by the sacred, in confrontation with the abject. This high literary realm is clearly very different from that of the gross-out comedy, in terms of both the

more challenging nature of the confrontation likely to be enacted in 'serious' fiction and the kind of audiences addressed. How well Kristeva's argument translates from one to the other remains open to question.

5   For a psychoanalytically-informed account in relation to the horror film see Creed 1993.
6   See Mellencamp 1983. For a very different account of language confusion in the Marx Brothers, however, arguing that it is rooted in culturally-historically specific factors resulting from the mass immigration of the late nineteenth century and early twentieth century, see Musser 1991.
7   See Seidman 1979; Bukatman 1991; Krutnik 1994.
8   Studlar thus argues against the version of psychoanalytic theory – based in notions of sadism and the aversion of castration-anxiety – that has predominated in Film Studies.
9   See Altman 1987 for a discussion of this issue in relation to the Hollywood musical.
10 See Frye 1957: 182–3; Babbington & Evans 1989.

Chapter Three

1   See also Tolstykh 1993 and Moss 1993.
2   See contributions by Lawton, Hames, Paul, Holloway and Goulding, in Goulding 1989.
3   See J. King 2000: 163; Espinosa 1983.
4   For analysis of the latter question in relation to audience and media reaction to the film, see Austin 2002.
5   For early British examples, see Medhurst 1986: 172.
6   See, for example, the different views offered by Hutcheon (1988) and Jameson (1984), although their focus is not generally on the comic varieties of parody on film.
7   See Gallagher 1986; Altman 1999; Neale 2000.
8   See Shklovksy 1965.
9   Figures from Internet Movie Database, www.imdb.com.
10 See Kolker 2000: 77, 88; McDonald 2000: 88–93.

Chapter Four

1   See Rowe 1995a; Davis 1978.
2   For some examples, see Garber 1993: 6–7.
3   See, for example, Fischer 1991.
4   See Riviere 1986; Heath 1986; Holmlund 1993; Butler 1993.
5   For a similar reading in relation to Marlene Dietrich, see Heath 1986: 57.
6   See Holmlund 1993 on Stallone.
7   I use the terms 'race' and 'ethnicity' here without accepting that such qualities exist as clearly distinct and measurable entities in the real world; that human cultures can, adequately, be categorised in these terms. 'Race' and 'ethnicity' are more usefully seen as cultural constructs, a fact that does not reduce the potency with which they are deployed, and hence the need to examine them at that level.
8   Mark Winokur reads the role-playing aspect of such performances more negatively, suggesting that the effort required to prove the ability of black performers to take on more authoritative roles, such as those of police officer or customs inspector, 'means that the roles are not perceived as automatically possible to them' (1991: 196).
9   See Guerrero 1991: 39–44, 82–6.
10 For a detailed analysis see Jenkins 1990.
11 Following the Chinese leader Deng Xiao Ping's attempt to reassure the population with the comment that, after the hand-over, horses would keep racing and dancers would keep dancing in Hong Kong.
12 For general discussions in the case of British cinema, see Higson 1995; Richards 1997; and, for the classic account of nation as 'imagined community', Anderson 1983.
13 These and the following figures are from the Internet Movie Database, www.imdb.com.
14 On this latter point see Dacre 1997.
15 See, for example, Ngangwa 1996.
16 For an earlier version of a similar argument see Durgnat 1969.

Chapter Five

1   For more analysis of the specific historical factors influencing the reception of comedy in the films of West, see Curry 1995.
2   A turn of events, positive or negative, gives rise to the production of emotion, according to

psychological theory applied to film by Ed Tan (1996: 56); the intensity of the emotion produced is related to the magnitude of change, strong emotions being created by rapid or abrupt change of the kind found in this and some of the other examples examined in this chapter.

3   For more on this process see Klinger 1989.

4   A problem likely to be recognised by anyone who has used early comedy with undergraduate audiences. There may, again, in some cases, be an exertion of the process of social distinction/ differentiation at work here, at some level: a rejection of the work of earlier eras as a way of asserting the 'superiority' of the contemporary period; something in which younger generations are likely to have a larger investment.

5   Roberta Pearson (1992) traces a shift from a 'histrionic' to a 'verisimilar' mode of performance in American cinema between 1908 and 1913.

filmography

Abbott and Costello Meet Dr Jekyll and Mr Hyde (1953, Charles Lamont, US)
Abbott and Costello Meet Frankenstein (1948, Charles Barton, US)
Ace in the Hole (aka *The Big Carnival*, 1951, Billy Wilder, US)
Ace Ventura, Pet Detective (1994, Tom Shadyac, US)
Adventures of Priscilla, Queen of the Desert, The (1994, Stephan Elliott, Aus.)
Affair to Remember, An (1957, Leo McCarey, US)
Ahí está el detalle ('There's the Detail', 1940, Juan Bastillo Oro, Mex.)
Airplane! (1980, Jim Abrahams, US)
Airport (1970, George Seaton, US)
Alien (1979, Ridley Scott, US)
All of Me (1984, Carl Reiner, US)
American Graffiti (1973, George Lucas, US)
American Pie (1999, Paul Weitz, US)
American Pie 2 (2001, James B. Rogers, US)
American Psycho (2000, Mary Harron, US)
American Werewolf in London, An (1981, John Landis, US)
Animal Crackers (1930, Victor Heerman, US)
Annie Hall (1977, Woody Allen, US)
Arie prerie ('The Song of the Prairie', 1949, Jiri Trnka, Cz.)
Arroseur arrosé L' ('The Waterer Watered', 1895, Louis Lumiere, Fr.)
Artists and Models (1955, Frank Taslin, US)
Atomic Café, The (1982, Kevin Rafferty, US)
At War With the Army (1959, Hal Walker, US)
Austin Powers: International Man of Mystery (1997, Jay Roach, US)
Austin Powers: The Spy Who Shagged Me (1999, Jay Roach, US)
Awful Truth, The (1925, Paul Powell, US)
Awful Truth, The (1937, Leo McCarey, US)
Bacalhau ('Codfish', 1976, Adriano Stuart, Brazil)
Bacal to Arms (1946, Robert Clampett, US)
Back to the Future: Part III (1990, Robert Zemeckis, US)
Ball of Fire (1941, Howard Hawks, US)
Bal poussière ('Dancing in the Dusk', 1988, Henri Duparc, Ivory Coast)

Bamboozled (2001, Spike Lee, US)
Bananas (1971, Woody Allen, US)
Battleship Potemkin (1925, Sergei Eisenstein, USSR)
Bean (1997, Mel Smith, UK)
Being There (1979, Hal Ashby, US)
Bellboy, The (1960, Jerry Lewis, US)
Belles of St. Trinians, The (1954, Frank Launder, UK)
Beverly Hills Cop (1984, Martin Brest, US)
Bhaji on the Beach (1993, Gurinder Chadha, UK)
Big (1988, Penny Marshall, US)
Big Momma's House (2000, Raja Gosnell, US)
Billy Elliot (2000, Stephen Daldry, UK)
Birdcage, The (1996, Mike Nichols, US)
Birth of a Nation, The (1915, D.W. Griffith, US)
Blair Witch Project, The (1999, Daniel Myrick, Eduardo Sanchez, US)
Blazing Saddles (1974, Mel Brooks, US)
Blockheads (1938, John G. Blystone, US)
Bluebeard's Eighth Wife (1923, Sam Wood, US)
Bob Roberts (1992, Tim Robbins, US)
Bonnie and Clyde (1967, Arthur Penn, US)
Bostonians, The (1984, James Ivory, US)
Bridget Jones's Diary (2001, Sharon Maguire, UK/US)
Bringing Up Baby (1938, Howard Hawks, US)
Britannia Hospital (1982, Lindsay Anderson, US)
Broadcast News (1987, James L. Brooks, US)
Buffalo Bill and the Indians, or Sitting Bull's History Lesson (1976, Robert Altman, US)
Bulworth (1998, Warren Beatty, US)
Bunny All at Sea (1912, George D. Baker, Laurence Trimble, US)
Bunny's Birthday Surprise (1913, US)
Butch Cassidy and the Sundance Kid (1969, George Roy Hill, US)
Butcher Boy, The (1917, Roscoe Arbuckle, US)
Caddyshack (1980, Harold Ramis, US)
Cage aux Folles (1978, Edouard Molinaro, Fr./It.)
Canadian Bacon (1995, Michael Moore, US)
Carrie (1976, Brian De Palma, US)
Carry On Cowboy (1965, Gerald Thomas, UK)
Casablanca (1942, Michael Curtiz, US)
Casino Royale (1967, John Huston, UK)
Cat and the Canary, The (1939, Elliott Nugent, US)
Catch-22 (1970, Mike Nichols, US)
Caught in the Draft (1941, David Butler, US)
Ceremonija ('The Ceremony', 1965, Bordo Dovnikovic, Yug.)
C' Est Arrivé Près de Chez Vous ('Man Bites Dog', 1992, Remy Belvaux, Andre Bonzel, Benoit Poelvoorde, Belg.)
Charme Discret de la Bourgeosie, Le ('The Discreet Charm of the Bourgeoisie', 1972, Luis Buñuel, Fr.)
Chasing Amy (1997, Kevin Smith, US)
Cheech and Chong's Next Movie (1980, Thomas Chong, US)
Chess Dispute, A (1903, Robert Paul, UK)
Chicken Run (2000, Peter Lord, Nick Park, US)
City Lights (1931, Charles Chaplin, US)
Cocoanuts, The (1929, Joseph Santley, Robert Florey, US)
Coffy (1973, Jack Hill, US)
College (1927, James Horne, US)
Comfort and Joy (1984, Bill Forsyth, UK)
Comicalamities (1928, Otto Messmer, US)
Con Air (1997, Simon West, US)
Cops (1922, Buster Keaton, Edward Cline, US)
Corny Concerto, A (1943, Robert Clampett, US)
Countryman and the Cinematograph, The (1901, Robert Paul, UK)
Crise, La ('The Crisis', 1992, Coline Serreau, Fr.)
Crocodile Dundee (1986, Peter Faiman, Aus.)
Cure for Pokeritis, A (1912, US)
Cure, The (1916, Charles Chaplin, US)
Daffy Duck Goes to Hollywood (1938, Carl Stalling, US)

Dai fu zhi jia ('It's a Wonderful Life', 1994, Clifton Ko, HK)
Dárek ('The Gift', 1946, Jiri Trnka, Cz.)
Day at the Races, A (1937, Sam Wood, US)
Dead Men Don't Wear Plaid (1982, Carl Reiner, US)
Demasiando miedo a la vida o Plaff ('Too Afraid of Life, or Splatt', Juan Carlos Tabío, 1988, Cuba)
Demolition d'un mur ('Demolition of a Wall', 1895, Louis Lumiere, Fr.)
Devil May Hare (1954, Robert McKimson, US)
Die Hard (1988, John McTiernan, US)
Diner (1982, Barry Levinson, US)
Dirty Dozen, The (1967, Robert Aldrich, US)
Disorderly Orderly, The (1964, Frank Tashlin, US)
Divorzio all'italiana ('Divorce Italian Style', 1961, Pietro Germi, It.)
Don't Be a Menace to South Central While Drinking Your Juice in the Hood (1995, Paris Barclay, US)
Double Crossed (1914, Mack Sennett, US)
Double Indemnity (1944, Billy Wilder, US)
Dream of a Rarebit Fiend, The (1906, Edwin S. Porter, US)
Dr Strangelove (1964, Stanley Kubrick, UK)
Duck Soup (1933, Leo McCarey, US)
Dumb and Dumber (1994, Peter Farrelly, US)
East is East (1999, Damien O'Donnell, UK)
Educating Rita (1983, Lewis Gilbert, UK)
Edward Penishands (1991, Paul Norman, US)
Erotic Witch Project (1999, 'John Bacchus', US)
Evergreen (1934, Victor Saville, UK)
Exorcist, The (1973, William Friedkin, US)
Explosion of a Motor Car (1900, Cecil Hepworth, UK)
Family Jewels, The (1965, Jerry Lewis, US)
Fantasia (1940, Ben Sharpsteen, US)
Fantome de la Liberte, Le ('The Phantom of Liberty', 1974, Luis Buñuel, Fr.)
Fast and Furry-ous (1949, Chuck Jones, US)
Female Trouble (1975, John Waters, US)
Finish of Bridget McKeen (1901, Edwin S. Porter, US)
Finzan ('A Dance Sung in a Hero's Honour', 1989, Cheick-Oumar Sissoko, Mali)
Fontan ('Fountain' 1988, Yuri Mamin, USSR)
Forget Paris (1995, Billy Crystal, US)
48HRs (1982, Walter Hill, US)
Four Weddings and a Funeral (1994, Mike Newell, UK)
Foxtrot Finesse (1915, Sidney Drew, US)
Foxy Brown (1974, Jack Hill, US)
Freaky Friday (1977, Gary Nelson, US)
French Connection, The (1971, William Friedkin, US)
Friday the 13th (1980, Sean Cunningham, US)
From Dusk till Dawn (1996, Robert Rodriguez, US)
Full Monty, The (1997, Peter Cattaneo, UK)
Galaxy Quest (1999, Dean Parisot, US)
Gee Whiz-z-z-z (1956, Chuck Jones, US)
General, The (1927, Buster Keaton, US)
Ghost Breakers, The (1940, George Marshall, US)
Goat, The (1921, Buster Keaton, Mal St. Clair, US)
Gods Must Be Crazy, The (1981, Jamie Uys, Botswana)
Goin' to Town (1935, Alexander Hall, US)
GoldenEye (1995, Martin Campbell, US)
Gold Rush, The (1925, Charles Chaplin, US)
Goodbye Charlie (1964, Vincente Minnelli, US)
Good Morning Vietnam (1987, Barry Levinson, US)
Gorod zero ('Zero City' 1989, Karen Sharnazarov, USSR)
Graduate, The (1967, Mike Nichols, US)
Great Dictator, The (1940, Charles Chaplin, US)
Great Escape, The (1963, John Sturges, US)
Great McGinty, The (1940, Preston Sturges, US)
Great Race, The (1965, Blake Edwards, US)
Gregory's Girl (1981, Bill Forsyth, UK)
Guest House Paradiso, (1999, Adrian Edmonson, UK)
Gulliver's Travels (1939, Dave Fleischer, US)

Hail the Conquering Hero (1944, Preston Sturges, US)
Hairspray (1988, John Waters, US)
Halloween (1978, John Carpenter, US)
Happiness (1998, Todd Solondz, US)
Happy Go Nutty (1944, Tex Avery, US)
Heathers (1989, Michael Lehmann, US)
Hallo Caesar! (1927, Reinhold Schünzel, Germany)
Help! Help! (1912, Mack Sennett, US)
High Anxiety (1977, Mel Brooks, US)
High Noon (1952, Fred Zinnemann, US)
His Girl Friday (1940, Howard Hawks, US)
Holiday (1938, George Cukor, US)
Home Alone (1990, Chris Columbus, US)
Hook (1991, Steven Spielberg, US)
Hori, Má Panenko ('The Fireman's Ball', 1967, Milos Forman, Cz.)
Horse Feathers (1932, Norman Z. McCloud, US)
Hot Rod and Reel (1959, Chuck Jones, US)
Hot Shots! (1991, Jim Abrahams, US)
Hot Shots: Part Deux (1993, Jim Abrahams, US)
How to get Ahead in Advertising (1989, Bruce Robinson, UK)
I Know What You Did Last Summer (1997, Jim Gillespie, US)
Immigrant, The (1917, Charles Chaplin, US)
In and Out (1997, Frank Oz, US)
Incredibly True Adventure of 2 Girls in Love, The (1995, Maria Maggenti, US)
Indiana Jones and the Temple of Doom (1984, Steven Spielberg, US)
Intolerance (1916, D.W. Griffith, US)
Irish Ways of Discussing Politics (1896, James H. White, US)
I soliti ignoti ('Big Deal on Madonna Street', 1958, Mario Monicelli, It.)
It Happened One Night (1934, Frank Capra, US)
It's a Mad, Mad, Mad, Mad World (1963, Stanley Kramer, US)
I Was a Male War Bride (1949, Howard Hawks, US)
Jack (1996, Francis Ford Coppola, US)
Jaws (1975, Steven Spielberg, US)
Jit (1993, Michael Raeburn, Zimbabwe)
Johnny Stecchino ('Johnny Toothpick', 1991, Roberto Benigni, It.)
Jour de Fête ('The Big Day, 1949, Jacques Tati, Fr.)
Judge Priest (1934, John Ford, US)
Jumping Jacks (1952, Norman Taurog, US)
Jumpin' Jack Flash (1986, Penny Marshall, US)
Kagi no Kag ('Key of Keys', 1964, Senkichi Taniguchi, Jap.)
Keep Your Seats Please (1936, Monty Banks, UK)
Kevin and Perry Go Large (2000, Ed Bye, UK)
Kindergarten Cop (1990, Ivan Reitman, US)
Kind Hearts and Coronets (1949, Robert Hamer, US)
Kingpin (1996, Peter Farrelly, Bobby Farrelly, US)
Know Thy Wife (1919, Al Christie, US)
Kramer vs. Kramer (1979, Robert Benton, US)
Lady Eve, The (1941, Preston Sturges, US)
Ladykillers, The (1955, Alexander Mackendrick, UK)
Last Action Hero, The (1993, John McTiernan, US)
Last Remake of Beau Geste, The (1977, Marty Feldman, US)
Lavender Hill Mob, The (1951, Charles Crichton, UK)
Lawrence of Arabia (1962, David Lean, US)
Left, Right and Centre (1959, Sidney Gilliat, UK)
Lethal Weapon (1987, Richard Donner,US)
Let Me Dream Again (1900, George Albert Smith, UK)
Liar Liar (1997, Tom Shadyac, US)
Life of Brian (1979, Terry Jones, UK)
Life is Sweet (1991, Mike Leigh, UK)
Little Big Man (1970, Arthur Penn, US)
Living in Oblivion (1995, Tom DiCillo, US)
Local Hero (1983, Bill Forsyth, UK)
Long Pants (1927, Frank Capra, US)
Love and Death (1975, Woody Allen, US)

Lucky Ducky (1948, Tex Avery, US)
Mabel's Married Life (1914, Charles Chaplin, US)
Manhattan (1979, Woody Allen, US)
Man in the White Suit, The (1951, Alexander Mackendrick, UK)
M*A*S*H (1970, Robert Altman, US)
Mask, The (1994, Charles Russell, US)
Masquerader, The (1914, Charles Chaplin, US)
Matar ou Morrer ('To Kill or Die', 1954, Carlos Manga, Brazil)
Matrix, The (1999, Andy Wachowski, Larry Wachoski, US)
Me, Myself and Irene (2000, Bobby Farrelly, Peter Farrelly, US)
Merzavets ('The Villain', 1989, Vaghif Mustafayev, USSR)
Mickey Blue Eyes (1999, Kelly Makin, US)
Miracle of Morgan's Creek (1944, Preston Sturges, US)
Modern Bo Biu ('Modern Security Guards' aka 'Security Unlimited', 1981, Michael Hui, HK)
Modern Times (1936, Charles Chaplin, US)
Monanieba ('Repentance', 1986, Tengiz Abuladze, USSR)
Monkey Business (1952, Norman Z. McLeod, US)
Monte Carlo or Bust (1969, Ken Annakin, UK/It./Fr.)
Monty Python's The Meaning of Life (1983, Terry Jones, UK)
Moon is Blue, The (1953, Otto Preminger, US)
Mrs Doubtfire (1993, Chris Columbus, US)
Mr Smith Goes to Washington (1939, Frank Capra, US)
Muerte de un burocrata, La ('The Death of a Bureaucrat', 1966, Tomás Gutiérrez Alea, Cuba)
Music Box, The (1932, James Parrott, US)
My Best Friend's Wedding (1997, P.J. Hogan, US)
My Wife's Relations (1922, Buster Keaton, Eddie Cline, US)
Naked Gun 2½: The Smell of Fear, The (1991, David Zucker, US)
Naked Gun 33 1/3: The Final Insult (1994, Peter Segal, US)
National Lampoon's Animal House (1978, John Landis, US)
Natural Born Killers (1994, Oliver Stone, US)
Nem Sansão Nem Dalila ('Neither Samson Nor Delilah', 1954, Carlos Manga, Brazil)
Neobychainyie prikliucheniia mistera Vesta v strane bol'shevikov ('The Extraordinary Adventures of Mr West in the Land of the Bolsheviks', 1924, Lev Kuleshov, USSR)
Network (1976, Sidney Lumet, US)
Nevinost bez saštite ('Innocence Unprotected', 1968, Dusan Makavejev, Yug.)
Night at the Opera, A (1935, Sam Wood, US)
Night of the Lepus (1972, William F. Claxton, US)
No Limit (1935, Monty Banks, UK)
Ninotchka (1939, Ernst Lubitsch, US)
Notorious (1946, Alfred Hitchcock, US)
Notting Hill (1999, Roger Michell, UK)
Nutty Professor, The (1963, Jerry Lewis, US)
Nutty Professor, The (1996, Tom Shadyac, US)
Nutty Professor 2: The Klumps (2000, Peter Segal, US)
O-Kay for Sound (1937, Marcel Varnel, UK)
Okno v Parizh (*Window to Paris*, 1994, Yuri Mamin, Rus.)
Old Mother Riley, MP (1939, Oswald Mitchell, UK)
One A.M. (1916, Charles Chaplin, US)
Ostre Sledované Vlaky ('Closely Observed Trains,' 1966, Jiri Menzel, Cz.)
Our Hospitality (1923, Buster Keaton, John Blystone, US)
Our Man Flint (1966, Daniel Mann, US)
Paleface, The (1949, Norman Z. McCleod, US)
Parenthood (1989, Ron Howard, US)
Parole Officer, The (2001, John Duigan, UK)
Passport to Pimlico (1949, Henry Cornelius, UK)
Patsy, The (1964, Jerry Lewis, US)
Pawn Shop, The (1916, Charles Chaplin, US)
Pee-Wee's Big Adventure (1985, Tim Burton, US)
Pérák SS ('Springer and the SS-Men', 1946, Jiri Trnka, Cz.)
Personal Services (1987, Terry Jones, UK)
Peti ('The Fifth One', 1964, Pavao Stalter, Yug.)
Pickaninnies, The (1908, US)
Pilgrim, The (1923, Charles Chaplin, US)
Pillow Talk (1959, Michael Gordon, US)

Pink Flamingos (1972, John Waters, US)
Planet of the Apes (1968, Franklin J. Schaffner, US)
Plan 9 From Outer Space (1959, Edward Wood, US)
Player, The (1993, Robert Altman, US)
Playhouse, The (1921, Buster Keaton, US)
Playtime (1963, Jacques Tati, Fr.)
Polyester (1981, John Waters, US)
Pool Sharks (1915, Edwin Middleton, US)
Porklips Now (1980, Ernie Fosselius, US)
Porky's (1981, Bob Clark, Can)
Postselui Meri Pikford ('The Kiss of Mary Pickford', 1927, Sergei Komarov, USSR)
Pretty Woman (1990, Garry Marshall, US)
Private Benjamin (1980, Howard Zieff, US)
Pulp Fiction (1994, Quentin Tarantino, US)
Rambo: First Blood Part II (1985, George P. Cosmatos, US)
Rastus in Zululand (1910, Arthur Hotaling, US)
Red-Headed Woman (1932, Jack Conway, US)
Red Hot Riding Hood (1943, Tex Avery, US)
Reefer Madness (1936, Louis Gasnier, US)
Repossessed (1990, Bob Logan, US)
Reservoir Dogs (1992, Quentin Tarantino, US)
Return of the Pink Panther, The (1975, Blake Edwards, US)
Rêve et réalité ('Dream and Reality', 1901, Pathé Brothers, Fr.)
Road to Morocco (1942, David Butler, US)
Road to Utopia (1945, Hal Walker, US)
Road Trip (2000, Todd Phillips, US)
Robin Hood: Men in Tights (1993, Mel Brooks, US)
Rock, The (1996, Michael Bay, US)
Ronin (1998, John Frankenheimer, US)
Rope (1948, Alfred Hitchcock, US)
Rosalie Goes Shopping (1989, Percy Adlon, Ger.)
Rowdy Ann (1919, Al Christie, US)
Ruka ('The Hand', 1965, Jiri Trnka, Cz.)
Sabotage (1936, Alfred Hitchcock, US)
Safety Last (1923, Fred Newmeyer, US)
Samson and Delilah (1949, Cecil B. DeMille, US)
Saturday Afternoon (1925, Harry Edwards, US)
Scarlet Letter, The, (1995, Roland Joffe, US)
Scary Movie (2000, Keenen Ivory Wayans, US)
Schindler's List (1993, Steven Spielberg, US)
Scream (1996, Wes Craven, US)
Scream 2 (1997, Wes Craven, US)
Scream 3 (2000, Wes Craven, US}
Searchers, The (1956, John Ford, US)
Secrets and Lies (1996, Mike Leigh, UK)
Serial Mom (1994, John Waters, US)
Series 7: The Contenders (2001, Daniel Minahan, US)
Sex and the Single Girl (1964, Richard Quine, US)
Shadow of a Doubt (1943, Alfred Hitchcock, US)
Shaft (1971, Gordon Parks, US)
Shallow Hal (2001, Bobby Farrelly, Peter Farrelly, US)
She Done Him Wrong (1933, Lowell Sherman, US)
Sherlock Jr. (1924, Buster Keaton, US)
She Wore a Yellow Ribbon (1949, John Ford, US)
Shoulder Arms, (1918, Charles Chaplin, US)
Shrek (2001, Andrew Adamson, Vicky Jenson, US)
Shriek If You Know What I Did Last Friday the 13th (2000, John Blanchard, US)
Silence of the Hams (1994, Ezio Greggio, US)
Silence of the Lambs (1991, Jonathan Demme, US)
Silent Movie (1976, Mel Brooks, US)
Silver Streak (1976, Arthur Hiller, US)
Sing as We Go (1934, Basil Dean, UK)
Sister Act (1992, Emile Ardolino, US)
Sixth Sense, The (1999, M. Night Shyamalan, US)

Sleepless in Seattle (1993, Nora Ephron, US)
Sliding Doors (1998, Peter Howitt, US/UK)
Snatch (2000, Guy Ritchie, UK)
Snow White and the Seven Dwarfs (1937, David Hand, US)
So Long Letty (1929, Lloyd Bacon, US)
Some Like It Hot (1959, Billy Wilder, US)
Son of Paleface (1952, Frank Tashlin, US)
Son of the Sheik, The (1926, George Fitzmaurice, US)
Sons of the Desert (1933, William A. Seiter, US)
South Park: Bigger, Longer and Uncut (1999, Trey Parker, US)
Spaceballs (1987, Mel Brooks, US)
Sperminator, The (1985, US)
Spy Hard (1996, Rick Friedberg, US)
Star Wars: Episode One – The Phantom Menace (1999, George Lucas, US)
Steamboat Bill Jr. (1928, Charles F. Reisner, US)
Stir Crazy (1980, Sidney Poitier, US)
Stripes (1981, Ivan Reitman, US)
Strong Man, The (1926, Frank Capra, US)
Sullivan's Travels (1941, Preston Sturges, US)
Sunset Boulevard (1950, Billy Wilder, US)
Sweet Sweetback's Baadasssss Song (1971, Melvin Van Peebles, US)
Swing Shift Cinderella (1945, Tex Avery, US)
Switch (1991, Blake Edwards, US)
That Fatal Sneeze (1905, Lewin Fitzhamon, UK)
That Sinking Feeling (1979, Bill Forsyth, UK)
There's Something About Mary (1998, Bobby Farrelly, Peter Farrelly, US)
Thing from Another World, The (1951, Christian Nyby, US)
This is Spinal Tap (1984, Rob Reiner, US)
Those Magnificent Men in Their Flying Machines (1965, Ken Annakin, US)
Three Ages (1923, Buster Keaton, Eddie Cline, US)
!Three Amigos! (1986, John Landis, US)
Three Kings (1999, David O. Russell, US)
Three Men and a Baby (1987, Leonard Nimoy, US)
Three Must-Get-Theres (1922, Max Linder, US)
Three on a Couch (1966, Jerry Lewis, US)
Throw Momma From the Train (1987, Danny DeVito, US)
Tillie's Punctured Romance (1914, Mack Sennett, US)
Titfield Thunderbolt, The (1953, Charles Crichton, UK)
To Be or Not to Be (1942, Ernst Lubitsch, US)
To Die For (1995, Gus Van Sant, US)
To Have and Have Not (1944, Howard Hawks, US)
Tootsie (1982, Sydney Pollack, US)
Top Gun (1986, Tony Scott, US)
To Wong Foo, Thanks for Everything! Julie Newmar (1995, Beeban Kidron, US)
Trading Places (1983, John Landis, US)
Trainspotting (1996, Danny Boyle, UK)
True Identity (1991, Charles Lane, US)
Trust (1991, Hal Hartley, US)
Tsrik ('Circus', 1936, Girgory V. Alexandrov, USSR)
Tsisperi mtebi anu arachveulebrivi ambavi ('Blue Mountains', 1983, Eldar Shengelaya, USSR)
Twins (1988, Ivan Reitman, US)
Uncle Josh at the Moving Picture Show (1900, Edwin S. Porter, US)
Unforgiven (1992, Clint Eastwood, US)
Up in Smoke (1978, Lou Adler, US)
Uuno Turhapuro (1973, Ere Kokkonen, Finland)
Vacances de Monsieur Hulot, Les ('Mr Hulot's Holiday', 1953, Jacques Tati, Fr.)
Veselye rebyata ('Happy Guys', 1934, Grigori Aleksandrov, USSR)
Vice Versa (1988, Brian Gilbert, US)
Viaje, El ('The Voyage', 1993, Fernando Solanas, Arg./Fr./Sp.)
Victor/Victoria (1982, Blake Edwards, US)
Vie est belle, La (*Life is Sweet*, 1986, Ngangura Mweze, Bernard Lamy, Zaire/Belg.)
Visiteurs, Les ('The Visitors', 1993, Jean-Marie Poiré, Fr.)
Vita è Bella, La ('Life is Beautiful', 1997, Roberto Benigni, It.)
Volga, Volga (1938, Grigori Aleksandrov, USSR)

Wag the Dog (1997, Barry Levinson, US)
Way Out West (1937, James W. Horne, US)
What's Up Tiger Lily? (1966, Woody Allen, Senkichi Taniguchi, US)
When Harry Met Sally (1989, Rob Reiner, US)
Whiskey Galore (1949, Alexander Mackendrick, UK)
Whoopee (1930, Thornton Freeland, US)
Who's Minding the Store (1963, Frank Tashlin, US)
Woman, A (1915, Charles Chaplin, US)
Wooing and Wedding of a Coon (1907, Selig Polyscope, US)
W.R. – Misterije organizma (W.R. – Mysteries of the Organism', 1971, Dusan Makavejav, Yug./W.Ger.)
Yentl (1983, Barbra Streisand, US)
You Can't Take It With You (1938, Frank Capra, US)
Young Frankenstein (1974, Mel Brooks, US)
You've Got Mail (1998, Nora Ephron, US)
Zelig (1983, Woody Allen, US)
Zid ('The Wall' 1965, Ante Zaninovic, Yug.)
Zipping Along (1953, Chuck Jones, US)

bibliography

Altman, R. (1986) 'A Semantic/Syntactic Approach to Film Genre', in B. K. Grant, *Film Genre Reader*. Austin: University of Texas Press.

____ (1987) *The American Film Musical*. Bloomington: Indiana University Press.

____ (1999) *Film/Genre*. London: BFI.

Anderson, B. (1983) *Imagined Communities*. London: Verso.

Apte, M. (1985) *Humor and Laughter: An Anthropological Approach*. Ithaca: Cornell University Press.

Austin, T. (2001) *Hollywood, Hype and Audiences*. Manchester: Manchester University Press.

Babbington, B. & P. Evans (1989) *Affairs to Remember: The Hollywood Comedy of the Sexes*. Manchester: Manchester University Press.

Bakhtin, M. (1984) *Rabelais and His World*. Bloomington: Indiana University Press.

Barr, C. (1993) *Ealing Studios*. London: Studio Vista.

____ (ed.) (1986) *All Our Yesterdays: 90 Years of British Cinema*. London: BFI.

Bazin, A. (1967) 'The Virtues and Limitations of Montage', in *What is Cinema? Volume 1*. Berkeley: University of California Press.

Bell-Metereau, R. (1993) *Hollywood Androgyny*. New York: Columbia University Press, second edition.

Bergson, H. (1956) 'Laughter', in W. Sypher (ed.) *Comedy*. Garden City: Doubleday.

Biró, Y. (1983) 'Pathos and Irony in East European Films', in D. Paul (ed.) *Politics, Art and Commitment in the East European Cinema*, Basingstoke: Macmillan.

Bogle, D. (1989) *Toms, Coons, Mulattoes, Mammies, and Bucks: An Interpretive History of Blacks in American Films*, New York: Continuum, updated edition.

Bondanella, P. (1983) *Italian Cinema From Neorealism to the Present*. Northam: Roundhouse Publishing.

Bordwell, D. & K. Thompson (1997) *Film Art: An Introduction*. New York: McGraw-Hill, fifth edition.

Bourdieu, P. (1984) *Distinction: A Social Critique of the Judgement of Taste*. London: Routledge.

Bowser, E. (1990) *The Transformation of Cinema: 1907–1915*. Berkeley: University of California Press.

Bukatman, S. (1991) 'Paralysis in Motion: Jerry Lewis's Life as a Man', in A. Horton (ed.) *Comedy/Cinema/Theory*. Berkeley: University of California Press.

Butler, J. (1993) *Bodies That Matter: On the Discursive Limits of Sex*. New York: Routledge.

Capra, F. (1927) 'The Gag Man', in G. Rickman (ed.) (2001) *The Film Comedy Reader*. New York: Limelight Editions.

Caputi, A. (1978) *Buffo: The Genius of Vulgar Comedy*. Detroit: Wayne State University Press.

Chamberlain, K. (2001) 'The Three Stooges and the *Commedia dell' Arte*', in G. Rickman (ed.) *The Film Comedy Reader*. New York: Limelight Editions.

Chanan, M. (1985) *The Cuban Image*. London: BFI.

Chapman, A. & H. Foot (eds) (1977) *It's a Funny Thing, Humour.* Oxford: Pergamon Press.

Charney, M. (1978) *Comedy High and Low: An Introduction to the Experience of Comedy.* Oxford: Oxford University Press.

Chiu-han Lai, L. (1997) 'Nostalgia and Nonsense: Two instances of commemorative practices in Hong Kong Cinema in the early 1990s', in *Hong Kong Cinema Retrospective: Fifty Years of Electric Shadows.* 21st Hong Kong International Film Festival: Urban Council of Hong Kong.

Christensen, J. (1993) 'The films of Edgar Shengelaya: From subtle humour to biting satire', in A. Horton (ed.) *Inside Soviet Film Satire: Laughter with a Lash.* Cambridge: Cambridge University Press.

Christensen, P. (1993) 'An ambivalent NEP satire of bourgeois aspirations: *The Kiss of Mary Pickford*', in A. Horton (ed.) *Inside Soviet Film Satire: Laughter with a Lash.* Cambridge: Cambridge University Press.

Corrigan, R. (ed.) (1965) *Comedy: Meaning and Form.* Scranton: Chandler Publishing.

Crafton, D. (1995) 'Pie and Chase: Gag, Spectacle and Narrative in Slapstick Comedy', in K. Karnick & H. Jenkins (eds) *Classical Hollywood Comedy.* New York: Routledge.

Creed, B. (1993) *The Monstrous-Feminine: Film Feminism, Psychoanalysis.* London: Routledge.

Crisell, A. (1991) 'Filth, Sedition and Blasphemy: The Rise and Fall of Satire', in J. Corner (ed.) *Popular Television in Britain: Studies in Cultural History.* London: BFI.

Crowther, B. (1967) 'Bonnie and Clyde Arrives', *The New York Times*, 14 August, in L. Friedman (ed.) (2000) *Arthur Penn's Bonnie and Clyde.* Cambridge: Cambridge University Press.

Creed, B. (1993) *The Monstrous-Feminine: Film, Feminism, Psychoanalysis.* London: Routledge.

Curry, R. (1995) '*Goin' to Town* and Beyond: Mae West, Film Censorship and the Comedy of *Un*marriage', in K. Karnick & H. Jenkins (eds) *Classical Hollywood Comedy.* New York: Routledge.

Dacre, R. (1997) 'Traditions of British Comedy', in R. Murphy (ed.) *The British Cinema Book.* London: BFI.

Daniel, F. (1983) 'The Czech Difference', in D. Paul (ed.) *Politics, Art and Commitment in the East European Cinema.* Basingstoke: Macmillan.

Davis, M. S. (1993) *What's So Funny? The Comic Conception of Culture and Society.* Chicago: University of Chicago Press.

Davis, N. Z. (1978) 'Women on Top: Symbolic Sexual Inversion and Political Disorder in Early Modern Europe', in B. Babcock (ed.) *The Reversible World: Symbolic Inversion in Art and Society.* Ithaca: Cornell University Press.

Deleuze, G. (1991) *Masochism: Coldness and Cruelty.* New York: Zone.

Desser, D. & L. Friedman (1993) *American-Jewish Filmmakers: Traditions and Trends.* Urbana: University of Illinois Press.

Diawara, M. (1992) *African Cinema: Politics and Culture.* Bloomington: Indiana University Press.

Dobson, P. (1994) 'Mirth of the Nations', in *Are we having fun yet? The Sight and Sound Comedy Supplement, Sight and Sound*, 4, 3.

Douglas, M. (1968) 'The Social Control of Cognition: Some Factors in Joke Perception', *Man* (new series), 3, 3.

____ (1984) *Purity and Danger: An Analysis of the Concepts of Pollution and Taboo.* London: Ark.

Durgnat, R. (1969) *The Crazy Mirror: Hollywood Comedy and the American Image.* London: Faber.

Dyer, R. (1992) *Only Entertainment.* London: BFI.

Eco, U. (1984) 'The Frames of Comic "Freedom"', in T. Sebeok & M. Erickson (eds) *Carnival!* Berlin and New York: Mouton.

Eidsvik, C. (1991) 'Mock Realism: The Comedy of Futility in Eastern Europe', in A. Horton (ed.) *Comedy/Cinema/Theory.* Berkeley: University of California Press.

Elsaesser, T. (1992) 'Author, actor, showman: Reinhold Schünzel and *Hallo Caesar!*', in R. Dyer & G. Vincendeau (eds) *Popular European Cinema.* London: Routledge.

Erens, P. (1984) *The Jew in American Cinema.* Bloomington: Indiana University Press.

Espinosa, J. G. (1983) 'For an Imperfect Cinema', in M. Chanan (ed.) *Twenty-Five Years of the New Latin American Cinema.* London: BFI/Channel Four.

Evans, P. & C. Deleyto (1998) 'Introduction: Surviving Love', in P. Evans & C. Deleyto (eds) *Terms of Endearment: Hollywood Romantic Comedy of the 1980s and 1990s.* Edinburgh: Edinburgh University Press.

Fischer, L. (1991) 'Sometimes I Feel Like a Motherless Child: Comedy and Matricide', in A. Horton (ed.) *Comedy/Cinema/Theory.* Berkeley: University of California Press.

Fowler, A. (1982) *Kinds of Literature: An Introduction to the Theory of Genres and Modes.* Oxford: Clarendon.

Freud, S. (1976) *Jokes and Their Relation to the Unconscious.* Harmondsworth: Penguin.

____ (1990) 'Humour', in *Art and Literature.* Harmondsworth: Penguin.

Frye, N. (1957) *Anatomy of Criticism: Four Essays.* Princeton: Princeton University Press.

____ (1984) 'The Argument of Comedy', in D. J. Palmer (ed.) *Comedy: Developments in Criticism.* Baskingstoke: Macmillan; original publication 1949.

Gallagher, T. (1986) 'Shoot-Out at the Genre Corral: Problems in the "Evolution" of the Western', in B. K. Grant (ed.) *Film Genre Reader.* Austin: University of Texas Press.

Garber, M. (1993) *Vested Interests: Cross Dressing and Cultural Anxiety.* Harmondsworth: Penguin.

Gehring, W. (1997) *Personality Comedians as Genre: Selected Players.* Westport: Greenwood Press.

____ (1999) *Parody as Film Genre: 'Never Give a Saga an Even Break'.* Westport: Greenwood Press.

Goldstein, J. & P. McGhee (eds) (1972) *The Psychology of Humor: Theoretical Perspectives and Empirical Issues.* New York: Academic Press.

Gomery, D. & R. Allen (1985) *Film History: Theory and Practice.* New York: McGraw-Hill.

Goulding, D. (1989) *Post New Wave Cinema in the Soviet Union and Eastern Europe.* Bloomington: Indiana University Press.

Gray, F. (1998) 'Certain liberties have been taken with Cleopatra: Female performance in the *Carry On* films', in S. Wagg (ed.) *Because I Tell a Joke or Two: Comedy, Politics and Social Difference.* London: Routledge.

Gross, E. (1990) 'The Body of Signification', in J. Fletcher & A. Benjamin (eds) *Abjection, Melancholia and Love.* London: Routledge.

Guerrero, E. (1993) *Framing Blackness: The African-American Image in Film.* Philadelphia: Temple University Press.

Gunning, T. (1990) 'The Cinema of Attractions: Early Film, Its Spectator and the Avant-Garde', in T. Elsaesser (ed.) *Early Cinema: Space/Frame/Narrative.* London: BFI.

____ (1995a) 'Crazy Machines in the Garden of Forking Paths: Mischief Gags and the Origins of American Film Comedy', in K. Karnick & H. Jenkins (eds) *Classical Hollywood Comedy.* New York: Routledge.

____ (1995b) 'Response to Pie and Chase', in K. Karnick & H. Jenkins (eds) *Classical Hollywood Comedy.* New York: Routledge.

Harries, D. (2000) *Film Parody.* London: BFI.

Hayward, S. (1993) *French National Cinema.* London: Routledge.

Heath, S. (1986) 'Joan Riviere and the Masquerade', in V. Burgin *et al.* (eds) *Formations of Fantasy.* London: Methuen.

Henderson, B. (1986) 'Romantic Comedy Today: Semi-Tough or Impossible?', in B. Grant (ed.) *Film Genre Reader.* Austin: University of Texas Press.

____ (1991) 'Cartoon and Narrative in the Films of Frank Tashlin and Preston Sturges', in A. Horton (ed.) *Comedy/Cinema/Theory.* Berkeley: University of California Press.

Hietala, V., A. Honka-Hallila, H. Kangasniemi, M. Lahti, K. Laine & J. Sihvonen (1992) 'The Finn-between: Uuno Turhapuro, Finland's greatest star', in R. Dyer & G. Vincendeau (eds) *Popular European Cinema.* London: Routledge.

Higson, A. (1995) *Waving the Flag: Constructing a National Cinema in Britain.* Oxford: Clarendon Press.

Hodge, R. & D. Tripp (1986) *Children and Television: A Semiotic Approach.* Cambridge: Polity Press.

Hobbes, T. (1651/1909) *Leviathan.* Oxford: Clarendon Press.

Holloway, R. (1983) 'The Short Film in Eastern Europe: Art and Politics of Cartoons and Puppets', in D. Paul (ed.) *Politics, Art and Commitment in the East European Cinema.* Basingstoke: Macmillan.

Holmlund, C. (1993) 'Masculinity as Multiple Masquerade: The "mature" Stallone and the Stallone clone', in S. Cohan & I. R. Hark (eds) *Screening the Male: Exploring Masculinities in Hollywood Cinema.* London: Routledge.

Horton, A. (1991a) 'Introduction', in A. Horton (ed.) *Comedy/Cinema/Theory.* Berkeley: University of California Press.

____ (1991b) 'The Mouse Who Wanted to F—k a Cow: Cinematic Carnival Laughter in Dusan Makavejev's Films', in A. Horton (ed.) *Comedy/Cinema/Theory.* Berkeley: University of California Press.

____ (1993) 'Carnivals bright, dark, and grotesque in the *glasnost* satires of Mamin, Mustafayev, and Shakhnazarov', in A. Horton (ed.) *Inside Soviet Film Satire: Laughter with a Lash.* Cambridge: Cambridge University Press.

Hunt, L. (1998) *British Low Culture: From Safari Suits to Sexploitation.* London: Routledge.

Hutcheon, L. (1985) *A Theory of Parody: The Teachings of Twentieth-Century Art Forms.* New York: Methuen.

____ (1988) *The Poetics of Postmodernism: History, Theory, Fiction.* New York: Routledge.

Jameson, F. (1984) 'Postmodernism, or the Cultural Logic of Late Capitalism', *New Left Review*, 146.

Jenkins, H. (1990) '"Shall We Make It for New York or for Distribution?": Eddie Cantor, *Whoopee*, and Regional Resistance to the Talkies', *Cinema Journal*, 29, Spring.

____ (1991) '"Don't Become Too Intimate With That Terrible Woman!": Unruly Wives, Female Comic Performance and *So Long Letty*', *Camera Obscura*, 25–6.

____ (1992) *What Made Pistachio Nuts? Early Sound Comedy and the Vaudeville Aesthetic.* New York: Columbia University Press.

Jordan, M. (1983) 'Carry On ... Follow that Stereotype', in J. Curran & V. Porter (eds) *British Cinema History.* London: Weidenfeld and Nicholson.

Kael, P. (1967) 'Bonnie and Clyde', *The New Yorker*, October 21, reprinted in L. Friedman (ed.) (2000) *Arthur Penn's Bonnie and Clyde.* Cambridge: Cambridge University Press.

Kant, I. (1790/1892) *Critique of Judgement.* London: Macmillan.

Karnick, K. & H. Jenkins (1995) 'Introduction: Funny Stories', in K. Karnick & H. Jenkins (eds) *Classical*

Hollywood Comedy. New York: Routledge.

Karnick, K. (1995) 'Commitment and Reaffirmation in Hollywood Romantic Comedy', in K. Karnick & H. Jenkins (eds) *Classical Hollywood Comedy*. New York: Routledge.

Keith-Spiegel, P. (1972) 'Early Conceptions of Humor: Varieties and Issues', in J. Goldstein & P. McGhee (eds) *The Psychology of Humor: Theoretical Perspectives and Empirical Issues*. New York: Academic Press.

Kerr, W. (1975) *The Silent Clowns*. New York: De Capo.

King, G. (1996) *Mapping Reality: An Exploration of Cultural Cartographies*. Basingstoke: Macmillan.

____ (2002) *New Hollywood Cinema: An Introduction*. London: I. B. Tauris.

King, J. (2000) *Magical Reels: A History of Cinema in Latin America*. London: Verso.

Kirk, K. & E. Heath (1984) *Men in Frocks*. London: Gay Men's Press.

Klein, N. (1993) *7 Minutes: The Life and Death of the American Animated Cartoon*. London: Verso.

Klinger, B. (1989) 'Digressions at the cinema: reception and mass culture', *Cinema Journal*, 28, 4, Summer.

Koestler, A. (1982) 'Joking Apart', in *Bricks to Babel: Selected Writings with Author's Comments*. London: Pan.

Kolker, R. P. (1988) *A Cinema of Loneliness: Penn, Kubrick, Scorsese, Spielberg, Altman*. Oxford: Oxford University Press, second edition.

____ (2000) *Film Form and Culture*. New York: McGraw-Hill.

Kramer, P. (1988) 'Vitagraph, Slapstick and Early Cinema', *Screen*, 29, 2.

____ (1995) 'The Making of a Comic Star: Buster Keaton and *The Saphead*', in K. Karnick & H. Jenkins (eds) *Classical Hollywood Comedy*. New York: Routledge.

____ (1999) 'A Powerful Cinemagoing Force? Hollywood and Female Audience since the 1960s', in M. Stokes & R. Maltby (eds) *Identifying Hollywood's Audiences: Cultural Identity and the Movies*. London: BFI.

____ (2001) '"Clean, Dependable Slapstick": Comic Violence and the Emergence of Classical Hollywood Cinema', in J. D. Slocum (ed.) *Violence and American Cinema*. New York: Routledge.

Kristeva, J. (1982) *Powers of Horror: An Essay on Abjection*. New York: Columbia University Press.

Krutnik, F. (1984) 'The Clown-Prints of Comedy', *Screen*, 4, 5.

____ (1994) 'Jerry Lewis: The Deformation of the Comic', *Film Quarterly*, 48, 1.

____ (1995) 'A Spanner in the Works? Genre, Narrative and the Hollywood Comedian', in K. Karnick & H. Jenkins (eds) *Classical Hollywood Comedy*. New York: Routledge.

____ (1998) 'Love Lies: Romantic Fabrication in Contemporary Romantic Comedy', in P. Evans & C. Deleyto (eds) *Terms of Endearment: Hollywood Romantic Comedy of the 1980s and 1990s*. Edinburgh: Edinburgh University Press.

Krzywinska, T. (1998–99) 'Masquerading the Phallus: Laughter and the Phallus/penis Analogue in Explicit Sex Films', *Diatribe*, 8, Winter/Spring.

Kuhn, A. (1985) *The Power of the Image: Essays on Representation and Sexuality*. London: Routledge.

Kuleshov, L. (1974) *Kuleshov on Film: Writings of Lev Kuleshov* (Ronald Leaco (ed.)) Berkeley: University of California Press.

Lacan, J. (1977) 'The Mirror Stage', in *Ecrits: A Selection*. London: Routledge.

Lau, J. (1998) 'Besides Fists and Blood: Hong Kong Comedy and Its Master of the Eighties', *Cinema Journal*, 37, 2, Winter.

Lawton, A. (1989) 'Toward a New Openness in Soviet Cinema, 1976–1987', in D. Goulding (ed.) *Post New Wave Cinema in the Soviet Union and Eastern Europe*. Bloomington: Indiana University Press.

Leab, D. (1975) *From Sambo to Superspade: The Black Experience in Motion Pictures*. New York: Secker.

Lent, T. O. (1995) 'Romantic Love and Friendship: The Redefinition of Gender Relations in Screwball Comedy', in K. Karnick and H. Jenkins (eds) *Classical Hollywood Comedy*. New York: Routledge.

Lévi-Straus, C. (1968) 'The Structural Study of Myth', in *Structural Anthropology*. Harmondsworth: Penguin.

Lindvall, T. & B. Fraser (1998) 'Darker Shades of Animation: African-American Images in the Warner Bros. Cartoon', in K. Sander (ed.) *Reading the Rabbit: Explorations in Warner Bros. Animation*. New Brunswick: Rutgers University Press.

List, C. (2000) 'Self-Directed Stereotyping in the Films of Cheech Marin', in G. Rickman (ed.) *The Film Comedy Reader*. New York: Limelight Editions.

Maltby, R. (1993) 'The Production Code and the Hays Office', in T. Balio, *Grand Design: Hollywood as a Modern Business Enterprise 1930–1939*. Berkeley, University of California Press.

Mast, G. (1979) *The Comic Mind: Comedy and the Movies*. Chicago: University of Chicago Press.

McCaffrey, D. (1992) *Assault on Society: Satirical Literature to Film*. Metuchen, NJ: Metuchen.

McCallum, J. (1998) 'Cringe and Strut: Comedy and national identity in post-war Australia', in S. Wagg (ed.) *Because I Tell a Joke or Two: Comedy, Politics and Social Difference*. London: Routledge.

McDonald, P. (2000) *The Star System: Hollywood's Production of Popular Identities*. London: Wallflower Press.

McGhee, P. (1972) 'On the Cognitive Origins of Incongruity Humor: Fantasy Assimilation versus Reality Assimilation', in J. Goldstein & P. McGhee (eds) *The Psychology of Humor: Theoretical Perspectives* and Empirical Issues. New York: Academic Press.

Medhurst, A. (1986) 'Music Hall and British Cinema', in C. Barr (ed.) All Our Yesterdays: 90 Years of British Cinema. London: BFI.

Mellencamp, P. (1983) 'Jokes and Their Relation to the Marx Brothers', in S. Heath & P. Mellencamp (eds) Cinema and Language. New York: American Film Institute.

Miller, F. (1994) Censored Hollywood: Sex, Sin, and Violence on Screen. Atlanta: Turner Publishing.

Miller, W. I. (1997) The Anatomy of Disgust. Cambridge, Mass.: Harvard University Press.

Moss, K. (1993) 'A Russian Munchausen: Aesopian translation', in A. Horton (ed.) Inside Soviet Film Satire: Laughter with a Lash. Cambridge: Cambridge University Press.

Musser, C. (1991) 'Ethnicity, Role-playing, and American Film Comedy: From Chinese Laundry Scene to Whoopee (1894–1930)', in L. Friedman (ed.) Unspeakable Images: Ethnicity and the American Cinema. Urbana and Chicago: University of Illinois Press.

____(1995) 'Divorce, DeMille and the Comedy of Remarriage', in K. Karnick & H. Jenkins (eds) Classical Hollywood Comedy. New York: Routledge.

Neale, S. (2000) Genre and Hollywood. London: Routledge.

Neale, S. & F. Krutnik (1990) Popular Film and Television Comedy. London: Routledge.

Nelson, T. G. A. (1990) Comedy: An Introduction to Comedy in Literature, Drama, and Cinema. Oxford: Oxford University Press.

Ngangwa, M. (1996) 'African Cinema – Militancy or Entertainment?', in I. Bakari & M. B. Cham (eds) African Experiences of Cinema. London: BFI.

Olson, E.(1968) The Theory of Comedy. Bloomington: Indiana University Press.

Palmer, D. J. (ed.) (1984) Comedy: Developments in Criticism. Basingstoke: Macmillan.

Palmer, J. (1987) The Logic of the Absurd: On Film and Television Comedy. London: BFI.

____ (1994) Taking Humour Seriously. London: Routledge.

Paul, D. (1983) 'Introduction: Film Art and Social Commitment', in D. Paul (ed.) Politics, Art and Commitment in the East European Cinema. Basingstoke: Macmillan.

Paul, W. (1991) 'Charles Chaplin and the Annals of Anality', in A. Horton (ed.) Comedy/Cinema/Theory. Berkeley: University of California Press.

____ (1994) Laughing Screaming: Modern Hollywood Horror and Comedy. New York: Columbia University Press.

Pearson, R. (1992) Eloquent Gestures: The Transformation of Performance Style in the Griffith Biograph Films. Berkeley: University of California Press.

Petric, V. (1993) 'A subtextual reading of Kuleshov's satire The Extraordinary Adventures of Mr West in the Land of the Bolsheviks (1924)', in A. Horton (ed.) Inside Soviet Film Satire: Laughter with a Lash. Cambridge: Cambridge University Press.

Purdie, S. (1993) Comedy: The Mastery of Discourse. New York: Harvester Wheatsheaf.

Ratchford, M. (1993) 'Circus of 1936: Ideology and entertainment under the big top', in Andrew Horton (ed.) Inside Soviet Film Satire. Cambridge: Cambridge University Press.

Riblet, D. (1995) 'The Keystone Film Company and the Historiography of Early Slapstick', in K. Karnick & H. Jenkins (eds) Classical Hollywood Comedy. New York: Routledge.

Richards, J. (1997) Films and British National Identity: From Dickens to Dad's Army. Manchester: Manchester University Press.

Rickman, G. (2001) The Film Comedy Reader. New York: Limelight Editions.

Riviere, J. (1986) 'Womanliness as Masquerade', in V. Burgin, J. Donald & C. Kaplan (eds) Formations of Fantasy. London: Methuen.

Rose, M. (1993) Parody: Ancient, Modern, and Post-Modern. Cambridge: Cambridge University Press.

Rowe, K. (1995a) The Unruly Woman: Gender and the Genres of Laughter. Austin: University of Texas Press.

____ (1995b) 'Comedy, Melodrama and Gender: Theorizing the Genres of Laughter', in K. Karnick & H. Jenkins (eds) Classical Hollywood Comedy. New York: Routledge.

Sandler, K. (1998) 'Introduction: Looney Tunes and Merry Metonyms', in K. Sandler (ed.) Reading the Rabbit: Explorations in Warner Bros. Animation. New Brunswick, NJ: Rutgers University Press.

Schatz, T. (1981) Hollywood Genres: Formulas, Filmmaking, and the Studio System. Austin: University of Texas Press.

Schopenhauer, A. (1818/1964) The World as Will and Idea, Volume 1. London: Routledge.

Schwartz, B. (2001) 'The Gag Man; Being a Discourse on Al Boasberg, Professional Jokesmith, his Manner, and Method', in G. Rickman (ed.) The Film Comedy Reader. New York: Limelight Editions.

Screen Digest, 12 December 1999.

Seidman, S. (1979) Comedian Comedy: A Tradition in Hollywood Film. Ann Arbor: UMI Research Press.

Shaviro, S. (1993) The Cinematic Body. Minneapolis: University of Minnesota Press.

Shklovsky, V. (1965) 'Art as Technique', in L. Lemon & M. Reir (eds) Russian Formalist Criticism: Four Essays. Lincoln: University of Nebraska Press.

Sikov, E. (1994) Laughing Hysterically: American Screen Comedy of the 1950s. New York: Columbia University Press.

Snodgrass, M. E. (1996) Encyclopedia of Satirical Literature. Santa Barbera: ABC-CLIO.

Smith, M. (1995) *Engaging Characters: Fiction, Emotion, and the Cinema*. Oxford: Clarendon Press.

Smith, S. (2000) *Hitchcock: Suspense, Humour and Tone*. London: BFI.

Stacey, J. (1994) *Star Gazing: Hollywood Cinema and Female Spectatorship*. London: Routledge.

Stallybass, P. & A. White (1986) *The Politics and Poetics of Transgression*. London: Methuen.

Stam, R., J. L. Vieira and I. Xavier (1995) 'The Shape of Brazilian Cinema in the Postmodern Age', in R. Johnson & R. Stam (eds) *Brazilian Cinema*. New York: Columbia University Press.

Stokes, L. O. & M. Hoover (1999) *City on Fire: Hong Kong Cinema*. London: Verso.

Studlar, G. (1988) *In the Realm of Pleasure: Von Sternberg, Dietrich, and the Masochistic Aesthetic*. Urbana: University of Illinois Press.

Styan, J. L. (1962) *The Dark Comedy: The Development of Modern Comic Tragedy*. Cambridge: Cambridge University Press.

Suls, J. (1972) 'A Two-Stage Model for the Appreciation of Jokes and Cartoons: An Information-Processing Analysis', in J. Goldstein & P. McGhee (eds) *The Psychology of Humor: Theoretical Perspectives and Empirical Issues*. New York: Academic Press

Tan, E. (1996) *Emotion and the Structure of Narrative Film: Film as an Emotion Machine*. Mahwah, NJ: Lawrence Erlbaum Associates.

Teo, S. (1997) *Hong Kong Cinema: The Extra Dimension*. London: BFI.

Thomas, D. (2000) *Beyond Genre: Melodrama, Comedy and Romance in Hollywood Films*. Moffat: Cameron & Hollis.

Thornton, S. (1995) *Club Cultures: Music, Media and Subcultural Capital*. Cambridge: Polity Press.

Tolstykh, V. (1993) 'Soviet film satire yesterday and today', in A. Horton (ed.) *Inside Soviet Film Satire: Laughter with a Lash*. Cambridge: Cambridge University Press.

Turner, V. (1982) 'Liminal to Liminoid, in Play, Flow, and Ritual: An Essay in Comparative Symbology', in *From Ritual to Theatre: The Human Seriousness of Play*. New York: PAJ Publications.

Turovskaya, M. (1993) 'The strange case of the making of *Volga, Volga*', in A. Horton (ed.) *Inside Soviet Film Satire: Laughter with a Lash*. Cambridge: Cambridge University Press.

Vieira, J. L. (1995) 'From *High Noon* to *Jaws*: Carnival and Parody in Brazilian Cinema', in R. Johnson & R. Stam (eds) *Brazilian Cinema*. New York: Columbia University Press.

Wagg, S. (ed.) (1998) *Because I Tell a Joke or Two: Comedy, Politics and Social Difference*. London: Routledge.

Waller, G. (1992) 'Another Audience: Black Moviegoing, 1907–16', *Cinema Journal*, 31, 2, Winter.

Ward, P. (2002) 'Animated propaganda cartoons in Britain during the First World War: issues of topicality and distribution', *Animation Journal*, forthcoming.

Wells, P. (1998) *Understanding Animation*. London: Routledge.

____ (2002) *Animation: Genre and Authorship*. London: Wallflower Press.

Winokur, M. (1991) 'Black Is White/White Is Black: "Passing" as a Strategy of Racial Compatibility in Contemporary Hollywood Comedy, in L. Friedman (ed.) *Unspeakable Images: Ethnicity and the American Cinema*. Urbana: University of Illinois Press.

____ (1996) *American Laughter: Immigrants, Ethnicity, and 1930s Hollywood Film Comedy*. Baskingstoke: Macmillan.

Youngblood, D. (1993) '"We don't know what to laugh at": Comedy and satire in Soviet Cinema (from *The Miracle Worker* to *St. Jorgen's Feast Day*', in Andrew Horton (ed.) *Inside Soviet Film Satire: Laughter with a Lash*. Cambridge: Cambridge University Press.

Zillman, D. & J. Bryant (1991) 'Responding to Comedy: The Sense and Nonsense in Humour', in J. Bryant & D. Zillman (eds) *Responding to the Screen: Reception and Reaction Processes*. Hillsdale, NJ: Lawrence Erlbaum Associates.

index

Abbott and Costello 207
Abdi, Akbar 37
abjection/the abject 65, 67–8, 82, 204, 219–20
absurd, logic of the 221
action films 43, 123, 141, 172–4, 180
Adlon, Percy 133, 212
African comedy 84
Alexandrov, Grigori 167, 213
Allen, Woody 22, 29, 36, 57, 121, 152–5, 200,
    207–8, 210, 214
Altman, Rick 3, 114, 203, 205, 208, 211–12, 217,
    220
anarchistic comedy 8, 22, 29–30, 40, 42, 81, 83,
    93, 154
animation/animated 21–2, 30, 97–9, 108, 115, 144,
    220–2
Arbuckle, Roscoe 'Fatty' 27, 36, 208
Aristophanes 55
Aristotle 4, 88, 203
army comedies 41, 89, 142, 145, 207
Atsumi, Kiyoshi 37
audiences 1, 3, 9, 17, 25–7, 29, 31–2, 36, 38–9,
    45, 49, 56, 59–60, 69–76, 81, 94, 97, 105–6,
    112, 117, 120–5, 131, 149–50, 153, 154–6, 161,
    166–7, 169, 172, 179–80, 184–5, 196–9, 201,
    204–6, 217, 220, 222
Australia 6, 53, 164, 220
Avery, Tex 21, 30, 88, 108, 117, 210, 212–13
Bakhtin, Mikhail 18, 67, 70, 75, 77–8, 84–5, 166,
    217
Balcon, Michael 158, 160
Barr, Charles 159–60

Bazin, André 44, 47, 204, 217
Bell-Metereau, Rebecca 134–5, 217
Benigni, Roberto 37, 39, 190, 210, 213
Bergson, Henri 5, 155, 204, 217
bisociation 15
black comedy 2, 13, 105, 185
Bleasdale, Alan 196
Boasberg, Al 31, 221
body 11, 15, 22, 26, 28, 34–5, 43, 47–8, 60, 63, 65,
    70–1, 76–7, 83, 85, 88, 100, 117, 125, 133–4,
    136, 139, 147–8, 175, 178
Bondanella, Peter 165, 217
Bourdieu, Pierre 72, 217
Bowser, Eileen 22–3, 27, 217
Brazil 102, 104, 112–13, 207, 211, 222
British comedy 10, 17, 148, 158–9, 161–3, 196, 218
Bugs Bunny 21, 30, 84, 144
Bulgaria 99
Bunny, John 23, 36, 130
Buñuel, Luis 15–16, 209–10
Cantinflas (Mariano Moreno) 37, 155
Cantor, Eddie 155, 219
Capra, Frank 31, 95, 210–14, 217
carnivalesque 66–7, 69–70, 73–5, 81, 84–5, 107,
    130, 171
Carrey, Jim 22, 32–3, 35, 40, 47, 67, 69, 77, 84
Carry On films 3, 74, 85, 109, 111, 115, 132, 199,
    208, 219
censorship 26, 74, 182, 218
Chamberlain, Kathleen 9, 217
Chaplin, Charles 9, 14, 23–9, 32, 36, 39–40, 45–8,
    50, 65, 77, 134, 164, 168–9, 208–12, 214, 221

227

Cheech and Chong 152–3, 208, 220
Chiau, Stephen 37, 155–6
childishness 18, 77
Christensen, Peter 96, 168, 218
Clampett, Bob 30, 207–8
class 13, 26, 29, 53–4, 56, 72–4, 106, 159–60, 163, 166
comedian comedy 32–9, 42–3, 64, 77–8, 81, 86, 129, 132, 145–6, 161, 166, 168, 221
comic quip 141, 172–5, 177
comic relief 172–80, 184
commedia all'italiana 164–5
commedia dell' arte 9, 217
Confessions series 163
Coogan, Steve 10, 37
Crazy Gang 25
Crosby, Bing 20–1
cross-dressing 133–8, 140–2, 148
Crowther, Bosley 181, 218
Cuba 18, 100–1, 209, 211, 217
cultural capital 72, 156, 222
Czechoslovakia 97, 99
Davis, Murray 5, 203, 205, 218
defamiliarisation 121
Deleuze, Gilles 73, 81, 218
DeVore, Dorothy 130, 142
Diawara, Manthia 166–7, 218
disgust 67–8
Disney 30, 99, 119, 154, 185, 197
disruption 7, 8, 19, 22, 24, 31, 40–1, 78, 115, 122–3, 132, 141, 145
Divine 69, 138
documentary 9, 103–4, 108–9, 115, 159, 189, 192
double entendre 182–3
Douglas, Mary 68
Dovnikovic, Bordo 98, 208
Drew, Sidney 23, 36, 209
Durand, Jean 164
Durgnat, Raymond 10, 16, 94, 198, 205, 218
Dyer, Richard 4, 218–9
Ealing comedy 95, 158–65, 217
Eastern Europe 18, 93, 97, 142, 218–20
Eastwood, Clint 114, 213
editing 17, 35, 43–5, 47, 101, 108, 179, 186
Edmonson, Adrian 74
Egypt 37, 166
Elfman, Danny 13
Elsaesser, Thomas 164, 218
Espinosa, Julio García 101, 205, 218 126–7, 140, 144, 152, 173–4, 176
extraneous inclusion 115, 118–19, 126
fantasy 9–10, 14, 20, 55–60, 84, 86, 106–7, 127, 140, 159, 160, 163, 169, 198, 203, 219–21
farce 4, 9–11, 29, 50, 56, 100, 105–6, 181, 183
Farrelly brothers, Peter and Bobby 18, 69, 71, 75, 209–13
Fetchit, Stepin (Lincoln Perry) 152
Fields, Gracie 25, 160, 162
Fields, W. C. 25, 36
Finland 213, 219
Fleischer brothers, Dave and Max 99, 209
Ford, John 2, 157, 183, 210, 212
Formby, George 25, 37, 160–3
Forsyth, Bill 163, 208, 210, 213

framing 11, 17, 42–3, 47–8, 60, 70, 98, 122, 176, 193
France 5, 16, 36, 164, 208
Freud, Sigmund/Freudian 5, 18, 77–8, 81, 89–90, 92, 195, 204–5
Frye, Northrop 5, 38, 55, 94, 218
gag-based comedy 17, 24, 26, 30–2, 126
Garber, Marjorie 138, 141–2, 205, 219
Gehring, Wes 114, 121, 125, 205, 219
gender 18, 56–7, 73, 86, 91–2, 129–44, 146, 148, 158, 163, 168, 193, 197, 199, 220–1
gender-bending comedy 129, 138, 140
genre 2–3, 20, 28, 39, 45, 51–3, 56, 58, 108–15, 119–23, 162, 164, 179, 199, 203–4, 217–22
Germany 164, 208
Goldberg, Whoopi 131–2, 145–6, 150, 152
Gray, Frances 132, 219
Greenwood, Charlotte 131, 219
Griffith, D. W. 119, 208, 210, 221
gross-out comedy 3, 17, 49, 61–77, 89–90, 92, 123, 129, 167, 195, 204
Gunning, Tom 25, 28, 49, 62, 204, 219
Harries, Dan 112, 114–16, 118–19, 121, 123, 219
Hartley, Hal 61, 213
Hawn, Goldie 41–2, 145
Hayward, Susan 164, 219
Hazlit, William 203
Henderson, Brian 22, 57, 219
Henry, Gale 130
Hepworth, Cecil 43, 209
Herman, Pee-Wee 77, 83
hierarchy of knowledge, 180
Higson, Andrew 162, 205, 219
Hitchcock, Alfred 108, 184–5, 210, 212, 222
Hobbes, Thomas 5, 203, 219
Hodge, Robert and David Tripp 9, 219
Hogan, Paul 6, 164, 211
Hong Kong comedy 155–6
Hope, Bob 20–1, 29, 31, 36, 39, 41–2, 77, 109, 111, 123–4
horror 2, 8, 16, 20, 77, 108, 115, 118, 131, 137, 188, 193, 196, 204–5, 220–1
Hui, Michael 37, 156, 210
Hungary 99
ideology 55–6, 91, 104, 110, 167, 169, 221
Imam, Adel 37, 166
incongruity 5–6, 8, 12–16, 44, 85, 115, 118, 133–5, 140–3, 153, 171, 186–7, 193, 195, 199, 203–4, 220
individualism 102, 169
industrial strategy 29
in-jokes 153
inversion 15, 17, 64–5, 115–16, 123, 127, 130–3, 137, 218
Iran 37, 181
Irish 28, 138, 157, 210
irritation 77, 81–2
Italy 39, 190, 208
Jacques, Hattie 132
Jagua 37, 64, 166
James Bond films 117, 121, 136, 174, 200
Jenkins, Henry 29, 31, 72–3, 131, 204–5, 218–21
Jewish humour 152–3
Jones, Chuck 14, 30, 208–10, 214
Kael, Pauline 181, 219

Kant, Immanuel 4, 14, 204–5, 219
Keaton, Buster 9, 13, 20, 25, 27–8, 36, 39, 44–6,
    77, 87, 119, 168, 208–12, 220
Keith-Spiegel, Patricia 220
Keystone 27, 36, 43–4, 56, 221
Keystone Kops 9, 23–4, 164, 181
Khamseh, Alireza 37
Klein, Norman 30, 99, 220
Koestler, Arthur 15, 204, 220
Kristeva, Julia 65, 204–5, 220
Krutnik, Frank 5, 20, 22–3, 25, 27, 31–2, 57, 59–60,
    83, 88, 184, 204–5, 220–1
Krzywinska, Tanya 122, 220
Kuleshov, Lev 44, 96, 204, 211, 220–1
Lacan, Jacques 81, 220
Langdon, Harry 21, 26, 36, 77, 79–80, 83–4, 130
Latin American 2, 18, 37, 94, 102, 218, 220
Lau, Jenny 109, 111, 156–7, 220
laughter 2, 4–5, 8, 14–15, 67–8, 88, 92, 130, 144,
    155, 167, 178, 185, 196, 199, 203–4, 217–22
Laurel, Stan and Oliver Hardy 12–13, 32, 48–9, 77,
    79, 101, 109, 111, 130, 187
Lawrence, Martin 134, 145, 147–8, 152
Leigh, Mike 195, 210, 212
Levi-Strauss, Claude 55
Lewis, Jerry 21–2, 36, 38–9, 41–2, 48, 64, 77, 81–3,
    86, 147, 188, 208–9, 213, 219–20
Linder, Max 36, 164, 213
Lindvall, Terry and Ben Fraser 144, 220
List, Christine 152, 220
literal isation 102, 115, 117, 123, 127
Lloyd, Harold 9, 27, 36, 39, 44, 47, 50, 96, 112
Lucan, Arthur 138
Lumière brothers 43, 207, 209
Lunacharsky, Anatoly 168
Makavejev, Dusan 75, 211, 219
Mancini, Henry 12
Martin, Dean 36, 38
Martin, Steve 32–5, 40, 45, 111
Marx Brothers 25, 29, 34, 36, 38–9, 51, 77–8, 95,
    149, 155, 221
Marx, Chico 19, 29, 46, 78, 89, 155
Marx, Groucho 19, 29, 46, 78, 89, 154–5
Marx, Harpo 19, 46, 77–8, 88–9
masochism 8, 81, 218
Mast, Gerald 25, 47, 204, 220
Mayall, Rik 74
McDaniel, Hattie 152
Méliès, Georges 43
melodrama/melodramatic 30, 34, 51–2, 62, 106,
    119, 167–8, 177, 179, 181, 195–6, 198, 204,
    221–2
Menander 55
misdirection 115–16, 123, 126
mode/modality 2–3, 5, 8–13, 25–6, 35, 38, 81,
    85, 94, 104, 110, 115, 153, 166, 172, 176, 181–2,
    188, 204, 206
Monroe, Marilyn 134, 136, 140–1
montage effects 35, 44, 47, 62, 96, 116, 141, 154,
    217
Murphy, Eddie 64, 145, 147, 152
Murray, Bill 42, 137
music 11–13, 41, 45–6, 62, 103, 108, 117, 131, 139,
    146, 170–1, 175, 177, 198, 222

music hall 24–5, 138, 159–60, 164
musical 2, 4, 25, 28, 30, 32, 36, 41, 96, 99, 162–3,
    167–8, 198, 205
Musser, Charles 56, 149, 154–5, 157, 205, 221
narrative 5, 8, 10, 15–17, 19–43, 48–51, 55–6, 59,
    61, 65–73, 78, 82–3, 86, 90, 105, 108, 112, 122,
    125–6, 128, 131, 133, 141–3, 146–9, 157, 160,
    162, 164, 176–8, 180, 184, 186, 188, 204
national identity 18, 144, 158, 220–1
Neale, Steve 5, 20, 23, 25, 27, 31–2, 57, 88, 184,
    204–5, 221
New Comedy 55
Nigeria 37, 166
nonsense comedy 155
Old Comedy 5, 55
Old Mother Riley (Arthur Lucan) 138, 211
Olson, Elder 9, 14–16, 221
Orwell, George 99
Palmer, Jerry 14, 16, 221
parody 3, 18, 28, 75, 96, 107–8, 141, 149–50,
    152–3, 155, 187, 195, 200, 205, 219, 223
Paul, Robert 208, 221
Paul, William 67, 73–4, 89, 205, 221
performative mode 32, 41
Perry, Lincoln 152
Petric, Vlada 96, 221
Plato 4, 88
Pope, Alexander 94
postmodern 120–1
pre-Oedipal 18, 77–9, 81–7, 89, 92
Production Code 30, 132–4, 182–4, 187, 220
pro-filmic event 46
propaganda 98–9, 103, 107, 109, 201, 222
Pryor, Richard 145, 147, 150, 152
psychoanalytical approaches 18
publicity materials 12, 65
Purdie, Susan 9, 221
race 18, 96–7, 115, 129, 146, 149–50, 168, 205
Ratchford, Moira 167, 221
ratings system 74
reconciliation 42, 53–5, 83, 86, 130, 138
reflexivity 119, 124, 126–8
regression 17, 63, 77, 82, 84, 86–8, 90, 130
reiteration 115, 123–4, 126, 133
Restoration comedy 55
Riblet, Douglas 36, 43–4, 221
Richards, Jeffrey 158, 160, 205, 221
ritual 40, 64, 222
Rock, Chris 145
role-reversal comedy 85–6
romantic comedy 1, 3, 9, 17, 28, 42, 50–62, 67, 73,
    84, 89–92, 105–6, 131, 204, 218, 220
Rose, Margaret 114, 221
Rowe, Kathleen 57, 131, 138, 140, 204–5, 221
Sägebrecht, Marianne 140
satire 3, 9, 12, 18, 93–128, 180, 188, 195, 218,
    221–2
Schatz, Thomas 120, 221
Schünzel, Reinhold 164, 210, 218
Schwartz, Ben 31, 221
Schwarzenegger, Arnold 13, 124, 141
science fiction 6, 8, 20, 128, 172, 199, 204
screwball comedy 51, 56–7
Seidman, Steve 86–7, 90, 204–5, 221

Sellers, Peter 38
semiology 6
Sennett, Mack 23–5, 27, 31, 36, 43, 119, 209–10, 213
Shakespeare, William 91
Shaviro, Steven 81, 203, 221
short films 119
Shumiatsky, Boris 167
Sikov, Ed 83, 95, 139, 221
silent comedy 31
Simms, Joan 132
slapstick 1, 9, 16, 21, 23–31, 36, 43, 50–2, 56, 73, 77, 81–2, 85–6, 88, 97, 100–1, 106, 130, 146, 156, 159, 164, 167–9, 177, 181, 187, 190, 218, 220
Smith, George Albert 43, 210
Smith, Kevin 208
Smith, Murray 203, 222
Smith, Susan 184–5, 222
Solanas, Fernando 102, 213
Solondz, Todd 195–6, 210
sound 21, 29–31, 33, 36, 52, 101, 117, 126, 171, 188, 192, 198–9, 211
Soviet Union 13, 93, 96–7, 99–100, 102, 107, 167–8, 219
special effects 1, 27, 147, 168, 199
Stallone, Sylvester 141, 145, 205, 219
Stalter, Pavao 99, 211
Stain, Robert, João Luiz Vieira and Ismail Xavier 112, 222
stars 23, 25, 27, 29, 32–3, 36–40, 47, 77, 81, 84, 95, 100, 119, 129–30, 147–50, 160, 167, 204
stereotypes 53, 130, 138, 143, 145–7, 149–53, 157, 197
Studlar, Gaylyn 82, 205, 222
Sturges, Preston 47, 95, 183, 209–11, 213, 222
Styan, J. L. 196, 222
subversion/subversive 8, 15, 17, 21, 34, 67, 71, 75, 81, 94, 132–4, 149, 152, 180
superiority theories 5
surrealism 15
suspense 10, 49, 125–6, 174, 184–5
Swift, Jonathan 94
Tan, Ed 8, 205, 222
Tarantino, Quentin 185, 188, 212
Tashlin, Frank 209, 213–14, 222
taste 61, 72, 87, 159, 181, 217
Tati, Jacques 14, 38, 47, 204, 210, 212
thematic oppositions 56
Tincher, Fay 130
transgression 8, 17, 63–92, 95, 123, 132
Trickster 64–5, 69, 88
Trnka, Jiří 97, 109, 111, 207, 209, 211–12
Tucker, Chris 145, 147, 152
Turhapuro, Uuno 165–6, 213, 222
Turovskaya, Maya 97, 222
unintentional comedy, 122, 189, 198–200
unruly woman 131, 133, 138, 144, 221
variety 24, 28, 155, 159, 164
vaudeville 24–5, 28–30, 34, 46, 52, 87, 219
Walters, Julie 133
Ward, Paul 99, 222
Waters, John 69, 72, 74, 138, 208, 210, 212
West, Mae 131
western 108–15, 119–20, 142, 157, 179
Wilder, Billy 207, 209, 213
Williams, Robin 32–5, 40–1, 83, 134
Windsor, Barbara 132–3
Winokur, Mark 168–9, 205, 222
Wisdom, Norman 37, 39, 77
Youngblood, Denise 167, 222
Yugoslavia 98–9
Zagreb school 98
Zaninovic, Ante 98, 215
Zimbabwe 53, 64